AMERICA'S GREAT WAR

AMERICA'S GREAT WAR

World War I and the American Experience

ROBERT H. ZIEGER

ROWMAN & LITTLEFIELD PUBLISHERS, INC.
Lanham • Boulder • New York • Oxford

ROWMAN & LITTLEFIELD PUBLISHERS, INC.

Published in the United States of America
by Rowman & Littlefield Publishers, Inc.
A wholly owned subsidary of The Rowman & Littlefield Publishing Group, Inc.
4501 Forbes Boulevard, Suite 200, Lanham, Maryland 20706
www.rowmanlittlefield.com

PO Box 317
Oxford
OX2 9RU, UK

British Cataloging in Publication Information Available

The hardback edition of this book was previously cataloged by the Library of Congress
as follows.

Library of Congress Cataloging-in-Publication Data

Zieger, Robert H.
    America's Great War : World War I and the American experience / Robert H. Zieger.
        p. cm. — (Critical issues in history)
    Includes bibliographical references (p. 251) and index.
        1. World War, 1914–1918—United States. 2. World War, 1914–1918—Social
aspects—United States. 3. United States—Politics and government—1913–1921. I. Title.
II. Series.

D570.A1 Z54 2000
940.4'0973—dc21   00-038742

ISBN 0-8476-9644-8 (cloth alk. paper)
ISBN 0-8476-9645-6 (pbk. alk. paper)

Printed in the United States of America

∞™ The paper used in this publication meets the minimum requirements of American
National Standard for Information Sciences—Permanence of Paper for Printed Library
Materials, ANSI/NISO Z.39.48-1992.

Contents

Series Editor's Foreword

Historians looking back on the twentieth century must conclude that contrary to all of its earnest declarations on behalf of internationalism, human rights, and tolerance, the century's great irony lay in its failure to resolve national, religious, and ethnic conflict. Indeed, the problems of nationalism, violations of human rights, and bitter, seemingly irrepressible religious and ethnic conflict continue undiminished into the twenty-first century. This observation is not to deride the Wilsonian idealism that found first expression in the First World War; instead it suggests that the historical forces of nationalism, ethnic and religious conflict, and wars of "self-determination" present complexities not as easily resolved as Woodrow Wilson hoped. These seemingly irrepressible historic forces were not surmounted by the Wilsonian insistence on self-determination, universal human rights, and an international organization to prevent future wars. Wilson's Fourteen Points provided the basis for the Armistice and set the initial agenda for the Paris peace conference. His vision of America as the redeemer of battle-scarred and morally corrupted Europe and his belief that America stood as a beacon in a new world order remained potent—and much contested—throughout the rest of the century.

The outbreak of war in Europe in August 1914 and its long duration, contrary to the expectations of most, who assumed it would be a short war, brought untold destruction and death that left the world traumatized. As the war continued, Wilson pursued a policy of neutrality to avoid American armed involvement. He hoped that American mediation would bring peace to Europe. As Robert Zieger explains, neutrality did not mean complete noninvolvement, as urged by Wilson's first secretary of state, William Jennings Bryan, and his allies. Noninterventionists such as Bryan held that the

United States should not be involved on any level in the European war. Instead, Wilson upheld the policy of neutrality that would allow the United States to find a resolution to the war by using its vast wealth and moral stature to maneuver the warring countries into a settlement, followed by new democratic world order in which such grotesque violence would be suppressed. Wilson believed, as Zieger writes, that "America could—must— seize the falling standard of European enlightenment and progress and save Europe from itself." At the same time, Americans found opportunities for profit as the war continued. At the outbreak of war in August, Wilson's State Department disapproved of extending American loans and credits to belligerents, but by October, such a policy seemed perverse as it became clear that the war might continue for months or years. Such a ban on financial arrangements entailed a catastrophic reduction in trade with America's chief prewar trading partners. In this context, Zieger concludes, "Americans increasingly came to couple their horror of the European catastrophe with the appreciation of the opportunities for profit and longer-range economic benefits that the war now offered." As we know, Wilson's attempts to mediate the war failed, and with the German's renewal of submarine warfare, America entered the war on the behalf of the democratic Allies in 1917.

The American contribution to the defeat of Germany was substantial. The First World War showed above all else that twentieth-century warfare was an economic struggle as much as it was a political struggle. America's potent economy provided the Allies with munitions, equipment, foodstuffs, and immense financial resources. The U.S. Navy played an important role in turning back the German submarine menace, and the huge influx of American troops was a key factor in blunting Germany's spring offensives and, especially, in the victorious Allied advance in the crucial summer of 1918. True, "only" 120,000 Americans died during their country's abbreviated participation in the Great War, but there is little doubt that without American manpower, Europe faced at least an additional year of war.

Drawing on the explosion of recent scholarship on the First World War, Robert Zieger offers the reader a powerful narrative and analysis of the international events that led to America's entry into the war and its profound consequences on the American home front. Zieger weaves a masterful narrative and interpretation of the effects of the war on progressive reform, racial and gender relations, civil liberties, labor and industry, and the emergence of America as a world power. Zieger's handling of these issues is skillful and richly informative, providing his readers with an opportunity to evaluate this traumatic event that left America and the world transformed. In doing so, Zieger invites readers to address the larger problems of nationalism and internationalism, ethnic and religious conflict and tolerance, and intervention and nonintervention in the twenty-first century.

Donald T. Critchlow

~

Preface and Acknowledgments

My grandfather, Alf Harman, was one of the last casualties of the Great War. On November 7, 1918, amid the false Armistice celebrations that gripped New York that day, the horse drawing the delivery cart he was negotiating through the streets of Manhattan shied and pitched him out. His head struck a street rail and his skull was fractured. He died the next day.

Shortly after Alf's death, his daughter, Grace, met my father, John. He had emigrated from Germany in 1912. As a schoolboy, he once saw the Kaiser. During the Great War, he was an enemy alien in New York City, looking for work, barred from going near the waterfront. In 1921, Grace Harman and John Zieger were married, effecting their own Anglo-German rapprochement, and went to live with my grandmother, Elizabeth Harman. In the years after the next world war, I remember vividly the exchanges between my grandmother and father, triggered by some item in the news. Having emigrated from England as a young woman in 1888, she was, I think, always a little unsettled by the presence in the household of this German who had married her daughter. Although he was a thoroughgoing Anglophile who despised even pre–Hitler German political culture, my father could not help twitting her about some folly of the royal family or some evidence of British imperial decline. But she invariably trumped him with "There'll always be an England," and I believe that he hoped she was right.

My father was convinced that had he stayed in Germany, he would surely have been among the 1.7 million of his countrymen killed in the Great War. His words to this effect—expressed so often and so casually as to have become a kind of family joke—came home to me powerfully in April 1995 when my wife, Gay, and I discovered one of the many German military cemeteries scattered about the countryside near Verdun and again this past summer when we came upon another at Belleau Wood.

There are cemeteries and monuments in Alsace, which Gay and I visited in 1995 to see at first hand where her mother, Annette Groelly Pitman, lived before she came to America in 1909. In Alsace you get a glimpse of how complicatedly European the Great War was. In 1914, of course, Alsace was part of the German Reich and most of it remained so throughout the fighting. As is the case in the village squares throughout France, war memorials abound in the Alsatian villages, listing the names of the dead. Only in these towns, the names are German, and it is not always clear on which side their bearers were forced to fight. Annette's husband (Gay's father), Verne Pitman, is the only member of either of our families to have actually participated in the Great War, if serving three months in the New Jersey National Guard (most of it in the hospital with influenza) counts as participation. We do have a splendid photograph of twenty-two-year-old Verne Pitman, puttees rolled, tunic buttoned, campaign hat upon his knee.

The American experience was so different and so relatively triumphant when compared with the experiences of our partners and enemies alike. Of the eight million soldiers killed during the war, "only" about 60,000 Americans died as a result of combat. U.S. troops were actively engaged for only about six months and knew only victory, first in helping to turn back the German drive on Paris, then in advancing at Soissons, St. Mihiel, and the Meuse-Argonne. Apart from some incidents of sabotage at munitions dumps and factories that were possibly attributable to German agents, America suffered no physical damage. The war, in fact, was good for business. For three years, the blood of Europe's youth nourished American industry and commerce. The United States became almost overnight a creditor nation while laying the foundation for becoming the "heir to empire," as the demands of war sucked wealth, and with it postwar power and influence, from Britain and the other countries of Europe. Americans never tired of proclaiming their distinctiveness, their freedom from the toils and tribulations of a Europe descended into madness.

Yet from the start America was implicated in Europe. Not only because American farms and factories provided the grisly matériel of warfare and because American investors extended the credits and bought up the loans that permitted the killing to continue. Not only because so many millions of Americans, such as those in my family and Gay's, had personal roots and in cases family members living in the warring countries. And not only rican ships were interdicted and sometimes sunk and American travelers killed in the deadly maritime war that raged after

1914. America was implicated because America was part of Europe. Europe's tragedy was America's tragedy because it was the tragedy of the West. Thus when novelist Pat Barker observes, "The Somme is like the Holocaust. It revealed things about mankind that we *cannot* come to terms with and cannot forget. It never becomes the past," she speaks not only of and for the British slaughtered as they strode into the German machine guns on July 1, 1916, but to all those involved with European civilization. Whether viewing the endless list of names of the dead at the Scottish War Memorial in Edinburgh, walking in Suresnes amid the gravestones of African American stevedores and laborers killed by influenza while serving in the segregated American Expeditionary Force, or counting the names on the memorials in tiny Provençal villages, you cannot help but feel implicated in and affected by this great human tragedy.

But it was also a *world* war, as the Indians, Moroccans, Senegalese, and Vietnamese who fought and toiled in Europe attested. Europe's folly distributed the suffering from Goose Bay to Auckland and from Saskatoon to Cape Town. Twenty percent of the conscripts in the American army were foreign born; 13 percent were African American. Despite being "heirs to empire," Americans showed little awareness of and less concern about how five years of war and revolution were both reshuffling the colonial deck and discrediting the colonial game.

I undertook to write this book in hopes that it would help students and general readers to gain a sense of the importance and tragedy of the Great War. The recent decline of communism broke a powerful link with the world of 1917–18, which seems in the past ten years to have grown remote from our own time in a way that was not the case in the previous half-century. It seemed important to tell members of a rising generation about the great events and developments that have shaped their lives. It is not so much that many of our current problems and challenges can be traced back to the era of the Great War—though they can. It is more that the threats to a sense of historical continuity, in the form of powerful electronic media and a cultural and political environment that ignores or trivializes the past, seem today unusually potent. The jerky old newsreel footage on the History Channel cannot substitute for the kinds of human connection that printed words can still convey best.

In a recent essay, historian Paul Kennedy puts the case forcefully. "The Great War is . . . not some distant problem about dead white males on and off the battlefields," he writes. "Its origins, course, and consequences are central to an understanding of the twentieth century." And in the words that capture something of my own motivation for teaching courses on the Great

War and for writing this book, he insists that "Any high school, college, or university that does not accord importance to teaching its meanings is short-changing the present generation of students and discrediting itself." *America's Great War* is the result of one historian's effort to come to terms with this profound chapter in human affairs.

When you write a book, you incur debts, and acknowledging them is a pleasure, not a duty. LeRoy Ashby, John Mahon, Pat Maney, Joe McCartin, Bob McMahon, Bill Skelton, Gary Mormino, and Mel Small read parts of the manuscript and offered equal measures of good advice and needed encouragement. Rowman & Littlefield's manuscript readers, Burton Kaufman and Kendrick Clements, likewise provided both challenging commentary and generous understanding. John Richard, Randall Stephens, and Alan Bliss did yeoman service as research aides. I am grateful to Don Critchlow for inviting me to participate in this series and especially to Steve Wrinn, my editor, for his enthusiasm and graciousness. Lynn Gemmell has been an exemplary production editor. I owe a special debt to my undergraduate students at the University of Florida, whose response to a work-in-progress has been invaluable in shaping the finished product. And finally, and always, the validation that my wife, Gay, offers, in this as in everything else, is beyond my ability to express.

Chronology

1914

28 June—Archduke Franz Ferdinand, and his wife, Duchess Sophie, are assassinated by Gavrilo Princep, in Sarajevo, Bosnia.

28 July—Austria-Hungary declares war on Serbia.

30 July—Russia mobilizes against Austria-Hungary and Germany.

1 August—Germany declares war on Russia.

3 August—Germany declares war on France.

4 August—Germany declares war on and invades Belgium; Britain declares war on Germany.

5 August—President Woodrow Wilson offers to mediate.

19 August—Wilson urges neutrality "in fact as well as in name."

5–14 September—Battle of the Marne; Allies halt German advance into France.

23 October—U.S. government okays commercial credit loans to belligerents.

1915

9–11 January—Woman's Peace Party is formed; Jane Addams is named president.

15 January—Commercial Agency Agreement is made between J. P. Morgan and Co. and the British government.

4 February—Germany proclaims "war zone" around British Isles.

10 February—Wilson declares that Germany will be held to "strict accountability" for submarine actions.

1 March—British order in council establishes virtual blockade of Germany.

25 April—Gallipoli landings begin.

26 April—Treaty of London is made, by which Italy agrees to enter the war on the Allied side.

28 April—International Congress of Women convenes in the Netherlands.

7 May—German submarine sinks the *Lusitania*.

10 May—Wilson makes his "too proud to fight" speech.

13 May—First *Lusitania* note.

8 June—William Jennings Bryan resigns as U.S. Secretary of State.

9 June—Second *Lusitania* note.

21 July—Third *Lusitania* note; U.S. will regard further sinkings as "deliberately unfriendly."

10 August—First Plattsburg training camp is opened.

15 August—U-boat sinks *Arabic*; two Americans are killed.

1 September—Germans pay indemnity for *Arabic* losses and pledge limits on submarine warfare.

October—First Allied unsecured public subscription loans are floated in the United States.

1 November—Anti-Preparedness Committee is formed (precursor to American Union Against Militarism).

4 November—Wilson speech calls for expansion of armed forces.

1916

8 February—German government instructs U-boat commanders to sink armed merchant ships.

21 February—Battle of Verdun begins.

22 February—House–Grey memorandum.

March–April—British government tightens blockade.

7 March—Gore–McLemore Resolution is defeated; would have restricted rights of Americans to travel on belligerent merchant ships.

8–9 March—Mexican irregular forces under Pancho Villa attack Columbus, New Mexico.

15 March—11,000 U.S. troops under General John J. Pershing enter Mexico in pursuit of Villa.

24 March— U-boat sinks French liner *Sussex*; several Americans are injured.

25 April—Irish patriots launch Easter Rebellion, seize Dublin Post Office.

4 May—Germany agrees to restrict submarine attacks ("*Sussex* Pledge").

31 May–1 June—Naval Battle of Jutland; German high seas fleet remains confined to North Sea.

14–17 June—Paris Economic Conference of Allies; U.S. is concerned about postwar economic discrimination.

18 June—National Defense Act enlarges U.S. Army.

1 July—Battle of the Somme begins.

18 July—News of British blacklist of U.S. firms stirs angry American response.

30 July—Black Tom explosion, New Jersey waterfront; causes massive destruction of munitions awaiting shipment to Allies.

29 August—Naval Act authorizes construction of new battleships and destroyers.

29 August—Congress creates Council of National Defense.

7 November—Wilson wins reelection.

7 December—David Lloyd George replaces Herbert Asquith as British Prime Minister.

18 December—Wilson appeals to belligerents to state peace terms.

1917

10 January—National Woman's Party begins picketing White House, demanding votes for women.

22 January—Wilson makes his "Peace without Victory" speech.

31 January—Germany announces implementation of unrestricted submarine warfare.

3 February—U.S. breaks diplomatic relations with Germany.

5 February—U.S. withdraws troops from Mexico.

28 February—Wilson releases Zimmermann Telegram to the press.

12 March—Wilson orders arming of U.S. merchant ships.

15–16 March—Czar Nicholas II abdicates; Provisional government takes power in Russia.

16 March— U-boats sink three U.S. merchant ships.

24 March—Cabinet meeting urges U.S. declaration of war.

2 April—Wilson asks for declaration of war against Germany.

6 April—Wilson signs declaration of war, passed by both houses of Congress.

14 April—Committee on Public Information, headed by George Creel, is established.

16 April—French General Robert Nivelle launches disastrous offensive.

29 April—First reports of mutiny among French troops on Western Front.

May—U.S. Food Administration is created.

10 May—British and U.S. naval commands inaugurate convoy system.

12 May—Wilson appoints General John J. Pershing to head the American Expeditionary Force.

18 May—Wilson signs Selective Service Act.

30–31 May—People's Council for Democracy and Peace, an antiwar coalition, is formed.

5 June—Draft registration begins.

15 June—Congress passes Espionage Act.

20 June—First Liberty Loan is launched.

26 June—First U.S. troops arrive in France.

1 July—Civil Liberties Bureau, precursor to American Civil Liberties Union, is formed.

12 July—Mass arrest, "deportation" of striking Bisbee, Arizona, copper miners.

13 July—German Chancellor Theobald von Bethmann-Hollweg is forced from office.

31 July—Battle of Passchendaele begins; British suffer massive casualties.

10 August—Lever Act is passed; provides emergency powers to control food and fuel supplies.

23 August—Violent racial outbreak involving black troops stationed in Houston, Texas; 20 people are killed.

23 August—Wilson creates U.S. Fuel Administration.

4 September—American Alliance for Labor and Democracy holds first convention.

5 September—Government raids of Industrial Workers of the World (IWW) facilities begin.

October—Revenue Act of 1917 is enacted.

24 October—Caporetto campaign begins; Italian army is routed.

7 November—Bolsheviks seize power in Russia.

7 November—Supreme War Council is created to coordinate Allied and U.S. military efforts.

12 November—Wilson addresses American Federation of Labor.

21 November—Inter-Allied Conference in Paris; lays basis for greater military coordination among Allies and the U.S.

5 December—Bolsheviks begin publishing secret treaty provisions.

26 December—Federal government takes over operation of railroads; U.S. Railroad Administration is created.

1918

8 January—Wilson issues Fourteen Points in address to Congress.

3 March—Treaty of Brest-Litovsk between Russia and Germany is signed.

4 March—Wilson appoints Bernard M. Baruch head of War Industries Board; General Peyton Marsh is named U.S. Army Chief of Staff.

11 March—First reports of influenza outbreaks, Fort Riley, Kansas.

21 March—Germans launch offensive in France against British forces along Somme River.

1 April—Federal trial of 101 IWW leaders begins in Chicago.

14 April—General Ferdinand Foch is named commander in chief of Allied (including U.S.) forces on Western Front; German offensive against British stalls.

18 April—National War Labor Board begins operations.

16 May—Congress passes Sedition Act.

20 May—Overman Act is passed; strengthens president's war powers.

27 May—Germans launch offensive along the Aisne River, France.

31 May—Germans reach Marne River, threaten Paris.

3–4 June—First major action for U.S. troops; helps stop German advance at Chateau-Thierry.

6 June–1 July—U.S. troops see in heavy action at Belleau Wood.

6 July—Wilson authorizes dispatch of U.S. troops to Siberia.

17 July—Wilson authorizes dispatch of U.S. troops to North Russia.

18 July—Allied Aisne-Marne offensive with 310,000 U.S. troops is a military turning point on Western Front.

8 August—British begin Somme offensive, make major gains.

19 August—British and Empire Ypres-Lys offensive pushes Germans back.

3–6 September—"Slacker" raids in New Jersey and New York round up thousands suspected of draft evasion.

12–13 September—U.S. forces capture St. Mihiel salient.

26 September—U.S. forces launch Meuse-Argonne attacks.

4 October—German Chancellor Prince Max asks Wilson for armistice based on Fourteen Points.

8 October—PFC Alvin York kills at least 20 German soldiers, captures 132.

5 November—Congressional elections result in GOP majority, control of Senate Committee on Foreign Relations.

9 November—Abdication of Kaiser Wilhelm II is announced.

11 November—Armistice goes into effect.

1919

18 January—Peace Conference opens in Paris.

29 January—Prohibition Amendment is ratified by states; goes into effect 20 January 1920.

6 February—Seattle General Strike begins.

15 February—Wilson leaves Paris, returns to the U.S.

24 February—Revenue Act of 1918 [*sic*] becomes law; raises corporate, upper income taxes.

2 March—Thirty-nine senators sign Round Robin urging separation of League from treaty.

15–17 March—America Legion is founded.

2 June—Attorney General A. Mitchell Palmer's house is bombed.

28 June—Treaty of Versailles is signed.

7 July—Germany ratifies treaty.

8 July—Wilson arrives in the U.S. and presents the treaty to Senate.

14–28 July—Lodge reads aloud all 246 pages of treaty to Senate.

27 July—Major racial violence erupts in Chicago.

28 July—Last U.S. troops pull out of North Russia.

31 July—Senate Foreign Relations Committee begins public hearings on Treaty of Versailles.

1 August—Department of Justice General Intelligence Division (precursor to FBI) is created.

19 August—Wilson meets with Foreign Relations Committee, agrees to interpretative reservations.

4 September—Wilson begins 8,000-mile tour, 40 speeches in 29 cities in 22 days.

22 September—Steel strike begins.

25 September—Wilson collapses in Pueblo, Colorado; returns to Washington.

October (early)—Mass killings of African Americans in Phillips County, Arkansas.

2 October—Wilson suffers stroke.

6 November—Senate Foreign Relations Committee proposes fourteen Lodge reservations.

7 November—Federally coordinated raids of alleged subversives begin.

19 November—Senate rejects treaty with fourteen Lodge reservations 39–55; then Senate rejects the original treaty, 38–53.

1920

2 January—Federal, state, and local authorities round up 10,000 radicals and suspected radicals.

1 February—Great Britain and France declare they would accept Senate reservations.

9 February—Senate votes to reconsider treaty and refers it to Committee on Foreign Relations.

19 March—Senate again fails to ratify treaty.

1 April—Last U.S. troops depart Vladivostok, ending Siberian intervention.

4 June—National Defense Act is passed; provides for volunteer army.

26 August—Nineteenth Amendment (women's suffrage) is ratified.

2 November—Republican Warren Harding is elected president.

Post-1920

2 July 1921—Joint Congressional Resolution declares that the war with Germany and Austria-Hungary is over.

18 October 1921—U.S. Senate ratifies separate treaties with Germany and Austria.

January 1923—Last U.S. occupation troops are withdrawn from Germany.

3 February 1924—Woodrow Wilson dies in Washington, D.C.

12 April 1934—U.S. Senate launches investigation of role of munitions makers in decision for war in 1917 (Nye Committee hearings).

26 June 1945—U.S. signs the United Nations Charter.

~

Introduction

Four broad themes emerge from my study of America's Great War. First, there is the theme of America's connection to Europe, obviously in terms of diplomatic, economic, and military affairs, but perhaps more profoundly with respect to culture and destiny. Second is the complicated relationship of the wartime experience to the Progressive era, of which it was a critical part. Third is the emergence of the National Security State. And fourth, suffusing the whole period, is the figure of Woodrow Wilson, whose assumptions, decisions, and behavior so deeply imprinted this period of American history.

This last point is perhaps most unexpected for someone such as myself, whose implicit assumptions have tended to marginalize individual actors and to stress underlying and impersonal forces as propellants of the historical process. And, of course, students of the Great War have no lack of such forces in their efforts to understand and interpret it. Capitalism, dynasticism, imperialism, statism, militarism, revolution, modernism, irrationalism—all these and others provide templates into which to fit the facts of the war, its origins, and its aftermath. But for Americans, although acknowledging the importance of long-range and underlying forces, their war was to an extraordinary extent "Mr. Wilson's War." It was Wilson whose response to the outbreak and course of the war in Europe combined such a potent mixture of Christian redemptionism, American exceptionalism, and determination to rescue European moral and cultural values from the folly of the Europeans. It was Wilson who defined the terms under which the American people went to war in 1917 and waged that war until the Armistice in November 1918. And as it was Mr. Wilson's war, it was Mr. Wilson's peace in that the course and the outcome of the domestic debate over the Versailles Treaty and the Covenant of the League of Nations were not about peace terms per se but rather about Wilson's distinctive vision of a new world order and of America's role in it.

The theme of America's connection to Europe is evident from the firing of the "guns of August" in 1914 until the anticlimactic declaration of an end to belligerency in 1921. The point is not simply that American goods and American finances and American policies played an increasingly central role in the course of the war. Nor that the overwhelming majority of Americans were descended from Europeans and that America's political, economical, and cultural traditions and institutions were largely European in origin. It is rather that in a profound, only partly understood, and elliptically articulated way, the Great War drove home the fact that America was Europe's offspring and successor. The one clear result of direct U.S. participation in the Great War was that the fighting ended in western Europe at least a year earlier than would have been the case without American belligerency. Americans, disdainful of Europeans and convinced of their own moral and material superiority, in effect, although at most only partly in intent, saved Europeans from the chaos and despair and perhaps even disintegration that continued warfare on the scale prevailing between 1914 and 1918 would surely have threatened. Americans tended to see their participation in the war as rescuing Europe ("We won't be back till it's over, over there"), but in pulling Europe back from the edge of the abyss into which it was slipping, America was simultaneously preserving the central engines of Western hegemony, which, for good or ill, were now its to operate.

Within the United States, the experience of the Great War reflected the diverse strands of the progressivism that dominated public discourse during the first two decades of the century. The Progressive impulse juxtaposed celebration of cultural experimentation and democratic enthusiasm on the one hand, with calls for discipline and order on the other. A hunger for social justice warred with a determination to promote social efficiency. Some progressives welcomed growing demographic and cultural diversity while others sought to bolster traditional white, Protestant, Anglo-American culture. Progressives of all stripes saw the war as an opportunity for social action. For liberal progressives, American belligerency necessitated the regulation of business, the promotion of the health, welfare, and education of the people, and the development of rational ways to resolve social conflicts, notably labor disputes. For their part, however, control progressives saw military necessity as a welcome opportunity to halt erosion of traditional values, promote common citizenship through social discipline, and rediscover the virtues of the patriots and pioneers of yesterday.

On the whole, the hopes of control progressives were more completely realized than those of liberal progressives. The ratification of the Eighteenth Amendment in January 1919, prohibiting the manufacture and sale of alco-

holic beverages, reflected in part war-buttressed moral, conservation, and efficiency concerns. Suppression of dissent and government propaganda and surveillance on the home front survived the end of fighting, and the Federal
Bureau of Investigation became one of the most powerful and popular government agencies. Military conscription and the mobilization of public support for military and foreign policy purposes, although not resulting immediately in permanent enhancement of the military establishment, gave
important impetus to the general default toward the government's definition
of "national security." The restriction of immigration, first owing to the logistics of the European war and then enshrined in legislation, further advanced
the agenda of control progressives.

In contrast, the hopes of liberal progressives were disappointed. The war's
end quickly aborted experiments in labor relations and social welfare programs. Modest measures affording the country's African American citizens a
degree of recognition and just consideration died even more rapidly. Women,
it is true, did achieve a long-sought reform with the ratification of the Nineteenth Amendment in August 1920, in part a result of war-born recognition
of women's services. Even so, however, broader questions of women's roles in
an urban, industrial society, haltingly addressed during the war in a series of
makeshift policies and agencies, only dimly echoed in the 1920s. The liberal
progressive goals of subjecting corporate power to closer regulation and providing greater public direction in the economy, partly realized during the war
through such agencies as the United States Railroad Administration and the
War Industries Board, were quickly frustrated. Savage assaults on civil liberties threatened liberal progressives' values at their wellspring.

Yet in the longer view, liberal progressives eventually drew positively upon
wartime initiatives. Even in the 1920s, pioneering, if short-lived, federal welfare legislation provided continuity with innovative wartime programs. If the
government rapidly retreated from even its hesitant and compromised gestures toward racial justice, an increasingly assertive African American community intensified its challenge to white political supremacy and cultural
hegemony. Great War–era reforms in labor relations, shelved during the next
decade, provided compelling models for the New Deal. The war-born threats
to civil liberties alerted some liberal progressives to the dangers of government intrusion and to the need for organized vigilance. The events of the
Great War era raised troubling questions about the wisdom of relying on government in the promotion of social progress, questions that men and women
of good hope continue to confront.

The National Security State was born during the Great War years. For the
first time in U.S. history, government forged powerful instruments of coercion

and repression in the service of military and foreign policy goals. It conscripted four million men. It regulated speech, publication, and assembly. It created potent means of investigation, surveillance, and punishment. It ran the railroads and subjected industry, agriculture, and energy to close regulation. It imposed direct taxes as never before. Along with private bodies that federal officials actively encouraged, its agents dominated public discourse and developed innovative forms of propaganda, persuasion, and repression. It ran roughshod over what had been a strong and vocal peace movement. For the first time in American history, facing no direct or tangible threat to the physical security of the country, the government effectively inculcated a kind of reflexive endorsement of military priorities among a people hitherto hostile or indifferent to military and foreign policy claims.

The National Security State that emerged during the era of the Great War, like the liberal progressive reforms, did not survive intact. In particular, the army quickly shrank to nearly prewar levels of strength. Reaction against the excesses of the Red Scare at least temporarily discredited the engines of repression and surveillance. During the 1920s, enthusiasm for arms limitation trumped advocacy of military and naval enhancement. But just as in the realm of domestic policies, the Great War left a legacy for the next generation of policymakers and opinion molders to draw upon in building a permanent National Security State.

America's Great War traces these themes and developments through the troubling and tumultuous years of the deadly conflict. Chapters one, two, six, and seven highlight the role of Woodrow Wilson in defining, articulating, and furthering his distinctive vision of America as its people faced cataclysmic events that no one—least of all Wilson himself—remotely anticipated during his successful 1912 run for the presidency. These chapters also stress the American relationship to Europe, both in terms of tangible matters such as trade, finance, diplomacy, and military action and in terms of the historical trajectory of Western civilization.

Chapter four, along with part of chapter three, focuses on the American military achievement during the Great War. Military service, especially combat, was the most profound experience in the lives of hundreds of thousands of young Americans, and I have sought in these sections to convey something of the distinctive character and course of the military effort. In my writing about the creation, training, and experiences of this remarkable new American army, the contradiction between its broad democratic and assimilative mandate, on the one hand, and the unrelenting racism that it exhibited on the other, stands out with particular force.

Chapters three, five, and seven focus largely on domestic affairs. It is in these chapters that the diverse and often conflicting strands of progressivism are most clearly revealed. Questions involving the mobilization of the public, the coordination of the economy, the control and regulation of labor, and the dynamics of class, race, and gender relations posed powerful challenges. American belligerency expanded the arena in which contending forces operated. Domestic conflict raged throughout the Progressive era, war or no war. Chapters three, five, and seven attempt to connect this internal turbulence to the emergence of the embryonic National Security State to which U.S. belligerency gave rise.

In the final chapter, I offer some judgments about the meaning of the Great War experience. I provide answers to these questions: How representative and legitimate a spokesman for American values and interests was Woodrow Wilson during the era of the Great War? Were U.S. policies from 1914 to 1917 unfairly weighted toward the Allies? Was the United States justified in declaring war on Germany? Was the settlement that Wilson brought home from France enlightened, or was it merely a victor's peace? Who was responsible for the failure of the U.S. Senate to ratify the Versailles Treaty and for the failure of the United States to join the League of Nations? Did the domestic wartime and postwar experience expose fatal flaws in the worldview of liberal progressives? And finally, where does the American people's experience during the Great War fit into the broader trajectory of the country's twentieth-century history?

In these concluding remarks, I write more as a citizen than as a historian. I relegate these questions and answers to a separate chapter because I do not believe that my answers are definitive or uncontested. For each of these questions, others with sharply different views will find ample material in *America's Great War* to support their positions. On the one hand, I want the narrative to stand on its own; on the other, I believe that readers have a right to see what I make of the story, if only to sharpen their critical responses.

To paraphrase Woodrow Wilson, it has been a fearful thing to lead the American people into war, into what in many respects remains the most terrible of all wars. It has been difficult to avoid imposing the values of the present on the actors of the past while not appearing to condone their sins and occasionally their crimes. At times, outrage has outweighed the historian's requirement of sympathetic understanding. Perhaps the men and women of 1917–18 will forgive these faults if *America's Great War* at all succeeds in bringing their story to their great-grandchildren.

ONE

~

A World at War
1914–1915

The United States was the unacknowledged specter that hovered over the courts and chancelleries of Europe during the fateful summer of 1914. The French, Russian, Austro-Hungarian, German, and British statesmen who led their countries into war following the assassination of the Archduke Franz Ferdinand on June 28 in Sarajevo made many errors, but their most serious miscalculation lay in their neglect of the American factor. Their virtually unanimous belief that the conflict would be short and decisive soon proved grotesquely wrong. They were equally mistaken in their failure to take notice of the United States as they weighed their options. To be sure, American diplomats and military leaders had played no role in the establishment of the alliance system that had dominated European affairs since the 1890s, and it was equally true that the minuscule American army, 3,000 miles away, could not affect the balance of military power. But it quickly became apparent that modern war was as much an economic contest as it was a diplomatic or military affair. Thus, with the world's most productive and rapidly developing economy, the United States, hitherto on the periphery of European diplomatic life, soon moved to the center.

Early Days

At the start of hostilities, official American opinion was confused and uncertain with respect to the legal and economic implications of the war, but in the fall of 1914, the U.S. government made critical decisions that directed its course over the next three years. Americans, President Woodrow Wilson urged, were to be "neutral in thought as well as in action," a sentiment that the people endorsed overwhelmingly. But what did "neutrality" mean in the context of global conflict? Did it mean that the United States must cut off all trade, or at least all trade in munitions and in the raw materials used in making arms and munitions, with all belligerents? Did it mean that the American government must abide by belligerents' definitions of what constituted contraband, or war-related trade, and thus submit to their efforts to control trade with their enemies? Was the American government bound to accept whatever methods of trade control a belligerent might impose, or did it have the right, indeed the obligation, to judge independently what forms of economic restriction it would recognize and what forms it would reject? If Americans did pursue trade, whether in munitions or food and other nonmilitary supplies, was it appropriate for American bankers to extend the usual kinds of short-term credits and loans that were standard practice in large-scale international transactions? Was it appropriate for private American citizens to extend unsecured loans to belligerents?

These were serious practical matters that demanded quick decisions as events so rapidly unfolded in the latter half of 1914. Implicit in these questions and yet larger than any of them was this broader one: would the United States break with its traditions and attempt to exert positive influence in the war-transformed world arena? Hardly articulated during the first months of the war, this question emerged forcefully as the savagery that gripped Europe threatened to discredit and perhaps to destroy Western world hegemony.

In 1914, the American government was not prepared to deal comprehensively with these questions. Events happened so rapidly that judicious deliberation was difficult. The assassination of the Austrian heir-apparent triggered an escalating crisis that within five weeks put vast armies in motion. The war itself, at least on the Western Front, where American attention was riveted, changed its character with equal speed. Within a matter of weeks, it was transformed from a war of motion to a bloody stalemate. If America was not a factor in the decision for war, and if the war would be short and decisive, as virtually all experts on both sides of the Atlantic believed, rulings and decisions on the part of the American government on practical matters of legal status and economic circumstance would be academic, and broader questions of the national role would never arise. But once the rival armies had fought to a standstill, these matters moved inexorably to the forefront.

For a few weeks in August and September, it did appear that military decision, at least in the west, would be swift and decisive. Powerful German armies smashed into neutral Belgium and swept into France. A small British force sent to Belgium was pushed relentlessly back. French armies along the Alsace-Lorraine border were decimated, suffering unimaginable losses. By the end of August, only three weeks after hostilities had begun, the Germans were hammering at the approaches to Paris. Nineteen fourteen, it seemed, was a reprise of the events of 1870, when Germany had crushed France in a war whose active phase lasted a mere ten weeks.

But 1914 was not 1870 after all. Allied resistance stiffened. Attenuated German supply lines could not keep pace with the advancing troops. Russian advances in the east drew German divisions away from the Western Front. Allied counterattacks drove the Germans back. In September and early October, the exhausted armies dug in across northern France, establishing parallel lines of trenches, neither side able to force a breakthrough. By November, although it was not always clear to rival generals still dreaming of a decisive stroke, the war of movement had ended and a war of attrition had begun.

Americans were fascinated and appalled by these terrible events. Expressions of gratitude for the existence of the Atlantic Ocean and of self-congratulation for America's traditional stance of noninvolvement in European affairs were almost universal. One Chicago newspaper offered "a hearty vote of thanks to Columbus for having discovered America," and a leading magazine reassured its readers that "We are in no peril of being drawn into the European quarrel." Even though international law and custom did not bar neutral nations or their citizens from selling arms or loaning money to belligerents, support for a ban on trade in munitions was widespread. The Department of State went so far as to rule that "loans by American bankers to any foreign nation which is at war are inconsistent with the true spirit of neutrality."[1]

In a short decisive war, the American response would have been of little significance. But once the battle lines had stabilized, as they did before the end of September, American resources and American policies suddenly loomed as of great consequence. A "war of attrition" meant keeping relentless pressure on the enemy, pounding his positions with high-explosive shells, probing endlessly for weaknesses, and then hurling huge masses of men forward. The Western Front—the zigzagging line of trenches that soon stretched from the Swiss border to the English Channel—sucked in hundreds of thousands of combat troops; vast numbers of laborers and construction workers, many of them recruited from Britain's and France's Asian and African possessions; and great numbers of horses, some for heavy hauling, others as a ready cavalry reserve poised to exploit an infantry-led breakthrough.

British arsenals and munitions works, designed to supply the needs of its small professional army, were quickly overwhelmed. In addition, the task of feeding millions of men and hundreds of thousands of horses was gigantic. The typical 17,000-man British division—of which there were more than forty on the Western Front by mid-1916—required the contents of twenty railroad cars each day to supply food and fodder for its men and horses. Allied purchasing agents swarmed into Canada, Australia, and the United States to line up consignments of meat, flour, cotton, and other staples and to negotiate contracts for the manufacture of arms and munitions. Calais, Boulogne, and other Channel ports were soon clogged with vast quantities of food, fodder, and war matériel.

North America quickly became a critical war zone, at least in an economic sense. Not only did its farmers and ranchers lead the world in grain and livestock production, but Canada and the United States had the great advantage of being only 3,000 miles away. Moreover, ties of consanguinity, language, and culture connected both the Dominion of Canada and the United States to Great Britain. The loyalty and economic cooperation of Canada, still formally a part of the British Empire, was not in doubt. Early in October, the first contingent of troops arrived in Britain. Eventually, 600,000 Canadians (from a population of eight million) served in the armed forces. Sixty thousand died in France. From the start, Saskatchewan wheat, Quebec lumber, and Ontario steel could be integrated into Allied needs, and by 1917, Canadian firms were producing more than a quarter of the shells that British guns fired in France.

But what of America? Could the Allies count on having the enormous productive capabilities of the United States available to them, and if so, under what terms and with what consequences? The economic power of the United States was beyond question. It led the world in production of steel, coal, wheat, and petroleum products. In the nineteenth century, the United States had been largely a supplier of bulk agricultural commodities and raw materials for Europe, but since the 1890s, a maturing American economy had begun to challenge its rivals in production of and trade in finished goods. American manufacturers of industrial machinery and a wide range of consumer goods increasingly encroached on British markets. In 1913, the United States accounted for 11 percent of world trade, and for the first time, the value of manufactured goods surged ahead of the value of agricultural products in America's exports.

True, the United States was still overall a "debtor nation." In the nineteenth century, Americans had relied heavily on European, and especially British, capital for the construction of its industrial and transportation infrastructure, and Americans still owed vast sums to foreign creditors. But the gap was closing, and since the late 1890s, the United States had enjoyed a favorable balance of trade and was steadily paying down its international obligations. By 1914 such financial houses as J. P. Morgan and Company held billions of dollars in investments abroad. Given the country's enormous agricultural, mineral, and industrial resources and its industrious and productive population, most observers believed that it was only a matter of time until the United States far surpassed its European counterparts, especially now that the bloody stalemate in France was consuming their resources at an astonishing rate. To what extent, if any, would the Allies—for it was only they who could hope to gain access to American goods and funds—be able to connect this American economy to their war effort?

In view of America's economic importance, the problematic nature of initial U.S. responses to the conflict soon became apparent. In August, Department of State disapproval of American loans and credits to belligerents seemed commonsensical, but by October, such a self-denying declaration seemed perverse as well as a departure from previous international custom and practice. If the war were to last months or years, a ban on such financial arrangements would mean a catastrophic reduction in trade with America's chief prewar trading partners. Moreover, even before August, the U.S. economy was suffering its worst depression since the dreadful 1890s. Initially, the outbreak of fighting in Europe disrupted trade and financial markets, worsening an already bad situation. As orders for materials, foodstuffs, and weapons began to pour in, however, Americans increasingly came to couple their horror at the European catastrophe with appreciation of the opportunities for profit and longer-range economic benefits that the war now offered. Now, in October, when American bankers asked Wilson's administration for clarification of its attitude toward loans, they got a different answer: short-term loans and credits by American financial institutions to belligerents in connection with trade were acceptable. The administration made a careful distinction between these kinds of "normal" credit arrangements and public subscription loans, of which it continued to disapprove, but even so, declares historian Paul Koistinen, this shift in policy "fundamentally alter[ed] financial relations with the Allies."[2]

In theory, of course, American firms and American financiers were also free to trade—and to finance that trade—with the Central Powers. Also in theory, Germany's powerful high seas fleet could challenge traditional British naval supremacy and could keep open the trading routes and thus tap into the American market. But in fact, trade and trade-related financial relations with "belligerents" meant in effect trade with the Allies alone. When war started, the Royal Navy acted quickly to bottle up the German fleet in the Baltic and North Seas, and within weeks, British ships had rounded up German merchantmen or driven them into port. The British acted with equal dispatch to deprive their enemies of neutral shipping as well, patrolling the North Sea and English Channel and laying minefields that forced merchant ships to come under British interdiction if they were en route not only to German ports but to those of the Netherlands and the neutral Scandinavian countries as well. Recognizing that even its powerful navy could not impose a traditional "close" blockade directly outside German ports, Britain relied on interdiction of merchant shipping on the high seas and lengthened the list of goods defined as contraband.

The British maritime actions raised important questions for the United States. Resting broadly on traditionally sanctioned wartime practices, these measures also asserted new rights for a belligerent naval power to monitor and interdict trade with its enemy. Britain's mining operations in effect enabled it to control all shipping bound for Germany and northern Europe. Moreover, as early as November, the British expanded the contraband list, soon including a wide range of "civilian" goods, including eventually food, using the dubious argument that the German economy was so controlled by the military that these goods now qualified as war matériel.

From the start, President Wilson and his advisers regarded these measures as problematic but negotiable. The massive mining of the North Sea approaches to Germany was, admittedly, an innovation, but it affected American shipping only marginally, since the English Channel route, by which U.S. goods normally went to Europe, remained open under British guidance. Enforcement of a remote blockade broke with established practice and evoked American objections. The Department of State attempted to gain British adherence to established international law with reference to search, seizure, and interdiction of shipping bound for Germany or for neutral countries within the German ambit. At the same time, Department of State Counselor Robert Lansing acknowledged that modern warfare called into question many of the assumptions on which international law was based, as codified in the 1856 Declaration of London. Eventually, after much haggling, the United States accepted the broad outlines of British policies while reserving the right to protest specific actions.

As was the case with the U.S. response to the economic challenges and opportunities that emerged in the early months of the war, its response to questions of naval and maritime issues was at once pro forma and fraught with long-range implications. At the time, given the supremacy of the Royal Navy, it seemed to American officials that the only maritime issues that would arise would be those involving Britain and its Allies. The Central Powers were thought to be relatively self-sufficient and moreover were not in a position to attempt to regulate or harass U.S. trade. Because Britain was by far America's largest prewar trading partner, and because the United States had a long and complex history of thrashing out maritime issues with the British, American officials saw nothing untoward about acceding to British regulations and leaving disputed matters to subsequent negotiations or the decisions of international tribunals. In a short war in which maritime issues were not expected to be central, American leaders asked themselves, why not accommodate the British? Why alienate America's most important trading partner in defense of abstract legal rights that were likely to have little practical effect?

However, on February 4, 1915, these issues took on a new dimension when the German government declared that the waters surrounding Great Britain constituted a war zone and announced its determination to retaliate against increasingly restrictive British measures by using the submarine, or U-boat (for *unterseeboot*). At the outset of the war, submarines had been a marginal weapon that was used primarily for harassment and intelligence gathering. These fragile vessels were not thought capable of sustained combat, but early in the conflict, German U-boats sank several heavily armored British battle cruisers, a feat that suggested that this new weapon might be an answer to the British blockade. Able to slip through British minefields and patrols to reach the open waters around Britain, submarines could attack merchant shipping, thus answering the British blockade of Germany with an attack on the Allies' lifeline.

Although it was not apparent at first, because German naval command instructed U-boat commanders to observe traditional practices of search and seizure, the entry of the submarine as a major weapon held profound implications for Americans with respect to both economic and legal issues. Strictly speaking, so long as Germany held to traditional rules of maritime interdiction, attacks on British merchant shipping could actually benefit American producers, since, of course, sinkings would increase demand for American goods. But it quickly became apparent that the submarine could not in fact observe traditional rules without jeopardizing its own safety. U-boats, it is true, did sometimes wait until the passengers and crew of a merchant vessel had boarded lifeboats before sinking it. But on the ocean surface, the submarine was extremely vulnerable to ramming and gunfire. Nor could German commanders easily distinguish which vessels bound for Southampton or Liverpool were in fact British, because captains routinely disguised the identity of their merchant ships by flying the flags of the United States or other neutral countries. Clearly, if submarines were to challenge British maritime supremacy, they would have to abandon traditional practices and fire their deadly torpedoes without warning. Although the Germans disclaimed an intention to attack neutral shipping per se, they warned American and other shippers that, in view of the British practice of flying false flags, no merchant ship in the war zone could consider itself free of risk. The British, declared German officials, had redefined traditional wartime maritime practices and had imposed an unprecedented blockade on Germany, claiming that new technology and new circumstances required the redefinition of neutral shipping rights. If neutral countries were not prepared to challenge these British innovations, they could not object when Germany did essentially the same thing.

Americans View the War

During this early phase of the war, Americans exhibited a wide range of attitudes and a broad sense of detachment from events in Europe. The facts of the war—the enormous destruction, the hideous casualty rates, the presumed consequences to the world of the victory or defeat of the Allied or Central Powers—were so monumental that few Americans could fail to acknowledge the war's importance. Still, the historic American stance of aloofness from European events and the simple fact that the war had no direct physical impact on America encouraged ambivalence and detachment. Even lurid British reports of German mistreatment of Belgian civilians and wanton destruction of libraries and churches elicited as much gratitude for American noninvolvement as they did outrage at the behavior of the Kaiser's troops.

The fact that millions of Americans had significant ties to one or another of the warring nations complicated public response to the war. More than one-third of the Euro-American population of the country was either foreignborn or had at least one parent who had been. Some retained citizenship in their natal land, and many cared deeply about the fate of their mother country. Historical memory of the French role in the American Revolution prompted pro-Allied feelings, as did a sense of common culture and common institutions with Great Britain. But then there were the ten million German Americans, many with family members in the Fatherland and many of whom openly supported the Fatherland's cause. Millions of Americans of Irish descent regarded Britain as the tyrant and, indirectly, Germany as the possible means of national liberation. Sicilians, Piedmontese, and others from the Italian peninsula often had only a vague sense of Italian national identity but followed the war news intently after Italy joined the Allies in April 1915.

Millions of former residents of the Austro-Hungarian and Russian empires had experienced little but deprivation and discrimination in their countries of origin. Jews from the Russian empire detested the czar, and Poles and Czechs hoped for an end to imperial rule and the creation of new national states.

These broad categorizations masked powerful crosscurrents of difference, dissent, and perspective. It was possible to love German culture while hating German authoritarianism and militarism, to cherish English literature while abhorring English snobbery and arrogance, to be Irish without wishing for British humiliation. Millions of so-called hyphenated Americans experienced the tragedy of the Great War less in terms of national aspirations and hatreds than in familial and personal loyalties and concern for relatives and loved ones still in Europe. In an era before public opinion polling, those interested in the attitudes of America's foreign-born residents carefully scrutinized the extensive foreign-language press and paid close heed to politicians representing distinctive enclaves of ethnic voters such as the Czechs of rural Nebraska, the Poles of Chicago, the Germans of Milwaukee and St. Louis, the Irish of Boston, and Jews, from diverse European countries, of New York City.

Among "Americans" too the response to the war was divided and divisive. During the two decades before the war, the United States and Great Britain had resolved many of their earlier diplomatic disagreements and entered into an informal but increasingly solid pattern of mutual agreement and support in world affairs. For many in government and journalism, and for those involved in academic, religious, and cultural pursuits among the eastern seaboard and in large cities in other parts of the country, sympathy for England was automatic and immediate. In the heartland of the Middle West, however, isolationism and suspicion of John Bull remained fierce. What of southerners, black and white? In the tenant shacks and the crossroads hamlets, even in the courthouses and legislative chambers, was this conflict anything but a distant, disagreeable rumor? People on the West Coast tended to be more worried about the so-called Yellow Peril supposedly posed by marauding (or simply migrating) Asians than about the fighting in Europe.

Political convictions also colored Americans' response to war. Those involved in the movements for women's rights, workers' rights, clean government, regulation of trusts, and general social improvement, viewed war as the enemy of reform. For these men and women, Europe's descent into barbarism involved not merely death and physical destruction on a massive scale; it marked a halt to the moral progress and social reform that they believed had characterized the past half century. But for others no less eager to improve national life, war, with all its horror, helped to instill a sense of order, discipline, and patriotism, qualities, they felt, sadly lacking in the hedonistic, polyglot, and chaotic America of the 1910s. These men and women envied Europeans for the opportunity they now had to rediscover the manly virtues of courage and honor that often seemed absent in the mechanized and effete modern world.

Early in the war, these crosscurrents of ethnic, political, and regional debate seemed to converge on two central points. Americans wanted to continue to profit from the war, and they wanted to remain out of the fighting. Whatever the sentiments of national feeling or hatred, Americans pursued eagerly the employment and profits associated with the war trade. And all but the most Anglophile or militaristic would have been appalled at the notion that their sons and husbands and neighbors might be sent across the Atlantic to join the carnage.

After a period of uncertainty at the very outset of hostilities, the American economy, buoyed by the war trade, boomed through 1915 and into 1916. Exports rose from just over $2 billion annually in 1913 to almost $6 billion in 1916. Allied orders for food, munitions, and other supplies quickly sopped up British and French capital invested in the United States and turned America almost overnight into a creditor country. Reliant initially on the liquidation of their securities in the United States for the financing of imports from America, the Allies in the summer of 1915 began efforts to borrow money directly from U.S. investors. The price of cotton—a crucial indicator of domestic health for a Democratic president reliant on southern votes and congressional leadership—soared between the onset of fighting and the 1916 presidential election. Producers of petroleum products, copper, nitrates, and other commodities prospered, and employment in the metal trades, arms factories, and food processing, mining, and transport sectors surged. Americans might deplore the killing and worry about distant relatives, but few wished for an end to the good times that war was bringing. Nor did the Wilson administration, whatever the ambivalence the president and his advisers might feel, want to forgo this prosperity or attempt to lead the public toward a conception of wartime policy that tried to combine prosperity and avoidance of the war trade. President Wilson was keenly aware of the fate of the previous Democratic president, Grover Cleveland, whose administration was shattered by the depression of the 1890s.

Americans were equally insistent on remaining out of the fighting. The more Americans learned of the scope and nature of the warfare in Europe, the more determined they were to stand clear. To be sure, preparedness advocates, led by military and naval leaders, seized upon the European war to advance plans for expanding and reequipping the armed forces. Civic and patriotic organizations promoting this cause flourished. But this militarizing sentiment was rarely connected to the notion of sending Americans to fight in Europe. Army war plans, for example, concentrated on repelling an amphibious assault on East Coast cities or on responding to a joint attack by Britain and Japan, allied by virtue of a 1902 treaty, through Canada and along the West

Coast. Even supporters of military enhancement stressed its positive domestic effects such as the establishment (in the words of one newspaper) of "wholesome discipline over the country's youth." Even as Congress cautiously considered measures to expand the army and the navy, virtually no one contemplated the actual dispatch of American troops to Europe.

The task of the president then was to devise policies that would at once ensure continued economic gain and also keep America out of the war. Wilson personally embraced both goals, but at the same time, he viewed America's role—and thus his own role—as not being confined to a clever combination of profit and avoidance. Wilson had brought to the presidency an expansive conception both of the role of the president and of the destiny of America, although in a distinguished scholarly career, he had rarely focused his attention to matters of foreign policy. At the same time, however, his intense religious feeling involved an ardent, demanding conception of American mission. He believed that America had a special dispensation, that it represented mankind's most advanced and enlightened achievement. It stood both within and apart from Western civilization, embodying the best of Western values and aspirations while remaining free from the venalities and corruptions of Europe. In seeking and achieving the presidency, Wilson had assumed that his principal task was the revitalization of American democracy and opportunity, the translation of its unique characteristics of Christian individualism and civic liberty into a new idiom that recognized the vast economic and social transformations of the post–Civil War era. As president, he pursued this mission energetically through reforms in the nation's tariff, regulatory, and banking structures and through his own eloquent calls for rededication and reform.

The European war posed a powerful, unanticipated challenge to Wilson's conception of America as an exemplar of political and moral virtue. A thoughtful student of the nation's past, he had recognized that a protracted continent-wide European war would have profound consequences for the United States, as the Napoleonic wars had had in the early nineteenth century. Wilson believed that as an emerging economic power and as the moral leader of the West, the United States would inevitably play a central role. Indeed, as the horror of the Great War intensified, he became increasingly convinced that as leader of the United States, he must use the growing importance of American resources to exert American leadership by negotiating an end to the killing. He felt this position should be used to help create a new international order, one based on reason and free intercourse and open and democratic relationships among nations. Suffusing these views was a very real, very deeply felt religious sensibility that, however arrogant or presumptuous it might seem to skeptics, actively and practically shaped the assumptions on which the president based his responses to the war.

Millions of Americans shared his belief in their country's special and even providential role in the world. But these ideas dictated no specific course of action. Many corporate leaders, for example, saw the war as an opportunity to expand American economic influence as European capital, needed to finance the war, retreated from undeveloped lands. Indeed, some spokesmen for America's economic elite waxed poetic in envisioning the opportunities, both economic and moral, that the war-bred breakdown in the world order promised. Thus, Willard Straight, an articulate and well-positioned advocate of aggressive U.S. efforts to take advantage of the war, believed that the expansion of American finance capitalism at the expense of European colonial powers could usher in a new golden age for the world. American enterprise, he insisted, was crucial in "helping China, for the better establishment of trade relations with South America . . . for international cooperation with backward countries . . . for more enlightenment at home and for higher commercial morality abroad." Straight, along with other influential supporters of former President Theodore Roosevelt, believed that trade with the Allies and exploitation of investment opportunities in underdeveloped lands offered the promise of nothing less than "a new political economy."[3]

But such effusions were not universal. Many Americans, including many members of Congress, no less convinced that their country was destined to exert moral and political leadership, drew precisely the opposite conclusions about war-related trade. Agrarian Democrats and middle-western Republican progressives had long coupled their critiques of domestic corporate hegemony with a denunciation of the munitions industry and its alleged role in fomenting international discord. Congressmen spoke of a "war trust" that had a vested interest in promoting conflict. Secretary of State William Jennings Bryan had long spoken out against munitions makers and advocates of military expansion and initially encouraged his legion of supporters in the Democratic Party to speak out against the trade in arms. Failure to embargo arms and munitions, declared Congressman Henry Vollmer of Iowa, would mark America "as the arch hypocrite among the nations . . . praying for peace . . . [while] furnishing the instruments of murder to one side only." Although Bryan himself opposed a congressional resolution in the fall of 1914 endorsing an arms embargo—in good part because agents of the German government were so clearly promoting it—there was widespread support for some sort of restriction on the munitions trade among newspaper editors and politicians.[4]

The debate over serving as a munitions supplier and financier of war was in many respects but a new chapter in a national debate dating back to at least the 1870s as to what sort of country the United States was to be. The swift rise of powerful corporations, the emergence of mass-production industries, and the relative decline of the individual autonomous producer in favor of the great industrialist and financial baron had triggered a wide-ranging, if not always clearly articulated, debate. Arguments about the locus of public authority, the relationship between powerful private corporations and the public weal, and the ways in which the local and regional elements in the national polity fit into the emerging corporate order dominated public discourse. Over the years, various groups had emerged to criticize the seemingly relentless drift of the republic toward vast accumulations of private economic power. The Greenbackers and the Knights of Labor in the 1880s, the Populists in the 1890s, and a wide variety of socialists and regionalists throughout the prewar period had opposed the corporatization and centralization of American economic life. Although rarely successful in electoral or programmatic terms, they kept alive a tradition of critical dissent and a sense that there remained real alternatives to monopolistic economic power and the systemic corruption of the political process by the wielders of wealth.

The America that witnessed the outbreak and rapid intensification of hostilities in Europe was a country in which this multifaceted debate remained vibrant. True, by the time Wilson took office in 1913, the grand alternative vision posited by the Populists twenty years earlier was no longer remotely plausible. No longer did leading elements in the labor movement put forth a different conception of political economy, as had been the case in the 1880s. But the character of the American political economy remained sharply contested, and in the 1912 campaign, all of the major presidential candidates, including the Socialist Eugene V. Debs, spoke pointedly and frequently about the ways in which the new economy might be subordinated to the public good through government intervention.

Those against the war trade drew upon these strands of dissent. For Republican Senator Robert La Follette of Wisconsin, Democratic Congressman Claude Kitchin of North Carolina, and for any number of lesser politicians, journalists, and clergymen, opposition to the enmeshment of American business in the Allied war machine was but the latest episode in the long struggle to tame the new economy and to make it serve the public interest. Americans, they believed, should turn away from Europe's madness. If European war interrupted normal trading patterns and thus brought temporary economic dislocation to America, a progressive government could help ordinary workers, farmers, consumers, and small businessmen. Enlightened government intervention, they believed, would achieve important progressive goals such as a more equal distribution of wealth, greater public regulation of business, and greater regional equity and balance in the economy. A progressive government would use the preoccupation of European powers as an opportunity to expand U.S. economic, diplomatic, and moral influence in Latin America and Asia, thus supplanting the corrupt and arrogant European empires and bringing victimized colonial peoples under the benign stewardship of the United States. In short, war in Europe did provide opportunities for Americans to prosper and to expand their influence, but these opportunities could only be realized by turning away from the arms trade and toward a more equitable and humane restructuring of America's political economy. So, declared reformer Basil Manly, schemes to encourage U.S. financing of armaments purchase were merely fronts for a "new imperialism," inevitably leading to "an aggressive foreign policy intended to protect every American dollar with a battleship and a regiment of soldiers." Even members of the financial community were distressed over the moral implications of U.S. financing and supply of the European bloodbath. Thus, in 1916, W. P. G. Harding, governor of the Federal Reserve Board, argued that the United States should use its decisive financial might to end, rather than prolong, the war, declaring, "The carnival of death and destruction has gone far enough and the United States should not act mindlessly to perpetuate it."[5]

All parties in this sporadic debate sought to influence the administration. President Wilson relied heavily on agrarian progressives in Congress, men who were reflexively distrustful of Wall Street. Until his resignation in June 1915, Secretary of State William Jennings Bryan articulated at the government's highest levels their concerns about the machinations of Big Business and Big Finance. Even after Bryan's departure, the president remained wary of leading financiers, many of whom helped to bankroll his political rivals in the Republican and Theodore Roosevelt–dominated Progressive Parties. Indeed, in his 1912 presidential campaign, Wilson had denounced involvement of the U.S. government in schemes of financial promotion in Asia and Latin America. Men such as Straight, who saw the war as an opportunity for the aggressive expansion of American influence through the vehicle of trade with (and increasingly, the financing of) the Allies, believed him an enemy of their long-term project.

For his part, Wilson understood both perspectives but embraced neither. His distrust of the bankers remained strong. At the same time, he rejected the approach urged by Bryan and the more vehement progressives. Implicitly, he drew a sharp distinction between a policy of nonintervention, which he believed that Bryan and his allies advanced, and his own policy of neutrality.

Wilson's America was firmly rooted in Western civilization. America was its exemplar, but America was also the inheritor of Europe's civilizing mission. Europe, it was true, had fallen victim to its chronic failings. This was now the decisive time in which America must seize the falling standard of European enlightenment and progress and save Europe from itself. America could only do this by sustaining its connection with Europe, by deepening and exploiting its importance to the old continent. America would be neutral insofar as taking sides in the deadly conflict that raged, but it would not be noninvolved. American would work ceaselessly to find some resolution to the war, to use its vast material and moral wealth to maneuver the warring countries first into a settlement of the war, then into a new peaceful, democratic world order.

Early in the war, neither Wilson nor his leading advisers actually thought consciously in these terms. True, as war broke out, the president issued a pro forma offer of mediation without expecting it to have any effect. At a press conference on August 3, 1914, shaken by the fatal illness of his wife, Ellen, he appeared remote and distracted. He affirmed his country's disinterestedness and pledged only that America "stands ready . . . to help the rest of the world" through its good offices. Yes, America stood above the battle, and in its very aloofness lay the possibility that it might eventually lead the warring countries to the bargaining table. But, as Wilson told an emissary sent in September to appraise the president of German outrages against Belgium, he as leader of a country "fortunately separated from the present struggle" could form no judgments or take no action in behalf or against any of the belligerents. He could only "pray God [that] very soon, this war will be over."[6]

Events in the first half of 1915, however, forced Wilson to formulate more concrete and definite policies. By January 1915, the economic relationships between American industrialists and bankers and the Allied governments had begun to assume vast dimensions. Allied purchases, at first chaotic and disorganized, soon became regularized through British arrangements with U.S. wholesalers, manufacturers, and most importantly, financial brokers. On January 15, 1915, the powerful American financial house J. P. Morgan and Company signed a Commercial Agency Agreement with the British government by which it entered into a wide range of purchasing and contracting arrangements with American firms in behalf of the United Kingdom. J. Pierpont Morgan's personal sympathies for the Allied cause were widely known—he had turned over his English estate for use as a military convalescent hospital—and soon House of Morgan officers were working directly with British military and financial experts on a wide range of manufacturing, transport, technical, and financial matters. One Morgan partner was assigned exclusively to keeping his British counterparts abreast of American political developments and serving as liaison between his Allied clients and the American government. Critics were quick to argue that this close enmeshment of the Allied war effort with private U.S. banking interests jeopardized the American government's claims to neutrality, although the president insisted that he remained as wary and critical of the financiers and corporate barons as in the past.

The *Lusitania* Crisis

But as the war moved toward its first anniversary, it was the other term in the economics-maritime rights axis of issues that most forcefully challenged the Wilson administration. On May 7, 1915, off the coast of Ireland, a torpedo launched by the German submarine *U-20* struck the huge British passenger liner *Lusitania*, with more than 2,000 passengers and crew aboard. The captain of the submarine later described what he saw moments after a huge explosion ripped through the liner when he peered at the stricken ship through the periscope: "It was the most terrible sight I have ever seen," Kapitanleutnant Walther Schwieger recalled. "The ship was sinking with unbelievable rapidity and there was a terrible panic on its decks. Desperate people ran helplessly up and down while men and women jumped into the water and tried to swim to empty overturned lifeboats." The German attack killed almost 1,200 people, among them 291 women and 94 children. For days afterward, their bodies washed up on the coast of southern Ireland. Among the dead were 128 U.S. citizens.

Naturally, the destruction of the *Lusitania* triggered a roar of protest. An Irish inquest jury charged the U-boat crew and its superiors in Germany "with the crime of wilful and wholesale murder." Newspapers and politicians denounced the Germans as barbarians, beasts, "baby killers." For their part, German political and naval leaders combined exculpatory justification and finger-pointing on the international scene with encouragement of the lionization of Captain Schwieger among the war-afflicted German populace.

And indeed in their defense, German officials could make telling points. After all, two weeks before the ship sailed from New York City, the German Embassy in Washington had published blunt warnings in all the city's newspapers, reminding passengers of the status of the waters surrounding Great Britain as a war zone. "Vessels flying the flag of Great Britain" the announcement had warned, "are liable to destruction . . . and . . . travelers sailing in the war zone on ships of Great Britain . . . do so at their own risk."[7] Moreover,

German officials declared, the violence and rapidity of the explosion caused by a single torpedo indicated strongly that the *Lusitania* was no innocent passenger ship but rather was carrying large supplies of munitions. More generally, German officials held that the illegal British "remote" blockade, which was already causing distress among the German people and entailed the wholesale violation of traditional neutral maritime rights, had made submarine warfare a necessity. Why had the American government permitted its citizens to travel into a war zone on a ship carrying munitions? Why, asked even many Americans, had the *Lusitania*'s captain ignored reports of U-boat sightings and acted in a manner seemingly oblivious to risk? Why had the Royal Navy not escorted the vulnerable liner in its passage through dangerous waters? Did not the obvious advantages accruing to the Allies with the sinking of the *Lusitania*, skeptics wondered, perhaps indicate that the British government may have hoped for such an incident?

The sinking of the *Lusitania* forced President Wilson and his advisers to confront the implications of their maritime policies. In several actions occurring before the sinking of the *Lusitania*, German U-boat and air attacks on both Allied and U.S. merchant vessels had killed several Americans, but the staggering loss of life involved in the sinking of this great passenger liner now necessitated a definitive American response. When Germany had announced the inauguration of a systematic submarine blockade of British waters, Wilson had warned that the United States would hold the German government to "strict accountability" for any violations of American rights. But what did "strict accountability" mean? Were American protests with reference to the conduct of submarine warfare commensurate with and parallel to U.S. objections to innovative British practices that also violated traditional neutral rights? Should protest against the German initiative be explicitly linked to calls for Britain to relax its interdiction of foodstuffs, loosen its control of neutral vessels, and forgo the *ruse de guerre* of flying neutral flags on its merchant ships? If the United States imposed "strict accountability" on the Germans, would it do likewise with respect to increasingly severe and high-handed British maritime measures? And what about the status of American citizens traveling as passengers or crew members on Allied merchantmen? Did "strict accountability" embrace them as well as those on American and other neutral commercial vessels?

During the ten weeks after the *Lusitania* episode, officials within the administration debated these issues. Secretary of State Bryan urged compromise and restraint, putting forth suggestion after suggestion designed to link response to *Lusitania* with efforts to persuade both the British and the Germans to forgo violation of traditional rights. The United States should, he believed, use its unique prestige and influence to persuade the British to abandon interdiction of foodstuffs and to place strict limits on its open-sea mine-laying operations even as the Germans were persuaded to curtail submarine operations. Bryan also proposed that the U.S. government issue an explicit warning to Americans to avoid travel on belligerent ships of any character, at least until an agreement had been hammered out.

Sympathetic to Bryan's intense antiwar feelings, Wilson nonetheless moved in a different direction. He insisted that if "strict accountability" meant anything, it meant that the German government must apologize for this heinous act, compensate American victims, and promise to avoid any similar outrage in the future. And it must do this independently of any action taken by the Allies. The United States would continue to pressure the British to modify their maritime policies and practices and the American government would continue to demand eventual compensation for cargoes illegally seized and ships wrongly detained. But the United States could not, Wilson believed, use 128 dead Americans as bargaining chips in protracted multilateral negotiations aimed at resolving the full range of maritime issues with all belligerents.

Wilson, backed vigorously by Department of State second-in-command Counselor Robert Lansing, made his position clear in three notes to the German government, issued on May 13, June 9, and July 21. The first affirmed the right of Americans to travel as passengers on merchant ships, demanded an explicit German disavowal of attacks on merchant ships, and called for a German pledge to abandon submarine warfare against commercial vessels, whatever flag they might fly. By its very nature, Wilson's note declared, submarine warfare constituted "a practice, the natural and necessary effect of which is to subject neutral nations and neutral persons to new and immeasurable risks" and must be terminated. In the second note, issued on June 9, Wilson waved aside German arguments that the British blockade was illegal, that the blockade was a cruel and even deadly attack on innocent civilians, and charges that the *Lusitania* was carrying munitions. The third American note of July 21 issued what amounted to an ultimatum, declaring that the United States would regard any subsequent sinkings as "deliberately unfriendly," which was diplomatic language that hinted strongly at a formal break in relations and perhaps eventual American belligerency against Germany. After failing to moderate the second note, Bryan resigned as secretary of state, thus removing from the administration the most forceful and prestigious voice favoring noninvention.[8]

The final episode in the *Lusitania* affair occurred on August 19. A U-boat torpedoed and sank the British merchant ship *Arabic*, resulting in the deaths of two Americans. The German government, while insisting on the legitimacy of its campaign against Allied shipping, quickly disavowed this sinking. It offered an indemnity and pledged to issue orders to submarine commanders to abandon unannounced attacks on merchant or passenger ships, thus implicitly agreeing to adhere to Wilson's stipulations. The reluctant German retreat, however, owed more to the peculiarities of the political and military situation in Germany than it did the eloquence of American protests or fear of U.S. reprisal. The German navy had only now begun to step up production of undersea craft capable of sustained open-sea warfare; it would take months to build a sufficient number of U-boats that could pose a serious threat to Allied lifelines. For the time being at least, avoidance of an open break with the United States was more important than inflicting marginal damage on Allied shipping.

As the first anniversary of the outbreak of war came and went, Americans could feel that their country had safely negotiated a perilous path. Although the *Lusitania* disaster had triggered widespread anti-German feeling and had increased demands for military preparedness and for direct confrontation with Germany, the government had seemingly forced an end to submarine attacks. Those who believed that a showdown with Germany was inevitable castigated the Wilson administration and a complacent citizenry for their lack of courage. Observed General Leonard Wood, a leading advocate of a tough line against the Germans, the government showed "Rotten spirit in the *Lusitania* matter." There was, he lamented, "Yellow spirit everywhere."[9] But most Americans hailed the resolution of the crisis. With Allied orders buoying employment, profits, and prosperity, the president's combination of resolution and patience seemed to be paying off. With little understanding of the inner deliberations of the German government and no knowledge of the frantic pace of U-boat construction taking place in the shipyards of Hamburg, Bremerhaven, and Kiel, the American people could continue to deplore the killing while prospering from the war.

TWO

~

War, Peace, War
1915–1917

In the nineteen months following the *Arabic* pledge, the Wilson administration continued to attempt to accommodate the desire of Americans to combine economic gain with nonbelligerency. Pressures mounted, however, to increase U.S. military and naval strength. At the same time, Woodrow Wilson continued to insist that America had an obligation to use its moral standing and diplomatic leadership to end the war. Particularly after his reelection in November 1916, the president renewed his attempts to lead Europe toward his cherished goal of "peace without victory." In the end, however, combining rigid definitions of America's maritime rights, heavy involvement in the Allied war trade, and nonbelligerency proved impossible. The escalating horror of the combat, the peculiar character of the military stalemate gripping Europe, and the determination of the belligerents to achieve decisive military victory frustrated these hopes. Early in 1917, the German government resumed submarine warfare in an effort to break the Allied blockade. In a matter of a few weeks during the winter of 1916–17, seemingly promising prospects of U.S.-led peace efforts gave way to a break in diplomatic relations with the German Empire. On April 2, 1917, Wilson asked Congress for a declaration of war.

Europe's Agony

By the spring of 1916, expectations of a quick, decisive war seemed a distant memory. A British explorer who had spent the previous two years isolated in the Antarctic asked the first of his fellow countrymen he encountered, "when was the war over?" "The war is not over," he was told. "Millions are being killed. Europe is mad."[1] On the Western Front, about two million British, French, and Belgian troops faced a roughly equal number of Germans across "no man's land," the desolate, shell-pocked terrain separating the two lines of trenches, sometimes less than a mile apart. To the east, vast but ill-equipped and ill-led Russian armies confronted German and Austro-Hungarian forces in a war more mobile but hardly less lethal. In February 1915, the British, relying heavily on Australian and New Zealand troops, launched an ill-prepared and dismally led amphibious assault against Central Powers ally Turkey on the Gallipoli Peninsula in Asia Minor. They hoped to open up southern supply lines to Russia and break the deadlock on the Western Front by attacking through the Central Powers' supposedly vulnerable underside. In April 1915, Italy joined the Allies, but hopes for a decisive breakthrough against Germany's Austro-Hungarian allies quickly collapsed in the mountains of southern Austria and northern Italy.

On the Western Front, the war grew ever more gruesome. Improvements in artillery and the proliferation of machine guns made offensive warfare a bloody business indeed. In February 1916, nearly a million German troops, supported by more than 2,000 heavy guns, assaulted French lines centering on the ancient fortress city of Verdun. In a battle that turned the surrounding countryside into a hellish landscape of ruin and death, French and German soldiers killed each other with a ferocity and hopelessness that soon turned the very name "Verdun" into a metaphor for the futility of modern combat. On July 1, in an effort to take the pressure off the beleaguered French, British commander Sir Douglas Haig hurled his partially trained and newly recruited mass army forward in a futile and protracted attempt to pierce heavily fortified German lines along the River Somme in northeastern France.

The toll of dead and wounded in these and dozens of other encounters soon reached astounding numbers. Some estimates put the number of French dead in the Battle of the Frontiers in the summer of 1914 at nearly 400,000. The Gallipoli campaign, which dragged on through most of 1915, cost the Allies 46,000 dead and another 200,000 wounded and missing, while at least 90,000 Turks died defending their homeland. In the ten months' struggle for Verdun, the Germans and the French lost more than 200,000. At the Somme, despite a seven-day bombardment that expended more than a million shells, Haig's forces were met with a hurricane of machine gun and artillery fire. On the first day of the five-month battle, 60,000 British and Empire soldiers fell, 20,000 of them killed, most within hours of going over the top. As the war ground on, month after month, death and suffering began to seem almost routine. On an average day, the war claimed the lives of 492 British soldiers, 852 Frenchmen, and more than 1,100 Germans. Moreover, the number of German civilian deaths attributable to the Allied blockade mounted steadily: well over 200 daily in 1915, more than 300 in 1916, and nearly 700 in 1917.

The horrific nature of the war hardened hearts and caused belligerents to demonize their enemies. Moreover, the peculiar disposition of forces on the Western Front also made peace unlikely, for by 1915–16 the two sides in the west seemed evenly matched. But two key additional factors militated against negotiated settlement: Allied belief in their long-term superiority, and German occupation of large parts of France and Belgium.

Any peace initiative would have to deal with a reality that combined German territorial gains and long-range Allied advantages. Allied leaders, able to draw on colonial manpower and on the enormous resources of the United States and the British Empire, believed that time was on their side. With the British blockade literally beginning to starve the German civilian population, they believed, it was only a matter of time before Germany and Austria-Hungary yielded. But meanwhile, of course, the Germans were in control of virtually all of Belgium and about one-fifth of France. In addition, the Germans continued to hold Alsace and Lorraine, taken from France forty-five years earlier. No French government could accept a settlement that left Alsace and Lorraine in German hands, much less one that ceded additional territory. At the same time, no German government could possibly conclude a peace that failed to include permanent territorial concessions and perhaps even complete subordination of Belgium to Germany. Why should the Germans give up what French and British armies had been unable to defend or take back?

The Growing American Stake

As deadly combat ground remorselessly on, the American economic involvement in the war deepened. As early as October 1914, the British government had ordered 400,000 rifles from American manufacturers. The signing in January 1915 of the Commercial Agency Agreement between the House of Morgan and the British government spurred intimate cooperation between Allied ordnance and technical experts and American munitions and arms makers, with Morgan representatives serving as conduits and facilitators. Morgan created an export department, headed by business executive Edward R. Stettinius, which oversaw contract arrangements between the Allies and the American suppliers. From 1915 to early 1917, Stettinius and his staff entered into more than 4,000 prime contracts on behalf of Allied governments, organized subcontractors, and in general closely scrutinized the financial and managerial aspects of Allied purchases. Meanwhile, Allied experts advised American manufacturers in the building of new factories and retooling of their operations. British inspectors now patrolled American plants, ensuring that manufacturing specifications were met, and traveled with shipments of munitions and weapons to East Coast ports to oversee security. Indeed, in 1916 when the British experienced difficulty in getting shipments of rifles and ammunition on time from Winchester and Remington, the House of Morgan helped to engineer a secret deal in which the British assumed de facto ownership of some American arms facilities.

The scope of these arrangements was staggering. Between January 1915 and April 1917, Morgan bought more than $3 billion worth of goods for the Allies. Under the Commercial Agency Agreement, Morgan soon became the world's largest single purchaser of goods, about 60 percent of which were arms and munitions and the remainder foodstuffs, raw materials, chemicals, machine tools, and similar items. By the time of the Battle of the Somme in July 1916, U.S. firms were supplying Britain with three-quarters of its light artillery shells. By the spring of 1917, U.S. plants were manufacturing more than 15,000 British and Russian rifles daily and had developed the capacity to produce machine guns, artillery shells, small arms cartridges, and gunpowder for the Allies on a staggering scale.

Purchases of these dimensions, of course, cost vast sums. To pay for weapons and munitions, the British liquidated overseas investments and sent gold to the United States. Morgan and other financiers extended commercial credit to the Allies, with Morgan by 1917 actually carrying nearly a half-billion dollars of only loosely secured British debt under the heading of "short-term" loans. In 1915, Morgan, along with other bankers, persuaded the American government that public subscription loans, wherein the financial houses would float unsecured loans to the general investing public in behalf of the Allies, did not violate the spirit of American neutrality. By the spring of 1917, the British had borrowed more than $2.7 billion in this fashion. And indeed by the fall of 1916, when British Treasury officials conducted a formal assessment of the economic and financial aspects of the war effort, they came to somber conclusions. The British, and hence the Allies generally, were irrevocably dependent on the United States both for munitions and other supplies and, most importantly, for the financial wherewithal with which to conduct the war. "Without American supplies," writes historian Paul Koistinen in summarizing their findings, "Britain could not continue the war; without American financing of almost $10 million a day . . . Britain would exhaust its reserves of gold and securities by March 1917. Its dependence was total. Cutting back procurement . . . would produce disaster in England."[2]

This trade in munitions and war supplies was, of course, extremely profitable for American manufacturers and provided high-wage jobs for tens of thousands of workers. Morgan and other banking and financial interests profited immensely from handling the purchasing and financing transactions. Reflexively pro-Allies and accustomed to intimate business and personal relations with British officials and financial leaders, American bankers also pursued both short- and long-term business goals. Most obviously, the arms trade and the financing of it was lucrative, although by the latter part of 1916, bankers and investors began to have second thoughts about lending vast sums to governments that might lose the war and perhaps prove unable to make good on their war-incurred debts.

In the longer-range view, however, corporate and financial leaders perceived in Allied dependency an exciting opening for U.S. world financial and economic leadership. American bankers and construction companies filled the void in areas formerly dominated by British interests, financing and carrying forth the construction of railroads, utilities, and industrial plants left uncompleted as British capital flowed out of these areas to finance the war effort. In November 1915, industrial and financial leaders founded the American International Corporation (AIC), which was designed to supplant the warring European colonial powers as a source of goods and capital in the underdeveloped areas of the world. That same year, the Investment Bankers' Association of America urged that the country "not lose the opportunity now offered to become a creditor instead of a debtor nation, and thus broaden the scope of our financial usefulness and interests the world over." Declared U.S. banking leader Frank Vanderlip of New York's National City Bank, "We have an opportunity now to become the wellspring of capital for the world," and a press account of AIC aims observed that Europeans were liquidating assets in undeveloped places and "In the control of these properties an immense opportunity exists for the new American enterprise."[3] In short, American supply and financing of the Allies, important in the short run for producing profits, high commodity prices, and employment, also promoted the long-run success, and indeed the hegemony, of the American economy.

President Wilson and his advisers understood these facts of economic and financial life and shared many of the assumptions and concerns of bankers and industrialists. Certainly, Wilson and Secretary of the Treasury William Gibbs McAdoo—who was also Wilson's son-in-law—appreciated that the war trade buoyed American prosperity. By the summer of 1915, for example, McAdoo, initially suspicious of public subscription loans to the Allies, had swung completely around and now urged the president to endorse a half-billion dollar loan that Morgan was floating in behalf of the British. "To maintain our prosperity, we must finance it. Otherwise, it may stop and that would be disastrous," he said.[4] Moreover, the president appreciated that the expansion of American finance at the expense of British interests could create the opportunity for a new American-led world order. American wealth would be used to dissolve the restrictive trade policies of the colonial powers and pave the way for open markets, which, Wilson believed, would inevitably be linked to free political institutions and a more peaceful world. The United States could use the war trade, paradoxically, as the lever to pry apart the old imperialistic order, reduce the artificial trade barriers that led to military and naval rivalry, and facilitate the wholesome commercial and moral leadership of the United States. Convinced that an Allied economic conference in June 1916, ostensibly held to facilitate the war effort, was in fact a thinly disguised effort to lay the basis for the postwar revival of British financial and commercial global influence at the expense of the United States, Wilson and his advisers were determined to use America's economic and financial power to resist efforts to revive the prewar power structure.

Sharing the broad perspective of financial leaders, Wilson by no means approved of the specifics of their activities. Banking and financial interests, he believed, merited close scrutiny. Under his Republican predecessors, they had too often and too successfully sought to use the government to advance their narrow interests. His domestic reform measures, notably the Underwood Tariff of 1913, the Clayton Anti-Trust Act of 1914, and the Federal Trade Commission Act of the same year, were premised on the need for federal monitoring and control of corporate and financial elites. Moreover, in his determination to meet the requirements of neutrality with respect to the war itself, Wilson was uneasy about the legitimacy of large-scale financial support of the Allies through private American loans. In 1915, he had rejected McAdoo's advice to lend explicit support for the 1915 Allied loan, and in the fall of 1916, at a time when the British financial situation was approaching crisis, he helped draft a widely publicized statement warning against overextension of credits to belligerents. Clearly, in Wilson's view, regardless of the outcome of the war, U.S. financial and economic dominance in the postwar world was assured. Overindulgence of the Allies through profligate American loans could only compromise his effort to assert the moral and political influence necessary for America to lead in ending the war and building a better postwar world.

The growing enmeshment of the American economy did not translate directly into uncritical support or sympathy for the Allies within the government. Wilson kept his options open, benefiting from the prosperity that the war trade and war financing brought, eager to exploit opportunities to expand U.S. economic interests and moral and political influence around the world, yet determined not to allow short-term economic considerations to dictate his policies. By late 1916, no one could doubt that the American economy was a prime asset to the Allied war effort—in a world war that consumed enormous resources, maritime power Britain could hardly fail to benefit disproportionately. But it was Wilson's vision of an American-led new world order, rather than any direct economic imperative, that drove U.S. policy.

Preparing for the Worst

War in Europe triggered an intense debate within the United States about the need to build America's military and naval strength. Many Americans believed that protracted conflict in Europe had created a dangerous world and that the United States, with its dynamic economy and extensive international trade, needed to bolster its armed forces. Patriotic organizations, military leaders, and security-minded publicists urged increased military appropriations, a larger army, and a more energetic and professional military establishment. Critics of military enhancement, however, were also active. A variety of religious, progressive, labor, and reform groups and individual supporters held that the lesson of the war was precisely opposite that which preparedness advocates put forth. In a world gone berserk, they believed, it was essential that the United States resist militarism. To do otherwise, declared editor Oswald Garrison Villard, would "deprive the world of the one great beacon-light of a nation unarmed and unafraid."[5]

A variety of overlapping groups and people pressed the case for "preparedness." Army and navy officers, sympathizers with the Allies, people who believed that an increasingly global economic and political environment required greater military capability, and those who believed that expanded military training would provide needed discipline among America's allegedly hedonistic and polyglot population, joined to press for expansion of the armed forces. These men and women worked through organizations such as the Navy League and the newly formed National Security League to advance their cause. The Preparedness movement boasted the support of prominent politicians, business and financial leaders, journalists, and well-known attorneys and publicists. Former President Theodore Roosevelt was the nation's foremost champion of an expanded military, producing a steady barrage of speeches and magazine articles urging the military cause and savaging those who raised doubts. Elihu Root and Henry L. Stimson, former secretaries of war, vocally lent themselves to the cause as well, and in New York, Chicago, and other large cities, business and civic leaders, professional men and women, and members of patriotic societies joined together to promote Preparedness. Local branches of the U.S. Chamber of Commerce participated enthusiastically in Preparedness activities. Army and navy officers, of course, saw in the world war an opportunity to press their claims for enlargement. Newspapers climbed on the bandwagon. Effective British propaganda depicting Germany as barbaric and inhumane, along with the dramatic exposure of several clumsy German espionage capers in the United States, further fueled the demand for expanded military readiness.

By the spring of 1916, Preparedness fever raged everywhere. In May, 135,000 supporters marched down New York's Fifth Avenue in a procession that lasted twelve hours. On June 3, 350,000 marchers in ten cities also took to the streets, 130,000 of them in Chicago, where telephone operators clad in red, white, and blue formed a moving American flag and the city's playground directors goose-stepped down State Street.

The case for Preparedness rested only in part on concerns about the physical security of the United States. A chamber of commerce spokesman declared that military training would aid in disciplining a selfish and inefficient work force; it would "take up this slack of idleness in the industrial field and substitute a period of helpful discipline for a period of demoralizing freedom from restraint." A common military experience would cure the working class of labor militancy and teach unruly immigrants the stern lessons of patriotic Americanism. Military service, declared one advocate, would "yank the hyphen out of America," and the *Chicago Tribune* predicted that it would "reduce the criminal rate, produce a higher type of manhood, and level class distinction."[6]

Nor were such views confined to employers and conservatives. Progressive journalist Ray Stannard Baker, no Wall Street stooge, found the street scene in large cities repellent, with "common people rolling carelessly and extravagantly up and down . . . in automobiles, crowding insipid 'movie' shows . . . drinking unutterable hogsheads of sickly sweet drinks or eating decorated ice cream at candy shows and drug stores!" Clearly, he felt, there was "Too much money, too easily had, too much pleasure, not earned," and Americans desperately needed the discipline and sense of purpose that Europeans were finding in their grim, but ennobling, struggle.[7]

Military men, business leaders, and journalists believed that the European war was toughening America's commercial rivals and inuring their populations to sacrifice and competitive struggle. Ignorant of the actual nature of the German war effort, in which a combination of mindless authoritarianism and fierce class and regional antagonism produced waste, inconsistency, and mounting domestic tension, Theodore Roosevelt and his militant followers combined fear and hatred of Germany with admiration for its reputed qualities of vigor and organization. One observer of the Preparedness phenomenon remarked, "I feel that those persons who most loudly curse Germany are most anxious that we should follow her lead."[8]

The drive for military preparedness took many forms. After the *Lusitania* sinking, a group of young New York lawyers and businessmen, most with Ivy League connections, launched a widely publicized effort to promote military training for private citizens, offering themselves as exemplars of patriotic leadership. Grenville Clark, a young Harvard-educated Wall Street lawyer, along with such luminaries as Elihu Root Jr., the son of the former secretary of war, and Theodore Roosevelt Jr., were outraged by what they deemed the weakness of President Wilson's response to German provocations and by his failure to promote military expansion. They soon enlisted the support of General Leonard Wood, one of the army's senior commanders and a controversial critic of the administration, in arranging for a special training camp for businessmen that was designed to inculcate military habits, familiarize potential officers drawn from the business and social elite with military life, and generally highlight the need for a trained and ready officer corps. The New York group secured use of a training camp in Plattsburg, New York, and in August 1915 sent its first contingent upstate to train under U.S. Army officers.

The "Plattsburg movement," as it became known, quickly caught on. The New York camp received extensive publicity, for among the initial 1,300 participants were the mayor and police commissioner of New York City, Harvard's football coach, and prominent businessmen, clergymen, and writers. For five weeks, trainees lived in tents, mastered the rudiments of drill and parade, and eventually fought mock battles against regular troops. The New York program inspired similar camps in California and Illinois, and by the fall of 1916, more than 16,000 men had trained in these encampments. Because of the origins of the Plattsburg movement and the money and time required for participation, the great majority of those involved were well-to-do, although General Wood and the camps' organizers did make some gestures toward recruiting a few lower-income men. Through 1916, the graduates of the camps joined eagerly in the national debate over Preparedness, lending their influential voices to the call for military expansion.

On one level a patriotic and public-spirited enterprise, the Plattsburg movement seemed to critics in the Wilson administration and among antiwar activists to have questionable and perhaps even sinister overtones. A Wilsonbashing speech by Theodore Roosevelt to the first Plattsburg contingent plunged the movement unwittingly into partisan politics. General Wood regarded the would-be officers as "a voice to the slumbering people of the country," and Clark, the young lawyer whose efforts had launched the Plattsburg movement, believed that he and his elite enthusiasts were "strengthening the nation internally against internal forces making for weakness and lack of national unity."[9] To their detractors, however, they were a self-appointed, undemocratic elite, playing soldier while assuming the right of the upper crust to exercise social control over their inferiors.

Nor was criticism of Preparedness confined to barbed references to the Plattsburgers. The national experience as perceived by millions of Americans did not privilege the claims of "national defense" or "preparedness." Quite the opposite, for distaste ran deep for strong central government and for the high taxes and coercive powers implied by military aggrandizement and conscription, especially among rural dwellers who comprised half the nation's population. Energetic and vocal labor, women's rights, and religious and reform groups regarded the military and its predominantly elitist and corporate supporters with suspicion. Millions of immigrants had fled conscription in their native lands, and the leader of the nation's largest trade union was "unalterably opposed" to military expansion, which, he believed, inevitably "means war." At the other end of the social scale, millionaire reformer Amos Pinchot issued a scathing attack on conscription, which he characterized as "a great commercial policy; a carefully devised weapon that the exploiters are forging for their own protection at home, and in the interest of American financial imperialism abroad." A variety of peace organizations mobilized to oppose Preparedness. Influential members of Congress vehemently opposed the expense of military and naval expansion dear to the hearts of Preparedness advocates. Thus declared Mississippi Congressman Percy E. Quin, no large professional standing army was needed, for "When our country really needs soldiers to defend it, millions of patriots will rush to arms and rally to the flag."[10]

The American Union Against Militarism (AUAM), which developed an impressive grass-roots campaign in opposition to Preparedness in the spring and summer of 1916, was the largest and most nationally prominent of many organized expressions of antimilitary sentiment. It distributed pamphlets, collaborated with antimilitary legislators, held forums, and used the press to spread its views. AUAM speakers toured the Middle West, addressing thousands of people, many of them working class. Imaginative as well as earnest, AUAM publicists concocted from papier-mâché a huge dinosaur that they named Jingo, using it, along with a trained parrot named General Wood, which repeatedly screamed "Preparedness!" to warm up audiences. The high-point of AUAM efforts came in May 1916, when Wilson received a delegation of its leaders in the White House, although they left disappointed at his unwillingness to endorse their views.[11]

Advocates of naval preparedness encountered less opposition than did those who stressed enhancement of the army. "[T]here is not the same controversy about the navy that there is about the army," Wilson observed. "The navy is obvious and easily understood." After all, it was American naval officer-historian Alfred Thayer Mahan who in the 1890s had written so persuasively about "the influence of sea power on history." America's extensive coastline, its newly acquired colonial possessions, and its growing involvement in international trade, to say nothing of the maritime character of the tensions it faced with both Britain and Germany, made naval enlargement popular. Already ranking among world leaders, the U.S. Navy had largely kept abreast of the rapidly emerging new naval technologies that were transforming sea power, even if it had not matched the rapid expansion of the British and German navies in the immediate prewar decade. A naval buildup would be relatively cheap, because manpower requirements for a modern navy were much lower than a comparable buildup of ground forces would entail. On February 3, 1916, President Wilson himself, now a grudging convert to some form of preparedness, highlighted the role of the navy, calling for building "incomparably the greatest navy in the world." In August 1916, Congress appropriated funds for the construction of new battleships as part of a three-year building program that was designed to enable the U.S. Navy to face any rival on at least equal terms.[12]

Expansion of the army, however, was a different matter. The United States had never maintained a large standing army in peacetime. After the Civil War, the role of the army had been largely one of patrolling the Indian frontier, which meant that relatively few troops were needed and those that were rarely had the occasion to operate in large integrated units. Unlike the European powers, the United States had no system of mass recruitment and no trained reserve. The country relied on state National Guard units for emergency duty, but these bodies were notoriously ill equipped, ill trained, and subject to political influence. In 1914, the U.S. Army was ranked by most experts at no better than nineteenth in the world in terms of size and capability. Its performance in the short Spanish-American War of 1898 had left much to be desired. Subsequent reforms had only marginally improved the army's antiquated systems of training, command, and supply. Voluntary recruitment was difficult and expensive. The U.S. Military Academy at West Point enjoyed a good reputation, but the glacial pace of promotion drove ambitious young officers out of the army. Difficulty in sustaining a cadre of capable officers in turn made any prospect of raising and training a mass army doubly problematic.

In the spring and summer of 1916, a frustrating campaign along the Mexican border revealed vividly the shortcomings of the army and especially of the National Guard. In March, President Wilson dispatched troops to protect Americans from raids by Mexican rebels under the command of a daring leader, "Pancho" Villa. In May and June, the president mobilized 110,000 National Guardsmen to augment the regulars as General John J. "Black Jack" Pershing crossed the Rio Grande and throughout the summer tried to track down Villa and his elusive guerrilla band in northern Mexico. This fruitless campaign exposed the army's inadequacies in its largest military engagement since the Spanish-American War. The performance of the National Guard units was particularly discouraging, as these undermanned outfits soon proved to be ill trained and poorly equipped, less a ready reserve than a grumbling and weakly coordinated patchwork of disparate state units. German observers in Mexico duly noted the army's problems, and policymakers in Berlin had additional reason to believe that if they did expand submarine warfare, the United States would be in no position to add significant military strength to the Allies.

The army's weakness was, of course, troubling, but was it a cause for particular alarm now? After all, even in 1916—perhaps especially in 1916—it was hard to specify exactly how a larger army would enhance the security of the United States. After all, Europeans were unlikely to break off fighting each other and mount an amphibious assault on Long Island. Perhaps because American journalists and other overseas observers failed to convey a realistic sense of the chaos and human devastation on the Western Front, proponents of army enlargement projected images of bold, confident European armies lusting after complacent America's wealth and plenty. They painted lurid pictures of massive ocean-borne attacks or forays up the Mississippi by battle-hardened, yet somehow unbloodied, enemies. In a 1915 book, for example, popular writer Hudson Maxim conjured up visions of 100,000 soldiers of vaguely specified foreign origin marching across the country while "our wives and our daughters and our sweethearts would be commandeered to supply the women" for them.[13] But in fact, by any rational measure, the very scope and intensity of the European war would appear to have reduced rather than increased the never-plausible likelihood of foreign invasion.

Much of the congressional skepticism about increasing the size of the army had to do with the cost. Owing in part to the higher standard of living and in part to the disrepute of the military, it was well over twice as expensive per soldier to recruit and maintain an army here than it was in Europe. America had never faced peacetime conscription, and it was impossible to generate popular enthusiasm for such a drastic step, especially since there seemed to be no remotely plausible threat to the physical security of the country. As one business newspaper observed, it was true that anything *might* happen: marauding enemies might storm the New Jersey coast and a volcano might cover Staten Island with molten lava. But neither seemed likely.

Through the first half of 1916, legislation to expand and modernize the army wound its way through the labyrinthine congressional legislative process. Wilson, although aware that he could not face reelection in 1916 without endorsing some enhancement of military capability, rejected ambitious plans for the creation of a massive new Continental Army, in part because he believed that powerful military buildup would compromise his efforts to broker a negotiated end to the war. In the end, army supporters had to settle for a modest gradual increase in the army's size over a five-year period, along with improvements in the funding and administration of the National Guard.

Wilson played a crucial role in the debate over Preparedness. Alarmed by jingoistic sentiments after the *Lusitania* sinking, he had at first sought to downplay the military aspects of emerging American policy, stressing instead the country's status as the one power that had not given in to war hysteria. In a speech a few days after the sinking, he even told an audience of 15,000 in Philadelphia, "There is such a thing as a man being too proud to fight. There is such a thing as a nation being so right that it does not need to convince others by force that it is right." He quickly qualified these sentiments, but despite his disavowals, they did indicate the gulf that separated him from an increasingly vociferous prowar faction. Moreover, although accepting the need to improve the nation's military posture, he rejected the plan of his secretary of war, Lindley M. Garrison, for the creation of a new Continental Army and in February 1916 replaced him with a fellow progressive with strong antiwar leanings, Newton D. Baker.

At the same time, however, with the fall election never far from his mind, Wilson did respond to concerns about military and naval policy. Early in 1916, he embarked on a speaking tour through the Midwest, endorsing naval expansion and supporting military reform. In May, sporting a jaunty straw boater hat and clasping an American flag, the president marched in New York's gigantic Preparedness parade. He worked with congressional leaders, including leading Democrats opposed to virtually any military expansion, for passage early in June of the Dick Act. This legislation instituted reforms in the administration of the army and in its relation to the National Guard and called for the eventual authorization of a threefold increase in the army's 1914 manpower levels. At the same time, however, Wilson rejected ambitious plans for the creation of a new reserve force of half a million men.

Indeed, Wilson handled the Preparedness issue shrewdly. His program of moderate army reform both muted calls for vast military expansion and appeased many congressional opponents of military expansion. Although the AUM delegation that met with Wilson felt that his support for the Dick Act indicated that he had caved in to militarist sentiment, in reality this legislation forestalled the sort of massive military buildup many Preparedness supporters urged. Whereas early in 1916 it seemed that Preparedness would be the key issue in the presidential campaign, by the fall, both parties were reduced to intoning generalities lest they be accused either of lack of patriotism or military adventurism. Meanwhile, the president aligned himself with the popular cause of naval power and succeeded in marginalizing both military enthusiasts and uncompromising pacifists, thus neatly removing national defense from contention during the close electoral campaign.

Reelection

Throughout most of 1916, Wilson combined efforts to ease diplomatic tensions with both sides, promote a peace settlement, and gain reelection. The most frequent maritime controversies actually involved British actions and not German U-boat attacks. Britain's increasingly restrictive (and patently illegal) blockade, as well as its arrogant imposition of a blacklist against American firms that traded, however indirectly, with Germany, led in the summer of 1916 to angry American protest and even at times to dark musings about the possibility of armed confrontation. In addition, the violent suppression by British troops of the Irish nationalists' abortive rising in March embittered thousands of Irish Americans, most of them loyal Democrats. "I am," Wilson declared in July, "I must admit, about at the end of my patience with Great Britain. . . . This blacklist business is the last straw." "Can we," he asked rhetorically, "any longer endure their intolerable course?"[14]

During the year and a half after the *Arabic* pledge, Germany adhered, however reluctantly, to its terms. This willingness to yield to American requirements had as much to do with German hopes for quick military victory and with awareness that the relatively small number of U-boats then available could not yet decisively affect Allied supply lines as it did with fear of American belligerency. For the time being, civilian leaders in Germany were able to counter the claims of naval leaders that the submarine was the key to victory, forestalling a break with the United States. However, even German leaders most determined to prevent American belligerency knew that the balance within the German government might shift quickly in favor of expanded submarine warfare.

But as early as February 1916, the fragility of the *Arabic* pledge became starkly apparent. The Germans, in ostensible retaliation over new British blockade measures, announced that after March 1, all armed enemy merchantmen would be sunk without warning. Because the Allies often disguised guns mounted on merchant ships and routinely masked their identities by flying neutral flags, the German announcement put all ships in the war zone and those aboard them, regardless of nationality, at risk.

This abrupt revocation of the *Arabic* pledge led to a sharp rift with the United States and revealed that division over maritime policy within the United States remained deep. Wilson responded to the new German policy with a stinging rebuke, holding that the United States could accept no unilateral changes in traditional maritime warfare, which did protect the rights of neutrals to travel on merchantmen of whatever status. To do so, he argued, would be to acquiesce in the diminishment of American rights under naked duress and would surely trigger ever bolder infringements. "Once accept a single abatement of right," he declared, "and many other humiliations would certainly follow." Critics in the United States challenged Wilson, arguing that the policy of the country could not be left in the hands of private citizens who foolishly insisted on traveling in the war zone. At the end of February, the House and the Senate both debated resolutions that would have warned citizens of the dangers of such travel and, in the case of the Senate measure, would have denied Americans so traveling of the protection of the U.S. government. Preliminary tallies showed strong support for these initiatives, but Wilson used party discipline and patronage to prevent votes on the more extreme Gore (Senate) Resolution and the milder McLemore (House) Resolution, which would have merely warned Americans of the dangers of traveling in the war zone. Stung by charges that he was attempting to provoke Germany, Wilson reaffirmed his commitment to keeping out of war: "In God's name," he expostulated to a congressional delegation, "could anyone have done more than I to show a desire for peace?"[15]

To those who charged that the administration was applying a double standard in its dealings with Britain and Germany, Wilson responded with a central distinction between the two sets of objectionable policies. German acts of submarine warfare killed people. British methods of interdiction, however high-handed and arbitrary, provided for the safety of passengers and crews and left disputes over the disposition of ships and their cargoes to eventual judicial determination and diplomatic negotiation. British policies often infuriated the president, and indeed in the fall of 1916, he declared that in view of the increasingly overbearing character of British maritime restrictions, "our relations with Britain were more strained than with Germany."[16] Although he admired British political culture, Wilson nonetheless regarded Britain as the linchpin of the traditional Europe-centered world order that generated the pathologies responsible for the carnage in Europe. Moreover, Wilson believed that Britain was using its maritime and naval supremacy not only to secure the defeat of Germany but to protect and even extend its long-range commercial and maritime preeminence. An Anglo-French economic conference in June 1916, held ostensibly to improve Allied economic mobilization, reinforced American fears that the British were already gearing up for postwar commercial and financial rivalry with the United States. In the long run, Wilson was convinced, worldwide British and American economic and financial interests would inevitably diverge. He further believed that the British Empire's subjects must one day achieve freedom and economic autonomy, inspired by the example of the United States.

But here and now, in the perilous world of 1915 and 1916, British policies, for all their arrogance and selfishness, were not incompatible with U.S. interests. And even more importantly, they were not lethal. For men of Wilson's background and sensibilities, nothing could be more dastardly than the calculated killing of civilians. Were British officials careless or even cynical in permitting the Lusitania to sail unprotected in a war zone? Perhaps, but in the final analysis, it was a German commander who fired the deadly torpedo and the German government that had given him his orders and praised his act. The savage warfare on the Western Front shattered many of the conventions of honorable combat. Wilson could do nothing about the airplanes that bombed cities or the poison gas that blinded or killed young soldiers. He could not prevent the ravaging of the countryside or protect the civilian populations of Belgium, Luxembourg, or northern France from German abuse. But he could use the moral and material weight of the United States to stop U-boats from sinking merchant vessels without warning. Obnoxious British maritime practices could be protested, adjudicated, and rectified, but there was no appeal from the deadly torpedo. Failure to use American influence to limit this horrific innovation in warfare would be to abdicate America's moral and legal responsibility.

Knowing that these arguments did not persuade all his critics but armed now with de facto congressional acquiescence in his policies, Wilson confronted the Germans directly when, on March 24, 1916, a U-boat sank the French steamer *Sussex*, whose victims included two Americans. On April 18, he issued an ultimatum: If Germany did not abandon its current methods of submarine warfare, the United States would sever diplomatic relations. Two weeks later, calculating that Germany did not yet possess a sufficient number of submarines with which to cripple the Allied war effort, the German government rescinded its order and backed down. On May 4, the Germans issued the *Sussex* pledge, which forswore attacks without warning on merchant and passenger ships.

This episode appeared to vindicate Wilson. Although critics argued that his categorical defense of private citizens' right to travel in war zones on armed ships stretched any reasonable definition of neutrality to the breaking point, the president insisted that the United States must uphold the full range of neutral rights. He pointed to the German retreat as evidence of the efficacy of his policy. During the rest of 1916, U-boats did sink some merchant vessels, with some loss of Americans' lives. However, the Germans claimed that these episodes were the result of foolish behavior on the part of the targeted ships or submarine commanders' errors of judgment and were not part of a concerted campaign. It was true that in the *Sussex* pledge, the Germans conditioned their willingness to bow to American demands with the stipulation that the British must stop their illegal blockading and interdiction policies. For its part, however, the Wilson administration, while separately protesting increasingly restrictive British policies, did not acknowledge this German qualification. Wilson refused to link German acquiescence to changes in Allied behavior. For the time being at least, this policy worked, and the submarine question remained largely a troublesome latent concern rather than an explosive source of contention.

This apparent vindication of his course served Wilson well as he sought a second term in the summer and fall of 1916. At the Democratic National Convention in June, platform speakers quickly discovered the strength of antiwar feeling among the party faithful. Keynote speaker Martin Glynn, former governor of Ohio, recited a long list of episodes from American history in which the nation had wisely refused to respond rashly to provocations. America, he intoned, had shown brave forbearance, just as President Wilson had done during the *Lusitania* and *Arabic* crises. The delegates erupted into cheers and forced him to repeat the answer to the rhetorical question he posed after recounting each historical episode. "What did America do?" he asked—and then provided the answer: "We did not go to war." The next day, the convention's permanent chairman, leather-lunged Senator Ollie James of Kentucky, fed the antiwar sentiment, orchestrating a reprise of the previous day's response. Thus was born Wilson's most effective slogan: "He kept us out of war!"[17] Democratic publicists and speakers repeated these words endlessly, contrasting the president's wise combination of prudent preparedness, articulate defense of American rights, and skillful diplomacy with the strident calls of militaristic extremists, whom they effectively, if unfairly, linked to the Republican candidate, Supreme Court Justice Charles Evans Hughes. Wilson's razor-thin victory in November was enough in his mind to validate his policies and to spur him to intensify his efforts to end the war through an American-brokered "peace without victory."

From the very start of the war, Wilson had put the United States forth as an agent of mediation. With the intensification of the fighting, he became increasingly convinced that the mindless killing and destruction were imperiling the very foundations of Western civilization and that his country—indeed, he himself—must play a crucial role in ending the killing and in rescuing the West. He sought repeatedly to maneuver the belligerents into American-sponsored negotiations, urging them to specify their minimal war aims, hoping that forthright stipulations about what each nation was fighting for would lead to a recognition of common ground and mutual give and take. He was convinced that virtually any meeting of the belligerents, however qualified or tentative, would trigger irresistible pressure on the part of the war-weary peoples of the belligerent countries to end the fighting.

During this period, Wilson undertook several initiatives, sometimes offering himself as mediator, sometimes simply calling on the belligerents to declare publicly their war aims. Of course, during his reelection campaign, the president reminded voters of his public efforts to bring about an end to the fighting, but several of his earlier initiatives were clouded in secrecy. On two occasions, believing that behind-the-scenes initiatives might be more effective in reaching European war leaders, he had sent his personal adviser and intimate confidant, Edward House, to Europe to serve as a go-between among the warring nations. However, although Europe's statesmen had listened politely to House and had piously proclaimed their desire to stop the bloodletting, the realities of the war undermined Wilson's hope that the war could be brought to a victoryless end.

Moreover, even House, who enjoyed Wilson's complete confidence, appeared to have misunderstood Wilson's genuine determination to maintain neutrality. During a trip to Europe in the winter of 1915–16, for example, House had quickly recognized the futility of American efforts to bring about "peace without victory." Indulging his own strongly Anglophile views, he had promoted a complex plan in which the United States would cooperate with Allied statesmen to isolate Germany, after which America would join the war on the Allied side. Indeed, in February 1916, at the height of the renewed submarine crisis with Germany, Wilson had even seemed to endorse this scheme, although not before he had effectively nullified the critical promise of U.S. belligerency. In the end, this ill-conceived plan, embodied in the House–Grey Memorandum of February 22, 1916, like all previous U.S. proposals, failed to bring the warring parties to the conference table.

Actually, prospects for an American-facilitated "peace without victory" were even bleaker than House had suspected. Wilson believed that no truly vital issues divided the rival countries, that territorial questions were susceptible to compromise, and that moral responsibility for the start of the war was widely shared. Increasingly, however, military and political leaders of the belligerent countries rejected these premises root and branch. Even as House visited the rival capitals in 1915 and early 1916, German military leaders and industrialists were drafting plans for permanent control over Belgium and Luxembourg as well as retention not only of Alsace and Lorraine but of rich iron- and coal-producing regions in occupied France. They had even more far-reaching territorial and economic ambitions in eastern and central Europe at the expense of Russia.

Meanwhile, the various Allies had entered into secret treaties that also advanced bluntly acquisitive war aims. For example, upon German defeat, the British would gain control of several of its African colonies. France would regain Alsace and Lorraine along with strategic areas along the Rhine River, as well as colonial territories. By the terms of the treaties, Russia and new ally Romania were to receive vast accretions of territory at the expense of Turkey and Austria-Hungary, and upon its entry into the war, Italy was promised gains in the Tyrol and Adriatic at the expense of Austria-Hungary. Attainment of these war aims—which could not be publicly declared—depended solely on military victory. And even if by some magic these agreements were to disappear, the French and Belgians were determined to force the Germans to pay the staggering costs that the destruction in the occupied territories wrought.

Although the House–Grey Memorandum appeared to be pro-Allied, British Foreign Secretary Edward Grey never sought to activate it by calling publicly for an American peace initiative. British and French expectations of military breakthrough remained strong. Moreover, the Allies actually were not then anxious to encourage the formal involvement of the United States in the war, either as belligerent or mediator. The British were satisfied for the time being with using America for munitions and supplies while denying these things to their enemies. Over the quarter-century before the outbreak of war, Britain's seemingly secure dominance in world trade and financial services had come under challenge, from bumptious America no less than from arrogant Germany. Would not the price of overt American participation in the war, even as a mediator, be American commercial, diplomatic, and financial dominance? How secure could the British Empire be in a world order in which naive but dangerous Wilsonian principles of national self-determination and equality of commercial opportunity held sway? The French were no less determined to keep the meddling Americans from interfering with their goal of root-and-branch destruction of German military power. Moreover, it was not entirely clear that Germany *would* reject calls for a conference. The Allied leaders' suspicion that perhaps Wilson's belief that virtually *any* conference would snowball into a mass popular insistence on peace without victory may have been well founded. They were loath to gamble, especially in view of their growing, if misplaced, military optimism. Thus, Allied leaders had plunged into the bloodletting of the ghastly summer of 1916 rather than follow this confused and ambiguous American initiative.

Last Chance for Peace

Wilson's election victory in November, along with the failure of the warring nations to break the bloody stalemate in 1916, encouraged the president to make a renewed effort to end the war. Perhaps now, after the staggering losses on both sides at Verdun and on the Somme, and after the naval Battle of Jutland in May and June had reconfirmed Britain's control of the high seas, the warring governments could be made to see the futility of further conflict. Convinced that the protraction of the war both imperiled Euro-American civilization and made eventual American belligerency ever more likely, Wilson was determined now to bring the adversaries to the conference table. He spent much of his time in the weeks after the election typing out drafts of a peace note, which he made public on December 18.

Over the next month, Wilson weighed the belligerents' responses. The Germans quickly endorsed his call for a conference, although their official communication bristled so aggressively with assertions of military dominance and insistence on Allied concessions that it seemed calculated to forestall rather than to facilitate negotiations. Early in January 1917, the joint Allied response was even more discouraging, rejecting out of hand Wilson's plea for a brokered peace and virtually calling for the overthrow of the German government as a precondition for talks. Wilson's December 18 note, seeking to find common ground on which to bring the warring countries together, had implied that the causes of the war lay in misunderstanding rather than calculation. The two sides, he believed, shared basic moral values that could provide a basis for settlement. But the Allied leaders had convinced themselves that Germany was evil incarnate and that their struggle was a holy crusade. They bridled at Wilson's even-handed allocation of blame for the start of the war and his implication of moral equivalency between the beleaguered Allies, on the one hand, and the savage Huns who had enslaved Belgium, on the other. Sir Robert Cecil, Britain's blockade minister, said that anything short of military victory "would leave the world at the mercy of the most arrogant and bloodiest tyranny that had ever been organized." It was Germany alone that had "murderously assaulted" European civilization. The Allies had to destroy German power "or . . . perish in the effort."[18] Wilson's Anglophile ambassador to Britain, Walter Hines Page, and even the secretary of state, Robert Lansing, stiffened British resolve to resist Wilson's initiatives, privately endorsing such bitter-end sentiments in communications with Allied officials.

His December initiative having failed, Wilson resolved to appeal over the heads of the governments of the belligerents directly to the peoples of the warring countries. He believed that so desperate was the hunger for peace among the populations of the combatants that an American appeal might compel their leaders to accede to his call for negotiations. And once at the conference table, he believed, the war leaders could not escape without arranging for an end to the killing lest their own people rise in protest.

Nor were Wilson's hopes entirely without foundation. Signs of war weariness appeared everywhere in the belligerent countries. The British, desperate for soldiers, were about to launch conscription in Ireland, an act sure to rekindle civil disorder there. Meanwhile, the French manpower reserves were practically exhausted and signs of disaffection were seeping into the army. In Germany, a combination of increasingly high-handed military leadership and strong socialist and trade union political influence were creating an increasingly volatile domestic situation. The British blockade caused massive hardship while the German economic effort faltered. Efforts to draft French and Belgian civilians for work in Germany triggered international protest and ended in logistical chaos. If Russia ever found a way to maximize its vast manpower and economic resources, the long-range situation of the Central Powers could be bleak indeed. Meanwhile, British (and hence Allied) dependence on American financing of war purchases mounted daily, giving substance to Wilson's periodic hints that he might attempt to use this dependency to force the Allies into negotiations.

On January 22, 1917, Wilson addressed a joint session of Congress, passionately pressing the American demand for "peace without victory." Any other outcome, he declared, would mean "a victor's terms imposed on the vanquished. It would be accepted [only] in humiliation," leaving "a bitter memory." Such a settlement "would rest . . . upon quicksand." With respect to the causes of the war and arrangements for territorial and financial matters, Wilson was silent. He did not mention German occupation of Belgium and northern France, nor did the speech touch upon the terms of the secret treaties among the Allies. It said nothing about reparations that occupying powers might be called upon to make. Rather, it sketched the broad concerns that Wilson believed had to be addressed if a settlement of the current hostilities was to lay the groundwork for lasting peace. He called for an end to military and economic alliances, for the limitation of armaments, for untrammeled freedom of the seas, and for the right of all peoples to choose the governments under which they would live. And he called for a "covenant of cooperative peace," an international organization that alone could foster and ensure "an organized common peace."[19]

It was a speech at once breathtaking in the audacity of its vision of a new world order and curiously detached from the bitter realities of Europe's battlefields. It was in essence an appeal not to the warring governments for any concrete program involving negotiations but rather to a broader, more amorphous international public. It invoked a new international order without hinting at how the war might be ended. In effect, Wilson was gambling that his vision would be so powerful and so convincing that the warring countries, each suffering from increasingly severe internal strains, must respond to the American initiative.

Perhaps Wilson intended that this broad outline of the results of a peace conference would be a stimulus to actual arrangements for talks. Having seemingly compelled the Germans to limit submarine warfare, perhaps now he could use America's commercial and financial power to bend the Allies to his purposes. Everything hinged on getting the belligerents to the conference table. There his leadership and his vision could bypass boundary disputes, silence recriminations over responsibility for the war's start, and sidetrack demands for reparations. By giving the war-weary masses an eloquent voice, Wilson could almost literally force the jaded statesmen into ending the fighting. Implicit in his speech was the notion, abhorrent to both sides, that the conflict was actually a kind of inter-European civil war whose causes and conduct were now irrelevant. The sacrifices of the living and the vindication of the dead, he implied, would lay not in territorial conquest or revenge against the enemy but rather in the creation of a new structure of peace and progress.

Whether Wilson could have followed this eloquent but abstract call for "peace without victory" with detailed efforts to bring the warring sides together—and thus to create the fluid situation that he believed would enable his leadership to work—remained moot. By January 1917 even the most obdurate British officials were growing despondent over the extent of their reliance on the United States. Declared a secret high-level British report in October 1916, "With respect to food, raw materials, steel, American supplies are so necessary to us that [American] reprisals [against British maritime restrictions] . . . would . . . practically stop the war." Declared British Treasury adviser John Maynard Keynes, "The sums which this country will require to borrow in the United States . . . are so enormous . . . that . . . in a few months' time the American executive and the American public will be in a position to dictate to this country on matters that affect us more dearly than [they do] them."[20] Might this British vulnerability have compelled the Allies to agree to talks? Would Wilson, who, after all, had okayed the pro-Allied (though now defunct) House–Grey Memorandum, actually use America's economic power and thereby perhaps incur the risk of German victory?

But in any event, Wilson never had to face these choices or to follow his high-minded appeal with detailed proposals for a conference. In public, the Germans had been marginally more responsive to his calls for a negotiated end to the war. But with German troops occupying Belgium, Luxembourg, and northern France, and with Germany and its allies having recently driven Romania from the war, the German government remained committed to military victory even as its diplomats encouraged talk of a presidential peace initiative. German shipyards had been turning out U-boats at a remarkable rate; by the end of 1916, more than one hundred were available for ocean-going patrols, compared with a mere twenty-three vessels, most of them unfit for rigorous service, that were in use when the war started. The military high command, dominated by de facto generalissimo Erich Ludendorff, became persuaded that only by unleashing the U-boats could Germany achieve victory, gain its basic territorial demands, and restore hope among the beleaguered German populace. On January 8–9, 1917, Ludendorff joined naval leaders in pressing the Kaiser to endorse a new program to achieve military victory. With the British economy overburdened and with French manpower reserves depleted, abandoning the *Sussex* pledge would unleash the U-boats and gain victory. The Americans, the German command acknowledged, would probably declare war on Germany, but it was difficult to see how the United States could supply more war matériel and financial aid to the Allies as a belligerent than it was already doing as a so-called neutral. True, the U.S. Navy would bolster Britain's submarine defenses, but the tiny U.S. Army provided no immediate manpower gain for the Allies, and by the time an American force could be raised, trained, and transported to Europe—itself, a risky and time-consuming operation—the German army would have beaten the demoralized and ill-supplied Allied forces in Europe. Indeed, to the extent that the Americans would need arms and munitions to supply their own forces, American belligerency might actually reduce the flow of military goods across the Atlantic.

If unrestricted submarine warfare were not authorized, Ludendorff implied, the suffering German population might crack under the brutal strain of the British blockade. The German people would turn against their leaders for failing to use the most potent available weapon to ease their distress and bring the war to a victorious conclusion. In vain, German Chancellor Theobald von Bethmann-Hollweg protested that assessments of the submarines' impact were grossly inflated and that American belligerency would mean the death knell, not only of the German cause but of the German Empire itself. For almost two years, he had held submarine enthusiasts at bay, but now he bowed to the claims of military and naval leaders. The campaign of unrestricted submarine warfare was to begin no later than February 1, 1917. Thus, even as Wilson prepared and then delivered his appeal for peace without victory, the U-boats were being fueled and armed, poised to strike at the Allies' maritime jugular. Late in the afternoon of January 31, 1917, Count Johann von Bernstorff, the German ambassador to the United States, delivered the proclamation of submarine warfare to U.S. Secretary of State Robert Lansing, who immediately advised Wilson to break diplomatic relations and seek a declaration of war.

And the War Came

Despite Germany's action, however, it took six weeks for the president to decide to ask Congress for war. During the first weeks of the new German policy, the absence of attacks on American merchantmen kept alive Wilson's hope that the announcement of unrestricted submarine warfare was a blustering threat rather than a lethal blueprint. Antiwar sentiment in America remained strong and Wilson still hoped to find a way to avoid belligerency. On February 3, 1917, he did sever diplomatic relations but continued to hope that the new German policy represented only a typically clumsy Teutonic effort to intimidate neutral shipping. In mid-February he authorized the arming of U.S. merchant ships, adopting thereby a policy of "armed neutrality." The dramatic release late in February of the "Zimmermann Telegram," outlining a secret German plot to encourage Mexico to join in a war on the United States with a view to reclaiming vast sections of the American Southwest, intensified anti-German feeling but failed to bring about an irrevocable decision for war. Even the sinking of three American ships, two of them without warning and with loss of American lives, on March 16–18 found the president still uncertain, even though these attacks demonstrated clearly that the German government had given its U-boat commanders a green light to wage war on U.S. merchant vessels.

Foremost in Wilson's mind were several broad, almost apocalyptical, concerns. It was imperative that the United States retain the moral authority and the practical capability of ending the war through mediation, forging a nonpunitive settlement, and erecting a new kind of democratic international order. American military involvement, he believed, would expand and protract the war, whereas the survival of Western world hegemony "rested largely on our ability to keep this country intact, as we would have to build up the nations ravaged by the war." Wilson saw America as the rescuer of Western, white civilization in a world increasingly threatened by a "yellow peril." He was convinced, he told his cabinet, that American belligerency would further discredit the West and undermine white hegemony in Asia. Repeatedly, in discussions with Lansing and in full cabinet meetings, Wilson referred darkly to America's duty to avoid belligerency to enable it to preserve "'white civilization' and its domination over the world." "He was willing to go to any lengths rather than to have the nation actually involved in the conflict," an impatient Lansing recorded after one meeting.[21]

In the end, however, Wilson chose war. The German declaration and implementation of unlimited submarine warfare went far beyond its earlier employment of the U-boat. At a climactic meeting on March 20, he found his cabinet united in the belief that the breaking of German pledges required a declaration of war. Armed neutrality, Wilson became convinced, merely delayed the inevitable. Failure to act now, he decided, would forfeit American influence. Negotiated settlement being impossible, America must now use its great economic and financial strength and perhaps even actualize its vast military potential to end the war and, more importantly, to enable it to play a leading role in a just and enduring postwar settlement. After the March 20 cabinet meeting, Wilson issued a call for a special session of Congress to meet on April 2. Several days later, he had legislation drafted to increase the size of the army. Naval installations were put on alert, leaves were canceled, and National Guard units were called to the colors. During the last week in

March, Wilson pounded away on his typewriter, attempting to find the combinations of words that would move a prosperous, secure nation to fierce belligerency.

Wilson understood the passions that modern warfare must unleash. He was a student of the Civil War and carried with him vivid memories of the gruesome aftermath of battle that he experienced as a child in Georgia. More than pre-August 1914 European statesmen and more than Theodore Roosevelt and other war enthusiasts, Wilson sensed something of the abject horror of the twentieth-century battlefield. He harbored no dreams of personal military glory, nor did he thrill to the beat of the drum and the cadence of marching soldiers. He regretted that the requirements of military mobilization would inevitably bolster the power and prestige of the large corporations that his prewar policies had sought to discipline. War meant the substitution of slogans for arguments, brute force for reasoned suasion. And indeed, Wilson himself had already begun to mobilize the emotions of the people in support of the government. As early as 1915, he had singled out German Americans as likely fomenters of disloyalty. "Such creatures of passion, disloyalty, and anarchy must be crushed out . . . the hand of our power should close over them at once."[22] Some of his advisers and confidants, perhaps projecting their own civil libertarian values onto him, detected in his anguished response to the crisis a foreboding that war would jeopardize precious individual liberties, but the president had already indicated his readiness to impose a stern and unforgiving patriotic orthodoxy.

In his war message of April 2, 1917, Wilson shelved any troubling thoughts and sought to convince the nation that duty to mankind and defense of national honor now required a declaration of war. It was not an easy task. The Germans had done nothing, after all, that threatened the physical security of the United States. Even recent German attacks on American vessels could seem remote and isolated episodes in the ongoing debate over the meaning of maritime neutrality in the unique context of modern warfare that had been raging since 1914. Moreover, Wilson's carefully nurtured image as a man of peace who had courageously stood against military hysteria made his conversion to war seem confusing and even suspicious. Was it not the president who in the wake of the egregious sinking of the *Lusitania* had spoken of a nation being "too proud to fight"? If war was not called for then, why was it imperative now? Although it was a foregone conclusion that Congress would honor his call for war, dozens of congressmen and some influential senators would oppose him. Beyond the formal vote, however, lay the problem of articulating a basis for belligerency, the need to establish a convincing case that would justify the appalling sacrifices that Wilson was calling on his fellow countrymen to make.

By all accounts, Wilson's speech was eloquent. Appearing on a rainy April evening before a joint session of Congress in the House chamber, with observers and journalists packing the galleries, the president laid out the case against the German Empire. In this thirty-six-minute speech, he devoted relatively little time to reviewing the maritime controversies and the sinkings that, after all, had precipitated the crisis of the spring of 1917. Rather, he stressed the militaristic character of the German government and the need to eliminate such a war-mongering autocracy. Repeatedly, he drew a distinction between the German people, whom he depicted as fellow victims of an arrogant government, and the bloodthirsty state under which they lived. Without endorsing the war aims of Britain, France, or Russia, he contrasted the broadly democratic character of the Allied governments with this German autocracy. The fact that once-autocratic Russia had just overthrown the czar and installed a regime pledged to democratic government strengthened his depiction of the war as a conflict between democracy and tyranny. Even so, Wilson stressed carefully that the United States entered into the conflict for its own, high-minded reasons, not as part of any formal alliance. To be sure, America would cooperate with the Allies, but the American people were not being asked to sacrifice so that Italy might acquire ports on the Adriatic or Britain obtain German colonies in Africa. "We have no selfish ends to serve," he declared. "We desire no conquest, no dominion."

If America had no material or territorial gains to pursue, then what were its citizens fighting for? Here Wilson cut loose from the specifics of U.S.–German disagreement and attempted to commit his countrymen to the creation of a new, American-led world order based on democratic principles. Wilson did not directly say so, but it was clear that victory would be defined not so much as the defeat of the German army as the destruction of the German regime. In effect, we would fight to overthrow a despotic and militarized government whose continued existence was incompatible with the establishment of a new democratic world order. We would fight, Wilson proclaimed amid a rising ovation, "to make the world safe for democracy."

Wilson closed with a sober and moving invocation of sacrifice and commitment. "It is a fearful thing to lead this great peaceful people into war," he intoned. "But the right is more precious than peace, and we shall fight for things which we have always carried dearest in our hearts." We would fight, he pledged, "for a universal dominion of right by such a concert of free peoples as shall bring peace and safety to all nations and make the world itself at last free." "The day has come," he concluded, "when America is privileged to spend her blood and her might for the principles that gave her birth. . . . God helping her, she can do no other."[23]

It was a moving and powerful speech. The House chamber erupted as cheering members of Congress and visitors leapt to their feet and waved American flags. Republican Senator Henry Cabot Lodge, a harsh critic of Wilson's earlier unwillingness to confront Germany, grasped his hand, declaring, "you have expressed in the loftiest manner possible the sentiments of the American people."[24] But in reality, Wilson's speech, for all its sober eloquence, evaded important questions and provided at best an uncertain basis for American participation in the war.

For example, the president's stress on the brutal and autocratic character of the German government raised questions about the wisdom of his policies over the previous two years. If the pathological character of the German state was truly the reason for American entry, why did Wilson take so long to recognize its irredeemable evil? Even in his sharpest protest notes demanding an end to submarine warfare, he had credited the German government with honorable intentions. If it was the very existence of Prussian militarism that imperiled the United States, was not Wilson admitting in effect that Roosevelt and other critics who had been arguing this very point since 1914 had been right and that he had been wrong all along? And if he had been wrong then, why should the American people assume that he was right now? If he now held that unannounced sinkings of merchant vessels was exposing the evil character of the German regime, had not the ruthlessness of the German occupation of Belgium in 1914 and the sinking of the *Lusitania* provided ample proof much earlier? Further, if it were true that America was to fight to achieve a transformed democratic world order, how did Wilson propose to bring about American participation in—much less leadership of—the new structure of world governance that alone could fulfill such a war aim?

Congressional critics such as Senators Robert La Follette of Wisconsin, George Norris of Nebraska, William Stone of Missouri, and others did not fail to raise these points. They suggested darkly that Wilson's sudden conversion to belligerency derived from the growing stake of the House of Morgan and other financial interests in the Allied cause. Were we not, Senator Norris asked, going to war "at the command of gold"? Others stressed the lack of actual threat to the United States, the dangers of military adventurism, and the desperate need of the United States to remain an island of nonbelligerent sanity in a world careening out of control.

Others challenged the very premises of Wilson's appeal to arms. The great problem of the twentieth century, African American leader W. E. B. Du Bois had declared a decade earlier, was the problem of the color line. Whether by outright physical control or hardly less effective economic hegemony, Europeans dominated vast areas of Asia, Africa, and Latin America. Clearly, a just world order such as that invoked by Wilson's war message could not simultaneously retain European domination and be truly democratic. Yet Wilson had repeatedly linked the desperate need to stop the fighting with the need to preserve Western world hegemony and to forestall ascension of the so-called colored races to leadership roles for which they were, in his view, unprepared. Moreover, even within the boundaries of the United States, Wilson was presiding over a blatantly racialized social and political order whose ruthlessly discriminatory character sharply intensified during his administration. By what verbal magic did the ruler of a colonial empire, the American president, turn a nation saturated in color discrimination at home and color dominance abroad into an exemplar of democracy?

Moreover, absent in Wilson's peace proposals of January or in his war message of April were references to economic matters. Apart from a general faith that free trade would spur benign economic development and undergird democratic international dealings, where was any consciousness of the brutal exploitation imposed on colored peoples by the "democratic" West? Wilson's utterances could be read as criticisms of the economic irrationality of colonialism, and it was true that under his leadership the United States had taken steps to prepare its one large colony, the Philippines, for eventual independence. But could the colonial subjects of the world, such as the people of the Belgian Congo or the Indian subcontinent suffering under direct European rule, or the masses in China or the peoples of Central and South America trapped in Western-imposed economic arrangements, see in Wilson's call for a new democratic structure of diplomacy anything more than new methods of colonial exploitation and control? The current war, Du Bois declared, reveals that "European civilization is now rushing furiously to its doom."[25] Was Wilson's bold new world order anything more than a desperate effort to prop it back up? Views such as Du Bois's, it is true, were not widely acknowledged in Wilson-era America, but anticolonial activists and Western radicals alike could see in the president's vision of a new world order the Americanization of traditional European economic and political hegemony rather than an end to racial and economic injustice.

Four days after his April 2 speech, Congress endorsed Wilson's call for war. In the House, Democratic Majority Leader Claude Kitchin of North Carolina broke with the president, as did Congress's only female member, Montana Representative Jeannette Rankin. In the Senate, a grief-stricken William Stone, chairman of the Senate Committee on Foreign Relations, concluded his speech by saying, "I shall vote against this mistake, to prevent which, God helping me, I would gladly lay down my life." But the vote was 82 to 6 in the Senate and 373 to 50 in the House. Declared editor Frank Cobb, "The old isolationism is finished. We are no longer aloof from Europe." Writing to a friend, the president acknowledged, "I never [before] felt the responsibilities of office more profoundly," but added, "there is a certain relief in having the task made concrete and definite." Indeed, the immediate task—the military defeat of Germany and its allies—was "concrete and definite," but what of the larger task, of building a new world order and defining an American role in it?[26]

THREE

~

Mobilizing for War
1917–1918

In mobilizing the American people for participation in world war, the government relied on a combination of voluntarism and coercion. It created a host of new agencies and bureaus, employed an army of clerks and secretaries, and intruded into virtually every area of private life. Congress passed sweeping legislation conscripting men into the armed forces and curbing political dissent. The federal government built shipyards and munitions plants and took over operation of the country's railroads. Legislation passed in August 1917 provided for the pegging of prices for wheat, cotton, and pork, the licensing of all large-scale producers and distributors of food, and the imposition of stiff jail sentences for a wide range of market transactions that were perfectly legal during peacetime. This law, the Lever Act, one newspaper declared, was "the most revolutionary measure ever enacted by an American Congress," and constituted virtual "state socialism," according to another.[1]

Despite its wide assumption of power, however, the government resorted more readily to voluntary methods of mobilization than it did to outright force. Military recruitment relied heavily on the willingness of men to step forward and register their eligibility for the draft. Throughout the war, industrial mobilization remained decentralized and was essentially voluntary. Patriotic appeals, negotiations with private parties, and massive publicity, rather than naked displays of power, characterized the U.S. war effort.

The actual pattern of American participation in the war pretty much reversed the expectations of President Woodrow Wilson and his advisers. At the outset of the war, Wilson hoped—indeed, expected—that the American contribution to German defeat would consist largely of supplying his co-belligerents with ever more generous financial credits and ever more bountiful shipments of munitions and war matériel. The U.S. Navy would bear the brunt of direct American armed participation. As late as November 1917,

Wilson clung to the hope of avoiding the dispatch of large contingents of U.S. troops to Europe. But events both in Europe and at home combined to confound these expectations. The American industrial and transport systems buckled under the strain of modern warfare even as a series of Allied disasters escalated the pressure to send American fighting men overseas. Thus, by the summer of 1918, more than one million American soldiers were actively involved in combat against Germany, but virtually all of their armor, artillery, transport, and airplanes were of British or French manufacture as were the majority of their machine guns. Even their rifles, although typically manufactured in the United States, were variations on the standard British design.

Making an Army

Shortly after Congress had declared war, one of Secretary of War Newton D. Baker's aides was testifying before the Senate Finance Committee as to the budgetary implications of American belligerency. After ticking off the expanded need for supplies and facilities, Major Palmer E. Pierce added that of course, "we may have to have an army in France." The committee chairman, Senator Thomas S. Martin of Virginia, looked up in amazement. "Good Lord!" he cried. "You're not going to send soldiers over there, are you?" But from the start of the U.S. involvement, America's new European partners had no doubt that they needed American troops, and plenty of them. French General Joseph Joffre, dispatched by his government to begin military liaison with the new belligerent, was blunt: "We want men, men, men."[2]

The measures that the Wilson administration employed to raise an army illustrated the mixture of coercion and persuasion that characterized the entire mobilization effort. Even before the declaration of war, Wilson had decided to employ conscription rather than voluntary enlistment to fill the ranks. In reaching this decision, he was influenced by both the experience of European belligerents, especially Great Britain, and ticklish domestic circumstances. At the outset of hostilities, the United Kingdom was the only one of the warring nations to rely on an all-volunteer army. But the staggering casualties of the early battles had decimated British forces. In addition, initial calls for volunteers had created chaos in war industries, as large numbers of skilled men, more useful as producers of weapons and munitions than as foot soldiers, enlisted. Thus, early in 1916, Parliament had passed legislation to authorize the country's first modern conscription, as much to ensure rational allocation of manpower as to fill the ranks, and Britain's example was not lost on American military planners.

Problematic traditions of volunteer-unit creation in the United States, as practiced during the Civil and Spanish-American Wars, also spurred quick adoption of conscription. In both these earlier conflicts, influential citizens had raised regiments on the basis of their own popularity or wealth or standing in the community, often gaining high military rank and exercising field command. The most famous recent example of elite-recruited troops was Theodore Roosevelt's raising and equipping of a regiment of "Rough Riders," a dashing cavalry unit that attracted massive publicity during the war with Spain in 1898. And now Roosevelt, an ex-president and an acerbic critic of Wilson, was loudly pressuring the government to authorize him to recruit an entire division or perhaps even two for service on the Western Front.

This was a bad idea by any measure. At best an enthusiastic amateur, Roosevelt would have been a disaster as leader of a 28,000-man division. The hoopla surrounding its establishment and outfitting would surely have disrupted more orderly recruitment. No, Wilson quickly decided, there would be no equivalent of the Rough Riders on the Western Front. As much as any single episode, the sharp rejection of Roosevelt's initiative and the prompt adoption of impersonal, bureaucratic methods of manpower mobilization dashed the notions of romantic knight errantry as the basis for military service.

But in opting for conscription, Wilson and his advisers were nonetheless mindful of the widespread suspicion of the federal government and of the military, as well as of the intense local parochialism of millions of their fellow citizens. Thus, the legislation submitted to Congress in April 1917 astutely placed responsibility for the actual drafting of men with some 4,648 local Selective Service boards composed of influential citizens, primarily business and civic leaders. In effect, these men would do the work of the Civil War–era influentials who had recruited and often privately outfitted regiments, but once they had selected the men to be drafted, these civilians would play no further role in the men's military service. The law, the Selective Service Act of 1917, as written in the office of the army's Judge Advocate General, removed the army itself—indeed, all direct agents of the federal government—from the thankless task of selecting specific men for the hazards and inconveniences of military duty, even as the national government tuned up its propaganda machine to encourage cooperation and honed its organs of enforcement and punishment to discourage resistance or noncompliance.

Conscription, however clothed with the mantle of local administration, was a drastic expedient. The country's last experience with the draft, during the Civil War, offered little grounds for optimism as to the degree of acceptance and compliance a citizenry unused to government coercion would award it. As many living people clearly recalled, the Union's draft law, shot through with loopholes, class-based deferments, and inept administration, had plunged the North into chaos in the summer of 1863, triggering the bloodiest and most destructive episode of urban insurrection in American history. In Congress, Speaker of the House James Beauchamp (Champ) Clark led the opposition to the law, declaring that to his fellow Missourians, "there is precious little difference between a conscript and a convict,"[3] although on May 18, with virtually unanimous Republican support in both chambers, the bill passed.

Wilson, Secretary of War Newton D. Baker, and military authorities defended the law as the only truly democratic method of raising an army. The president asserted that the draft was "in no sense a conscription of the unwilling." It was, in fact, a "selection from a nation which has volunteered in mass," and he characterized June 5, the day on which millions of young Americans were to come forward to register, as a "great day of patriotic devotion and obligation." Baker urged state and local officials and chambers of commerce to promote registration as an expression of exuberant patriotism.[4]

Baker and other military and civilian authorities had initially feared widespread resistance to the draft. After all, the America of 1917 was riven by class, ethnic, and ideological conflicts. In vast parts of the country, the only tangible evidence of the federal government was the local post office, and that was often merely a window in the general store. Because there was no danger of enemy invasion, authorities worried that the call to arms would reveal disloyalty, resistance, and even violent refusal to comply.

The actual response of the American people on June 5, a Tuesday, exceeded the most optimistic hopes of Baker and his military advisers. Amid hastily organized local festivities, parades, pageants, and processions, some ten million men between the ages of twenty-one and thirty came forward to register before more than 135,000 local board officials. From across the land, reports of enthusiastic and patriotic compliance flooded in. Ocala, Florida, was typical. Civic officials organized a parade of almost one thousand citizens. To the strains of "The Star Spangled Banner" and "Dixie," members of fraternal orders, women's clubs, and service organizations marched down Fort King Avenue, the black contingents following the whites. Particular highlights were "eighteen lovely young girls and matrons dressed in . . . regulation Red Cross costumes" and "the little boys of the primary department of the Ocala High School" performing complex military tactics to the delight of the crowd. There was no sign of dissent or resistance, as 503 Marion County men, equally divided between white and black, registered, though a disapproving reporter did note that the crowd's attention sometimes wandered in the Florida heat during the inspiring oratorical presentations.[5] The actual selection of draftees, launched with lottery drawings beginning on July 20, likewise met with overwhelming and even cheerful compliance.

Throughout the conflict, this structure of conscription served well. By the beginning of 1918, it became clear that initial troop projections had been far too low. The impending withdrawal of Russia from the war, the horrendous British losses in the fall of 1917 campaigns, the rout of the Italians in October 1917 at Caporetto, and the demoralized state of the French army made an enormous infusion of American troops imperative. In January 1918, Congress declared all men between the ages of eighteen and forty-five draft eligible and Selective Service boards were instructed to step up inductions. By the end of the war, almost 24 million men had been registered, more than 4 million were selected, and 2.8 million were inducted, more than 70 percent of them in 1918. It was still possible for men to volunteer, but only for service in existing regular or National Guard units or for service in the navy. In all, almost 4.5 million men served in the U.S. armed forces during the period of the Great War, with the army reaching a peak strength in France of more than 2 million men as the war ended.

The achievement of the administration and the response of the citizenry were remarkable. Even so, there was a dark underside to this largely successful experiment in army building. As many as three million men, 11 percent of the age-eligible pool, evaded the draft, most without penalty. Resistance flared in some places. In Oklahoma, posters in rural counties declared that this was a "Rich man's war [and a] Poor man's fight," and urged that "Now is the time to rebel against this war with German boys." Clashes between authorities and draft opponents there led to a dozen fatalities. In big-city immigrant enclaves, where political radicalism meshed with Old World hatred of militarism, police and self-appointed patriots assaulted antidraft demonstrators: "Soldiers Crack Slacker Heads in Street Row," headlined the *Chicago Tribune* on registration day. When the lottery numbers were drawn in July, the *New York Times* reported that "the majority of New Yorkers of conscript age" responded enthusiastically to their country's call, whereas "The grumblers and slackers kept quiet."[6]

Some men refused on religious or ethical grounds to serve in the armed forces. The authors of the Selective Service Act of 1917 made provision for those whose long-established religious beliefs forbade active military service, and Secretary of War Baker eventually broadened the permissible grounds for conscientious objector (CO) status to include those with "personal scruples against war." In fact, the vast majority of inductees initially claiming CO status eventually agreed to serve in arms-bearing capacities. The most famous case of conversion from religious pacifism to willingness to fight was that of Alvin C. York, an evangelical Protestant from Tennessee. He received kindly counsel from his superior officer and was given leave to return to his hometown to reflect on his initial decision to refuse to fight. Eventually convinced that bearing arms was not incompatible with his religious faith, York soon became an outstanding soldier, and on October 8, 1918, he single-handedly killed or captured more than 150 Germans in what French Marshal Ferdinand Foch called "the greatest thing accomplished by any private soldier of all the armies of Europe."[7] Not all who at first refused armed service received such considerate treatment; rather, they succumbed to powerful psychological pressure and even physical abuse. Many of them no doubt hoped that they would wind up in clerical, medical, or transport roles. In the end, more than 80 percent of the 20,000 men claiming CO status who were inducted through the draft boards agreed to serve under arms.

Those COs who did not often faced harsh and punitive treatment. About two-thirds of these men were willing to accept noncombatant army service or agreed to army-assigned civilian duty. Most of these men were put to work driving ambulances, serving as medical orderlies, or performing clerical duties. Others were "furloughed" by the army to do agricultural work.

Most of the 1,500 or so who refused absolutely to subject themselves to military discipline were imprisoned. Baker instructed that such men were to be segregated from the felonious members of the prison population and to be treated with "kindly consideration," but in reality, absolutist conscientious objectors frequently endured physical abuse. Some died in prison as a result of exposure to damp, unsanitary conditions and neglect of medical needs, and several committed suicide. At Fort Riley, Kansas, General Leonard Wood encouraged his officers to humiliate and abuse COs. When one launched a hunger strike in protest, Wood permitted him to be tortured and force fed. At nearby Fort Leavenworth, members of a Russian pacifist sect, who had come to the United States in the 1870s as a refuge from czarist conscription, were shackled, forced to stand for hours at a time, forbidden to read, write, or talk, and routinely abused by the guards. Occasionally, however, a CO got lucky. Thus, civil libertarian Roger Baldwin found that the New Jersey jail to which he was sent was presided over by an Irish American warden whose hatred for Great Britain caused him to look kindly on those such as Baldwin who refused to fight alongside it. About 500 absolutist COs were tried under military law, receiving punishments ranging from the death penalty (for 17 of them) to lengthy prison sentences. No one was actually executed, however, and within two years of the Armistice ending the fighting, all COs had been released. As

with other aspects of conscription, the short duration of active U.S. military involvement saved the country from having to test the limits of its tolerance. Although the actions of General Wood and other military authorities gave a frightening foretaste of what might lie in store for recalcitrant citizens, the war was over before such draconian measures took full force.

Certainly, in the summer of 1918, the stepped-up demand for ever more soldiers revealed the coercive reality behind the government's initial reliance on patriotic persuasion and citizen compliance. That summer, federal agents, in league with local law officers and citizen vigilantes, conducted widely publicized sweeps along city streets. They publicly humiliated men of apparent draft age dressed in civilian attire, especially those whose appearance and demeanor suggested working-class status.

Local Selective Service boards, ostensibly run by disinterested and impartial civic leaders, compiled a mixed record. They began with a built-in class and ethnic bias, for few ordinary working men, trade unionists, representatives of immigrant communities, or African Americans of any sort were selected to run them, nor, of course, were women appointed. Favoritism was less a function of personal interest than of reflexive class and/or ethnic predilection. Racial bias was particularly noticeable in the patterns of induction, especially in the South, where exemptions on occupational or hardship grounds were much more readily granted white registrants. Indeed, overall, about a third of black registrants were drafted, as compared with one in four of whites. The law exempted aliens, and in cities with large immigrant populations, resentment against them quickly spilled over into racist outrage. "While the flower of our neighborhood is being torn from their homes and loved ones," one inner-city board fulminated, aliens—"miserable specimens of humanity"—"remain smugly at home." Declared California Senator Hiram Johnson, "The draft law was being administered in such a fashion as to make it unfair, unequal, partial, and discriminatory."[8]

Despite these limitations, however, the system achieved its primary purpose, providing men for the army. Exemptions for those performing critical industrial and agricultural labor helped to mitigate class bias. Blacks may have been overselected but were less likely—again because of the prejudice that permeated both military and civilian circles—to be assigned to combat duty. The promise of expedited citizenship proceedings encouraged immigrants to register. Above all, the system did produce the critical mass of men needed to fill the ranks and to create, by mid-1918, a vast American military presence in Europe.

Even so, the efficacy of American-style Selective Service was never fully tested. Owing to the short duration of the American phase of the war, only about one-eighth of those registered actually served in the armed forces, a far lower proportion than that prevailing among the Continental belligerents. Americans served largely during a period of movement and triumph and were not called on to endure the rigors of trench warfare for extended periods. Whether America's relatively lax system could have functioned efficiently if confronted with the circumstances that faced the British, French, and German people for more than four years remained a question that mercifully needed no immediate answer. The aggressiveness of the "slacker" raids, the government's encouragement of vigilante action, and the emotional patriotism of even the most respectable newspapers provided a hint of the possibilities for brutality and infringement on personal liberties had a true manpower crisis developed.

Mobilizing the Economy

Mobilizing the economy proved more difficult than mobilizing manpower. For the duration of its participation, the United States failed to produce significant quantities of the weaponry and matériel needed for modern warfare. Hampered by indecision about what kind of gun to produce and by French reluctance to share information about their fabled "75" cannon, American arsenals and factories produced no usable field artillery, to say nothing of heavier ordnance. Despite Secretary of War Baker's announcement of a billion-dollar program of aircraft construction, U.S. factories built fewer than one-fifth of the planes flown by American pilots, with the vast majority of these useless in combat. American troops were entirely dependent on French and British tanks and never had enough of them. Before the war's abrupt end, American shipyards, despite the construction of massive new facilities, built few new merchantmen and fewer naval vessels. U.S. production of explosives and gunpowder lagged, with huge new facilities coming on line almost literally only as the guns fell silent in Europe.

A variety of factors lay behind these failures. In addition to the sheer magnitude of the task, military men, the Wilson administration, and industrial leaders contributed to the weak performance of the economy. The U.S. Army clung to archaic systems of procurement and weapons development even as the war raging in Europe rendered traditional tactical doctrines obsolete and introduced a whole new generation of armaments. Until at least January 1917, Wilson was focused on brokering an end to the war and regarded full-scale military planning as likely to undermine his diplomatic efforts. Business leaders promoted preparedness but resisted any hint of authoritative government direction of economic resources. During the war itself and for a generation afterward, participants in economic mobilization debated why the vaunted American industrial machine had performed so poorly. Few, however, disputed that it did fail to deliver.

The country never did develop a coordinated system of allocation, production, and procurement. Before the United States entered the war, Wilson only reluctantly embraced preparedness and indeed worried that enhancement of U.S. military power might send the wrong message to the European belligerents. Moreover, the president remained suspicious of the large industrial and financial enterprises that would inevitably dominate large-scale military production. Even after his military advisers recommended against it, the president continued to believe that production of weapons and munitions should be a government monopoly. Although Wilson and his chief advisers, Secretary of War Baker and Secretary of the Navy Josephus Daniels, did encourage private citizens in efforts to promote military–industrial cooperation before the United States entered the war, the administration avoided planning for mobilization of the country's industrial and scientific resources in the event of war.

Before the United States entered the war, Baker, like Wilson loath to contemplate large-scale dispatch of American troops to Europe, failed to prod the military to confront the requirements of modern warfare or to revamp its wasteful and inefficient procurement procedures, even after the *Lusitania* sinking in May 1915. Leonard Wood, former army chief of staff, did urge massive military upgrading, but he disapproved of the administration's peace-seeking efforts and was a confidant of Wilson's bitter political rival, Theodore Roosevelt. Even within the military establishment, Wood's was a singular voice, for the army clung to its decentralized and duplicative patterns of procurement and devoted little time or effort to weapons design. Military research and development was sporadic and ill funded, depending on inspired maverick officers and public-spirited inventors and entrepreneurs rather than on systematic assessment and development of military hardware. Because army manuals featured reliance on the rifleman as the key to the aggressive tactics they promoted, few officers looked systematically into the role of the tank, the machine gun, or the airplane, despite the lessons so abundantly available on the Western Front.*

Those who did attempt to apply the lessons of the European conflict to America usually thought in terms of repelling an invasion and not of sending

*For a fuller discussion of army doctrine, see below, pages 86, 87, 95, 98, 102.

two million men to France. Thus, in May 1915, the *New York Times* published an interview with fabled inventor Thomas Edison. Alarmed by the sinking of the *Lusitania*, Edison urged that an armada of submarines and surface ships be built, stocked, and held in coastal locales in readiness for activation in the event of attack. The army would train 40,000 drill sergeants and then fur-lough them to civilian occupations. When invasion impended, these men would train citizen volunteers, who would be rushed to the coast in thousands of commandeered private automobiles. Huge machines would dig as many as fifty lines of trenches for them to man. Government factories and arsenals would stockpile huge supplies of the most modern weapons and munitions ready for instant use. The great inventor, a popular folk hero widely credited with virtually occult powers, believed that "with our unlimited supply of the most intelligent and independently thinking individual fighters in the world, we would be invincible." And best of all, he believed, this program could be carried through on the cheap. Huge expenditures on standing armies were unnecessary.

Army officials refrained from commenting on the practicality of dispatch-ing millions of hastily trained volunteers in tens of thousands of Model T's to defend the Carolina coast, nor did the navy publicly call attention to the problems involved in maintaining vast fleets of ships in battle-ready condi-tion, presumably without full staffing or costly sea maneuvers. The feature of Edison's much-discussed interview that did prompt immediate action was his call for an inventory of industrial facilities capable of producing weapons and his suggestion for creation of a joint government–private consortium to receive and evaluate ideas for weaponry from private citizens. Edison believed that in a crisis, individual inventors such as himself would emerge to create the technological means by which any invader, no matter how powerful, would be repelled. "If any foreign power should seriously consider an attack upon this country," he predicted, "a hundred men of social training quickly would be at work here upon new means of repelling the invaders. I would be at it myself."[9]

Edison's statements invoked all the cherished national beliefs. They com-bined a reliance on individual genius, a commitment to patriotic citizen sol-diery, a faith in technology, and derogation of expensive standing armies and intrusive government. And they meshed with the perspectives of the presi-dent and his chief civilian advisers. In particular, Secretary of the Navy Daniels was intrigued, for here were the germs of a plan for preparedness that would undercut the warhawks and demonstrate the administration's concern for national defense while avoiding costly armaments. Later in the summer of 1915, Daniels met with Edison and worked with him to establish the Naval

Consulting Board (NCB), a nongovernment body charged with receiving and winnowing suggestions from private citizens that were designed to enhance safety at sea and better enable the U.S. Navy to defend America in the event of war. Serving on the board were representatives of national technical and engineering societies, most of them recently established organizations that reflected the growing role of technical expertise in industry and the determination of engineers to play an increasingly active and influential role in public life.

Although Edison and Daniels initially conceived of the NCB as a means of promoting defensive technologies consistent with the administration's determination to remain at peace, several of its members advanced more ambitious agendas. In particular, Howard Coffin, a Hudson Motors executive and president of the Society of Automotive Engineers, had long urged fellow industrialists to emulate their German counterparts by adopting common technical standards and eliminating waste and inefficiency. For all his envy of German efficiency, however, Coffin shared with many other business and professional leaders strong pro-Allied sympathies and believed that America would inevitably be drawn into the war on the side of Britain and France. In 1915, Coffin declared that "Twentieth-century warfare demands that the blood of the soldier must be mingled with from three to five parts of the sweat of the men in the factories, mills, mines, and fields of the nation in arms," adding that the war was "the greatest business proposition since time began."[10] For Coffin and others recruited onto it, the NCB provided an excellent opportunity to promote expanded business–military cooperation.

Throughout the period from late 1915 until the U.S. declaration of war in 1917, Coffin and other Preparedness advocates promoted the integration of American industrial capacity with its war-making needs. First through a subcommittee of the NCB called the Industrial Preparedness Committee (IPC) and then through the Council of National Defense (CND), which Congress created as a public body in the National Defense Act of June 1916, leading industrialists, engineers, medical men, and academics continued to press the case for readying American industry for the rigors of modern warfare. Of particular importance was the CND's Advisory Council consisting of business, labor, industrial, medical, and engineering leaders, among them Coffin. Starting in October 1916, the Advisory Council began a detailed inventory of the country's scientific and industrial resources, a project that Coffin had actually started earlier, using his personal funds, while serving on the NCB. This inventory was conducted to permit the government to plan needed military production and to acquaint manufacturers with the methods and tools that full-scale munitions development would entail. The CND also initiated an elaborate state and local network of advisory and information-gathering bodies, often working through local chambers of commerce.

In one sense, all this activity did represent an effort to anticipate and prepare for industrial mobilization. It certainly reflected a growing movement among business, professional, and government leaders to find ways of mutual collaboration in case of war. It reflected one significant strand of the Progressive era, the drive for efficiency combined with an effort to find the basis for harmonious relationships between private business and public authority, while shunting aside an equally significant theme of Progressive reform, the determination to curb corporate power and influence. Its elaborate state-and-local structure of organization, however, proved cumbersome and unrealistic, reflecting as it did older notions of how the economy functioned rather than the increasingly national operations of large-scale producers.

These pre-1917 activities also reflected the Wilson administration's efforts to project itself both as sincere seeker of peace and vigilant guardian of national defense. Preparedness advocates could find in the work of the CND, as in the less formal support of Daniels and Baker for the private efforts of Coffin and the others, evidence of the government's concern for national defense. At the same time, even the CND confined itself largely to fact-finding and inventorying, defendable as prudent precautions but hardly evidence of militarization of the economy. Had the United States not entered the war or had its participation been confined to naval action and financial support for the Allies, these measures might well have sufficed. But the vast demands of large-scale U.S. military participation quickly laid bare their inadequacy.

The inefficiency and traditionalism of the army and the War Department contributed to the procurement and supply problems. At the time of the declaration of war, the U.S. Army was a small, sclerotic operation, with a command structure and administrative organs reflecting its post–Civil War role as a subduer of the Indian tribes. Army leaders faced chronic problems of attempting to pry funds from a niggardly Congress and a citizenry that distrusted and feared the military. Acquisition of supplies remained divided among separate army bureaus, each of which curried favor with congressional patrons. The National Defense Act of 1916, partly in response to congressional suspicion of military aggrandizement, actually reduced the ability of the army's small general staff to oversee the ordinary activities of the army, including purchasing and weapons development. Secretary of War Baker, reflecting the decentralist perspectives of the Wilson administration, paid little heed to those officers who warned that the staggering demands of modern warfare would require the drastic upgrading of the general staff and centralized coordination of transport, supplies, and finances.

The contrast with the U.S. Navy is instructive. Dating back at least to the 1880s, the navy had enjoyed a relatively positive public reputation. Whereas the army drew controversial assignments, such as occupying the post–Civil War South, fighting Indians, breaking strikes, and suppressing insurrectionaries in the Philippines, the blue water navy proudly carried the national flag into foreign lands. Congress appropriated funds for modern warships with a generosity that the army's advocates could only envy. Even the Wilson administration, determined to keep the army on a short leash, supported new ship construction in the Naval Appropriations Act of 1916 on a comparatively lavish scale. As a result of its ongoing technological upgrading and its proportionately larger budgets, the navy had developed close and sympathetic relations with key suppliers. Moreover, the navy's relatively small manpower needs meant that a far larger proportion of its expenditures went for equipment and munitions, thus facilitating a more centralized and efficient system of procurement. Although hardly prepared for the kind of war that the growing importance of the U-boat heralded, the navy at least had a method in place for handling in a coherent fashion the new demands placed on it.

Not so with the army. Throughout at least the first year of American involvement, the transport, purchasing, and weapons procurement activities of the army proved a nightmare of overlapping efforts, duplication of functions, and lack of coordination. At the outbreak of war, the various army bureaus scrambled to buy up all sorts of goods, from rifles and bullets to canned vegetables to office furniture, that no doubt would soon be in short supply. The army's chief administrative officer quickly stockpiled more than twelve thousand typewriters, filling the basements of various government buildings. "There is going to be the greatest competition for typewriters around here," he declared, "and I have them all."[11]

During the first nine months of the war, the situation continued to deteriorate. One high-ranking army officer, stopping in June 1917 in Washington en route to France, observed the administrative chaos with amazement. "If we really have a great war," he predicted, "our War Department will quickly break down."[12] Out in the field, the situation was no better. Troops trained without weapons or even uniforms. Army bureaus and military chiefs bid against each other for supplies and equipment, unchecked by Baker. The CND had no formal authority to reform military procurement. Not until January 1918, when Baker had to withstand days of harsh congressional questioning, did the administration respond to what by then had become a true crisis in military production and procurement. The eventual passage of the Overman Act, on May 20, 1918, which gave the president theoretically sweeping powers to commandeer economic resources, along with a long-delayed shake-up in the army's central administration, began to put military production and allocation on a systematic basis.

Indeed, in the months following Baker's testimony, both the civilian and the military aspects of economic warfare began to improve. On the civilian side, a new federal agency growing out of the CND, the War Industries Board (WIB), had been struggling since its inception in July 1917 to streamline war-related manufacturing. WIB representatives, many of them supplied and paid by business organizations such as the U.S. Chamber of Commerce, could recommend, cajole, and publicize, but even after the passage of the Overman Act, they had no direct authority either to force industrialists to follow their advice or military procurement chiefs to agree to centralized coordination of orders. In March 1918, however, Wilson elevated Wall Street speculator Bernard M. Baruch, who had been serving as a member of the board, to its chairmanship, and Baruch brought energy and direction to the board in its efforts to gain overall coordination of the wartime economic effort.

Baruch soon proved an effective arm twister who used a combination of patriotic appeal, sympathetic understanding, and threats of direct government takeover to impel otherwise competitive firms toward government-led cooperation. Getting businessmen to agree to produce fewer and simpler models of consumer goods provided a relatively painless way to save matériel and transportation space. Changes in bicycle design, for example, saved an estimated 2,000 tons of steel. The agreement of shippers to use lighter and less bulky packaging materials freed up more than 17,000 freight cars. The simple expedient of getting thread manufacturers to agree to wind an additional 50 yards on each spool resulted in making 600 railroad cars available for other uses.

In general, however, Baruch's charm and persuasiveness worked best in industries that were vulnerable by virtue of their fragmentation or lack of coordinated political and economic influence to government's inducements and threats. When it came to the giants of the economy, such as steel and autos, Baruch sometimes talked tough, but invariably the WIB backed off from decisive showdowns. The administration was committed to an ideal of business–government collaboration and to avoidance of "Prussian" methods of economic coercion. And even under the Overman Act, the authority of the president actually to commandeer a given firm, much less a vast industry such as automobiles, was in question. When vehiclemakers balked at the WIB's appeal that they curtail passenger vehicle production, Baruch warned that if automakers resisted, "we've got to close the automobile industry." "You will take your medicine" in the form of denial of the materials they would need for car production, he promised. In reality, however, Baruch knew that he could not force the steelmakers to curtail shipments to Detroit or even rely on the railroads to cooperate in bringing the automakers in line. In the end, the WIB settled for relatively minor concessions from the automakers, who continued to produce passenger cars throughout the conflict. As was the case with the operation of the draft, the shortness of the duration of U.S. belligerency did not test the jerry-built structure of American mobilization to anything near its breaking point, and the American industrial machine was able to clatter along largely without centralized direction.[13]

One key sector of the economy, however, demanded more drastic measures. By the fall of 1917, chaos gripped the nation's railroads. Military bureaus and private manufacturers competed for storage space and freight cars, and the railroads' half-hearted gestures at private coordination soon proved catastrophically inadequate. Raging blizzards tore through the Middle West and, along with subzero temperatures, exacerbated transport difficulties and fuel shortages. Behind the railroad crisis lay the enormous demand for coal, which supplied more than 90 percent of the nation's industrial, commercial, and residential energy needs. Thousands of coal cars clogged tracks, sidings, and switching yards. As early as December 1917, thousands of unloaded cars jammed eastern freight terminals and sidings, and shortages of rolling stock left tons of fuel, food, and war supplies piling up in other parts of the country.

Even railroad officials called for federal intervention, although they opposed outright government operation. Initially, President Wilson's order on December 26 creating a United States Railroad Administration (USRA) charged with operating the rail network seemed to be a step in the direction of "war socialism," with the government taking direct control of key functions and facilities. Progressive reformers saw in federal operation an opportunity to rid the country of an inefficient and predatory private monopoly and to institute a scientifically designed program of efficient and public-spirited management. And it was true that under its director general, William G. McAdoo (who retained his post as secretary of the treasury), the USRA did what the railroads separately could not do. It consolidated terminal facilities, coordinated traffic and routing, dipped into the federal treasury to improve rolling stock and equipment, and satisfied the restless railroad unions with generous wage settlements. With the arrival of spring, the transport logjam broke, and by May 1918, the USRA was transporting an average of 625,000 troops a month on some 9,000 special trains in addition to meeting the intensified wartime industrial demands.

Even so, progressive hopes for permanent change in the ownership structure of the rail network were disappointed. In fact, from the outset, the Wilson administration made it clear that federal operation was strictly a wartime measure. The president promised rail executives that railroad profits would continue at prewar levels, and in March 1918, Congress passed the Federal Control Act requiring a rapid postwar return to private hands. Railroad executives actually provided the great bulk of the management of the USRA-run railroads. With the investigative and regulatory functions of both the federal Interstate Commerce Commission and state bodies curtailed during the war, the USRA was able to pay for its generous wage settlements and capital equipment purchases with record high freight-rate increases, gaining for the railroads revenue structures for which they had long, but unsuccessfully, lobbied. Thus, even in the case of the most drastic exercise of federal power in the economic realm, cooperation between business and government and incentive rather than coercion remained the central component of the Wilson administration's efforts.

No sectors of the economy better illustrated the pattern of heightened federal power, reliance on voluntary methods of inducement, and tub-thumping exhortation and patriotic appeal than agriculture and fuel. On August 10, 1917, Congress passed the Lever Act, which granted the president wide power to regulate supplies and prices of food and fuel, and created new agencies: the U.S. Food Administration and the U.S. Fuel Administration. Through the remainder of the war, Food Administrator Herbert Hoover and Fuel Administrator Harry Garfield worked to increase agricultural and coal production, eliminate hoarding and profiteering, encourage conservation, and regulate prices. Implicit in the legislation under which these agencies operated was the prospect of virtually unlimited power, to which the new federal agencies sometimes actually resorted. In response to the rail-coal crisis of 1917–18, for example, Garfield ordered the temporary closure of thousands of factories to free up coal cars and break transport bottlenecks in the Northeast.

On the whole, however, both men relied primarily on persuasion, manipulation, and indirect controls. Farmers throughout the Middle West were skeptical of U.S. entry into the war in any event, and Hoover believed, "Although Americans can be led to make great sacrifices, they do not like to be driven." Garfield's factory shutdown order had triggered a huge public outcry: "The Fuel Administration," declared the *New York Tribune*, "has lost its head." By the spring of 1918, however, the Fuel Administration, relying on hundreds of coal company managers recruited temporarily into government service, had devised effective plans for reducing interzone movement of coal. These plans relied on close cooperation between the federal body and coal operators who found in this sort of regulation at least temporary relief from the chronic boom-and-bust cycles of production and market glut normally characteristic of the soft coal industry.[14]

Even before the Lever Act, Hoover had been at work devising plans for the coordination of key agricultural commodities. Not only did the United States have to feed the vast new army it was creating, it also had to meet the increasingly desperate shortfalls in available food supplies that its war partners were facing. The collapse of Russia in the fall of 1917 all but eliminated a major Allied supplier. U-boat attacks claimed thousands of tons of British shipping, much of it carrying food and fiber. Poor growing conditions in America's heartland in 1916 and the summer of 1917 cut harvests of wheat by 8 percent in comparison with prewar averages. "Food will win the war," was the Food Administration's slogan, but of course the converse—the war could well be lost on the farms of America—was equally pertinent.

Hoover never issued the kind of compulsory directive to which Garfield had resorted in relieving the winter coal crisis. But along with the businessmen, publicists, academicians, and managers eager to serve under this engineer-cum-humanitarian, he did devise expedients that in their overall thrust amounted to federal compulsion. Hoover established a licensing system, denying farmers and middlemen direct access to overseas markets. He encouraged record wheat production by creating a government corporation that, in effect, required farmers to sell their product to it at a (high) pegged price. He worked with farm organizations and processing, banking, and commercial leaders to curb speculation in grain futures and to encourage stepped-up production and more efficient storage and transport of the bumper crops harvested in the summer of 1918. Hoover regarded the Food Administration's policy of working with and through these commercial and agricultural leaders as evidence of "grass roots" mobilization, but in effect they gave select people and enterprises—usually well established and influential before the war—the government's sanction in subordinating smaller farmers, processors, and banks to their interests.

Indeed, to many people, Hoover's reliance on "voluntary" compliance with Food Administration policies and plans masked the essentially compulsory nature of its actions. The de facto suspension of market forces placed the government in every wheat field, grain silo, and kitchen. Patriotic enthusiasts and public officials alike operated as if the Lever Act had given the government compulsory powers. "The Government has a definite program for war purposes on the food question," state and federal prosecutors in Indiana told suspected violators of Food Administration directives. "Are you for it, or against it?"[15]

Hoover's methods were least controversial in the area of conservation. By eating oatmeal instead of wheat cereal, by growing a vegetable garden, and by cleaning one's plate, citizens could feel themselves to be an integral part of the patriotic effort. A U.S. Food Administration card, distributed to millions of housewives, advised Americans to "Go back to simple food. . . . Pray hard, work hard, sleep hard, and play hard. Do it all courageously and cheerfully." Food Administration agents enlisted twenty million housewives to agree to keep a wary eye on neighbors and storekeepers who appeared not to be following the government's conservation and inflation-fighting rules. Hoover promoted meatless days, wheatless days, and other means of reducing food wastage. Posters, films, and placards relentlessly hammered home the message. U.S. Food Administration page fillers peppered women's and agricultural periodicals: "Food is sacred. . . . Wheatless days in America make sleepless nights in Germany. . . . If U fast U beat U boats. . . . Serve beans by all means."[16] Fuel Administrator Garfield was not far behind, mobilizing a vast army of volunteers to teach fellow citizens the virtues of saving fuel, using schoolchildren to distribute tags to be attached to the family coal shovel with fuel-saving tips, and restricting outdoor commercial lighting.

The combination of incentives and propaganda paid off in the form of greater production. Soft coal production surged upward, reaching record levels in 1918, and wheat production and resultant exports to the Allies, despite a crippling drought in the summer of 1918, expanded by nearly a third, although the food conservation program had at best mixed results. Even so, increased grain, meat, and coal production during the conflict laid the basis for crises of oversupply in both agriculture goods and coal after the war. Once the guns fell silent, Hoover found himself faced with the problem not of conserving scarce supplies and discouraging consumption but rather of disposing of the vast stockpiles of pork, lard, flour, and other commodities that his exhortations had helped to bring forth from America's farms. Meanwhile, wartime demand for soft coal brought marginal, low-efficiency mines into production, even as it spurred consumers to switch to oil burning. The sudden ending of the war returned the chronically volatile bituminous coal industry to chaotic prewar conditions, beginning a decade-long crisis of oversupply, bitter labor relations, and desperate poverty in many coal-mining regions.

Exhortation and public relations also played a central role in the Wilson administration's plans for financing the war effort. Throughout the period of American belligerency, fierce debate raged in Congress and in the country at large about how to pay for the war. Believing that the country had gone to war "at the command of gold," that is, to rescue bankers and financiers from the massive defaults that would inevitably follow Allied defeat, antiwar legislators, joined by colleagues who supported the war effort but believed that wartime conditions should be used to achieve Progressive and egalitarian ends, urged that at least half the staggering cost of the war be paid for through taxation. Congressional progressives, led by Senator Robert M. La Follette of Wisconsin, sought to impose steep taxes on corporate profits and the personal incomes of wealthy people, forcing the affluent to sacrifice heavily through the "conscription of wealth." Wartime taxation thus might blaze a trail toward more egalitarian public finance and toward a downward redistribution of wealth. Bankers and orthodox economists, however, countered that punitive corporate and excess-profit taxes would cause investors to divert funds into unproductive tax havens while disturbing the country's capital markets.

Initially, President Wilson and Secretary of the Treasury McAdoo appeared sympathetic with the progressives. In his war message Wilson called for a sharp increase in taxation, and a week after the declaration of war, McAdoo said that "fifty percent of the cost of War should be financed by" taxation. Tax legislation was notoriously contentious, and the plans of congressional leaders to impose high corporate and steeply graduated personal income taxes quickly became bogged down in the House and Senate Finance Committees. In truth, however, only steep regressive tax increases, impinging significantly on the buying power of millions of ordinary citizens, could have curtailed mass purchasing power, and this was a step that the administration, for perfectly understandable and even admirable political reasons, was unwilling to take. By the time the War Revenue Act became law in the fall of 1917, early estimates of the costs of the conflict had skyrocketed, making amendments to this law immediately necessary and even more protracted debate a certainty. Business, agricultural, financial, and labor representatives testified before congressional committees, simultaneously affirming their patriotism while explaining why it was really in the national interest to tax lightly their particular industry or activity. "Our endeavors to impose heavy war profit taxes," declared California Senator Hiram Johnson, "have brought into sharp relief the skin-deep dollar patriotism of some of those who have been loudest in declamations on war and in their demands for blood."[17]

McAdoo quickly realized that borrowing was both more expedient and more expeditious than taxation. Under his direction, the government launched a series of highly publicized and emotional "Liberty Loan" drives to encourage Americans to buy war bonds. McAdoo initially hoped that widespread citizen participation in war bond drives would dampen inflationary pressures. As ordinary people cut current consumption to buy Liberty bonds and stamps, demand for civilian goods would decline, thus helping to keep prices in check. In financing, then, just as in military recruitment and food and fuel conservation, this was to be a "people's war." McAdoo recruited movie stars and patriotic speakers to address monster rallies. He enlisted Boy Scouts in bond purchase schemes. "We went direct to the people," he recalled, "to businessmen, workmen, farmers, bankers, millionaires, school-teachers, laborers" with passionate patriotic appeals. Nor did McAdoo balk at pointing the finger of public scorn at those who did not participate. "A man who can't lend his government $1.25 per week at the rate of 4 percent interest," he proclaimed in the fall of 1917, "is not entitled to be an American citizen."[18] And in fact, response to the loan drives was impressive, as each was oversubscribed; altogether the five campaigns raised almost $20 billion, 30 percent of it from people earning less than $2,000 a year.

Resort to such massive borrowing was necessary in part because within four months of the onset of American belligerency, McAdoo was forced to quadruple his early estimates of expenditures. In April 1917, he had estimated the cost of the war at $3.5 billion for the first year, with the Revenue Act providing about half. But late in July he ratcheted this estimate upward, now projecting outlays of more than $15 billion. In April, Congress, under the assumption that it would provide about half the funds necessary, had quickly and with hardly any dissent authorized the Treasury to float loans without specifying monetary limits. But as the vast dimensions of the government's needs became starkly clear, and with the tax legislation wending its tortured way through Congress, the ratio of borrowing to taxation leapt from one to one to five to one.

In important respects, McAdoo's program for financing the war amounted to a series of ad hoc expedients. It did raise the needed money without alienating taxpayers or disrupting financial markets. But in his hopes of creating a system of public finance that would simultaneously connect ordinary citizens directly to the war effort, raise massive amounts of money, and check inflation, McAdoo was only partly successful. Indeed, certain aspects of the Liberty Loan program actually served to fuel inflationary pressures. The peculiar pattern of interest rates and tax-free features available to purchasers of Liberty (and later, Victory) bonds tended to dump millions of dollars of government bonds into banks included in the new Federal Reserve System. Once there, these bonds served as collateral for bank loans to other businesses and private citizens, thus drastically increasing the country's money supply and hence stimulating demand for scarce goods.

All in all, the United States financed about 23 percent of its direct war expenditures through taxation and the rest through borrowing. The amount raised from taxes for Great Britain was around 20 percent; for Italy, 16 percent; and for Germany, less than 2 percent. Even this relatively good performance, however, meant that too much disposable income was available in the United States to chase relatively scarce goods. Thus, consumer prices did rise significantly, increasing by about 18 percent between 1916 and 1920.

Here too, though, the increase was less than was the case with Britain, Italy, or France, and less than was the case during the American Civil War. Could the government have continued to avoid painful taxation and a more coercive approach to commanding financial resources in a more protracted period of U.S. belligerency? Fortunately for Wilson and McAdoo, in fiscal matters, just as in military recruitment, the abrupt end of the war precluded the need to confront this difficult question.

For all the often-strident public debates over public financing, the most important long-range fiscal aspects of American belligerency were the sheer magnitude of its cost and the increasing reliance on the new income tax as the primary source of federal revenue. In the last fiscal year before U.S. entry, the total budget of the federal government was less than $800 million. In contrast, during fiscal years 1918 and 1919, the war cost the American people an average of almost $43 million a day, or about $15.5 *billion* annually, a rate of expenditure nearly twenty times higher than during peacetime. Moreover, the recently adopted federal income tax, which in fiscal 1916 accounted for only about 16 percent of all federal revenues, by 1918 was providing nearly 60 percent. More than the details of the mixture between taxation and borrowing, it was the vast scale of federal expenditures, along with the replacement of excise and customs duties as the chief source of revenue, that constituted the enduring fiscal legacy of U.S. involvement in the Great War.[19]

Mobilizing the Public

The federal government's mobilizing of the economy may have been clumsy and flawed, and its mobilizing of the army may have been hasty and wasteful. But in mobilizing public support for the war, the government performed brilliantly, although often in ways that seemed to subvert Wilson's public vision of America's role in a new world order. It was this area of mobilization, which reflected the techniques and values of the nation's powerful strain of commercial republicanism, that revealed America's true genius. Here private citizens, official bodies, and civic and educational institutions came together to form the kind of partnership in behalf of national goals that Progressive reformers, business leaders, and policy intellectuals often urged but rarely achieved in the more general realms of political economy. Both government leaders and private citizens employed the language and techniques of public persuasion drawn from the world of commercial advertising in the service of exalted goals of national purpose and human betterment. Yet the mobilization of public opinion and the government–private party collaboration that achieved it raised important questions of individual integrity, government accountability, and the relationship between salesmanship and public values that lingered long after the guns had fallen silent.

Because the United States was not under direct attack and the nation's war aims were as abstract as they were high minded, Wilson and his cohorts quickly understood that the government would have to make a conscious effort to enlist the people's enthusiastic support. War underlined the dangers of the many vexing problems of ethnic, class, and regional conflict that for the past generation had rocked the country. How could a nation with weak central government powers, widespread antimilitary feeling, endemic labor strife, and bewilderingly polyglot population be brought into unified action? Could the government find ways to rally the American people without resorting to the coercion and repression against which it purported to be fighting? Could it marshal journalists, educators, religious leaders, and scholars to promote the national cause without fatally compromising their ethical and professional standing? Could the government make use of the country's potent private advertising and publicity organs without encouraging the corruption of the language of civic purpose by these essentially profit-seeking organizations?

In the realm of information, as in other aspects of mobilization, the government relied on a combination of coercive legislation, voluntary compliance, and propaganda. At Wilson's behest, Congress passed several laws, notably the Espionage Act of June 15, 1917, and the Sedition Act of May 16, 1918, giving the government officials wide powers to suppress free expression. The Trading with the Enemy Act of October 1917 added to the government's ability to punish unfriendly opinions. Prosecution of violators, encouragement of private vigilante action against dissenters, and denial of mailing privileges to antiwar publications, along with military crackdowns against those accused of printing or disseminating information about ship or troop movements, weapons, or military plans, became commonplace.* Declared New York Senator Elihu Root shortly after Congress declared war, "We must have no criticism now."[20]

But Wilson did not want government control of information to be purely, or even primarily, negative. Newspapers, motion pictures, public gatherings, and public spaces all provided opportunities to enlist the people in the great crusade. A week after the declaration of war, Wilson issued an executive order creating the Committee on Public Information (CPI), a new agency charged

*For a fuller discussion of civil liberties in the era of the Great War, see pages 194–203.

with portraying the "absolute justice of America's cause [and] the absolute selflessness of America's aims." To head it, he chose *Rocky Mountain News* editor George Creel, a long-time Wilson political supporter who believed that America's vast network of newspapers, libraries, schools, universities, and citizen associations could be used to promote the country's war aims and policies. At the same time, the CPI would provide newspapers with accurate information about the war's progress. It would abjure conscious falsehoods and forswear direct censorship, relying instead on the selection and distribution of news to shape its public presentation.[21]

From its beginning, the CPI both disseminated its own propaganda and coordinated the propaganda activities of other federal (and some private) agencies. The CPI meshed its activities with professional advertising and public relations organizations to produce and distribute posters, billboards, pamphlets, and slogans for agencies such as the Food Administration, the Red Cross, and the Selective Service System. CPI artists and writers collaborated closely with the Department of the Treasury in Liberty Loan campaigns. The Division of Civic and Educational Publications, headed by historian Guy Stanton Ford, enlisted scholars to produce pamphlets, syllabi, and study guides for use by editors, school teachers, and professors. The Division of Pictorial Publicity, headed by popular artist Charles Dana Gibson, created posters and illustrations designed to recruit workers into war industries, encourage food conservation, persuade citizens to subscribe to war bond drives, and most dramatically, promote Selective Service registration and enlistment in the armed forces. The nation's libraries served as outlets for CPI materials, as did churches, schools, service clubs, and business and professional associations.

The most distinctive and widely publicized activity associated with the CPI was the "Four-Minute Men" program. The brainchild of Chicago businessmen, the idea of the Four-Minute Men was to use local citizens to bring the war home to all segments of the population in a particularly vivid and insistent way. Reasoning that people attending motion-picture showings constituted a kind of captive audience, businessman Donald Ryerson hit upon the device of providing patriotic speakers who would address an audience during reel changes, a process that usually took about four minutes. Because at least ten million people attended motion-picture shows each day, Ryerson and his friends calculated, these brief speeches would soon reach a vast audience, including especially working-class and foreign-born people, who at that time comprised a huge segment of motion-picture audiences.

The limited time available for these speeches turned out to be an asset. With relatively little preparation, amateur orators, supplied with printed materials by the CPI, could master the significant details relating to specific topics such as draft registration, Liberty Loan appeals, or American war aims. In a ritual initiated in Chicago theaters even before the declaration of war and soon repeated throughout the country, as soon as a reel ended, the projectionist flashed a slide on the screen, instructing patrons to "Please remain seated. A representative of the government is to deliver an important message." A second slide revealed the identity of the speaker—usually a prominent local business or professional man—and the subject. The speaker then strode to the front of the audience and delivered his carefully rehearsed speech. He quickly got to the point, rattled off carefully selected facts, reiterated his central message, and strode off just as the film resumed. One experienced four-minute speaker instructed newcomers to the program: "Use short sentences. . . . Avoid fine phrases. . . . Be natural and direct. . . . Finish strong and sharp . . . and always—Stick to . . . the four-minute limit."[22]

By war's end, more than 75,000 speakers had been recruited. Branching out from movie houses to lodge meetings, union locals, churches, service clubs, schools, and other places of public assembly, these patriotic orators delivered more than 750,000 talks before an estimated 314 million listeners. Following recommendations from local business and civic leaders, the CPI relied largely on middle-class and relatively well-educated citizens who could be expected to follow the standard format and to avoid political partisanship or class or ethnic controversy. The CPI made special pains to recruit African American clergymen, teachers, and community leaders and established a special department for Work Among the Foreign Born. A Women's Division, featuring female speakers, targeted matinee audiences, women's clubs, and church groups. Four-Minute Men worked with teachers to promote conservation and Liberty Stamp purchase among school children and to train junior Four-Minute Men for classroom and assembly orations. On Indian reservations, in Italian and Lithuanian neighborhoods, and among skeptical midwestern farmers, the Four-Minute Men hammered home the messages of patriotism, sacrifice, and obligation, generating Liberty Bond sales, donations to the Red Cross, and enthusiasm for the war effort. One Alaskan logged more than 60,000 miles to address 64,000 people in the northern territory. Declared Creel, this massive program, carried forth with minimal governmental expense, amounted to "a vast enterprise in salesmanship, the world's greatest adventure in advertising."[23]

Rallying support for the war by inundating the people with snappy slogans and crisp speeches certainly generated enthusiasm. At the same time, however, the application of techniques of salesmanship and public relations to the business of "selling" the war raised disturbing questions. Reflecting their business and professional status, Four-Minute speakers inevitably cast the government's appeals in inherently class-bound language and context. Some local recruiters worried about this problem. The program's Los Angeles chairman, for example, lamented his inability to find "four or five men from the ranks of labor" to speak to working-class audiences. He was troubled that "our speakers may be said to come [exclusively] from the upper class, but it does require trained minds to present subjects in four minutes."[24]

But the problem of the class and ethnic character of the Four-Minute Men program went deeper than inability to recruit working-class speakers. Both the format and implicit subtext of Four-Minute speeches projected a business approach to themes of patriotism, national purpose, and the meanings of citizenship. In the America of the 1910s, workers and employers fought, sometimes savagely, about the definitions of these terms. For persons of foreign birth or parentage, the very terms "Americanism" and "patriotism" were problematic. The Four-Minute Men presentational template bent the overtly universalistic message of Wilsonianism into a class- and ethnic-freighted medium. Educated and successful business and professional men ventured into the recreational space of workers and immigrants, bearing the assumption that *these* Americans were inherently suspect in their commitment to the war. Four-Minute Men employed a rhetorical mode that echoed the hucksterism and commercialization of value that these same speakers, in their "civilian" identities, used to sell soap and cigarettes.

In the 1910s, alternative versions of Americanism, as reflected in the widespread popularity of such socialist leaders as Eugene V. Debs and in the sharp industrial conflict that punctuated these years, were widespread. Working-class Americanism prized civil liberties, valued international solidarity, stressed class division, and even embraced notions of cultural pluralism. The fiery oratory of a strike rally, the whistle-stop appeal for workers' votes of a Gene Debs aboard the Red Special, the stump speech at a county fair or St. Patrick's Day celebration by an aspiring politician—with the American flag waving amid defiant union banners and embroidered slogans in a dozen languages: *these* public scenes were as much a part of 1910's America as was the salesman's pep talk or the service club's anodyne rituals. Now, however, the Four-Minute Men, with the official imprimatur of a crusading government, appropriated patriotism and Americanism and, in their distinctive idiom, both inflated their emotive importance and threatened to trivialize their content.

There were other disturbing problems associated with the CPI's efforts and with the administration's other propaganda activities. Although Creel continually stressed the need to present positive and edifying material, official propagandists often could not resist the impulse to demonize the enemy and to feature lurid and even inflammatory definitions of the national crusade. Under the leadership of Gibson, a real Germanophobe, the Division of Pictorial Publicity churned out vivid, horrific posters, usually depicting a generic German soldier with evil countenance and feral expression. In his war message, Wilson had sought to draw a sharp distinction between the German people and their vicious and militaristic leaders. "We have no quarrel with the German people. We have no feeling towards them but one of sympathy and friendship," he intoned. But CPI posters supporting Liberty Loan drives featured scenes of brutal Germans ravishing and murdering helpless Belgians. One spoke of "the vicious guttural language of [German] Kultur." In Germany, the poster proclaimed, the academic degree "A.B." "means Bachelor of Atrocities." Another depicted the consequences of Prussian victory—bombs from German airplanes falling on a defenseless America as the Statue of Liberty, surrounded by a New York City in flames, continues to hold high the torch of freedom.

Nor did the historians and other scholars in the Division of Civic and Educational Publications avoid hyperbole and distortion. Enlisting some of the most distinguished members of the historical profession, the "Ford Division" (as it was dubbed after its head, Guy Stanton Ford of the University of Minnesota) produced an estimated 75 million pieces of literature purporting to explain the origins of the war, the reasons for American entry, and U.S. war aims. A flood of pamphlets, written in an accessible scholarly idiom and replete with imposing bibliographies and citations to documents, found its way into libraries, classrooms, and private homes. Ford rejected contributions that appeared too obviously propagandistic. "I should be very reluctant to father anything which sank to the level of vituperation and calling of names," he declared. Even so, some Ford Division publications stepped over the line, featuring, for example, inflammatory accounts of an imagined German invasion of the United States. Indeed, the author of *American and Allied Ideals* frankly admitted it being "distinctly propagandistic." Even purportedly objective and dispassionate treatments often betrayed the authors' nationalistic zeal in ways that conflicted with President Wilson's view that any lasting postwar settlement would have to acknowledge the vitality and legitimacy of a strong, if demilitarized, Germany. According to scholar Wallace Notestein, for example, it was not merely the Kaiser or the military caste that impelled German aggression; rather, expansionism at the expense of peaceful neighbors was rooted in German culture, indeed in the very language of the German people. A *War Cyclopedia*, edited by three distinguished scholars, purported to be an unbiased, factual handbook for general reference, but through selection and omission, it actually presented a highly partisan and one-sided introduction to the war and America's role in it. Toward the end of the war, prominent American scholars gave the stamp of approval to documentary material claiming to prove the existence of a German conspiracy to spread revolution throughout Eastern Europe that even zealous Allied propagandists dismissed as crude forgeries.[25]

The point is not that the government should have been expected to produce only scrupulous and objective material for public dissemination. The whole reason for having a CPI was to promote the administration's version of the war. Everyone expected advertising and public relations men to appeal to emotion and to play fast and loose with the facts. But the use of scholars, especially when writing in the sober voice of the academy and employing the paraphernalia of footnotes and annotations to mask one-sided or even inflammatory presentations, is another matter. They compromised their professional integrity and academic credibility and contributed significantly to the corruption of public discourse. The role that many leading academics took on as partisan propagandists was particularly alarming because many of these same men were simultaneously serving as advisers to the government in its planning for the postwar European order, a role that presumably called for nothing short of rigorous objectivity and avoidance of wishful thinking and cultural stereotyping.

In important respects, the campaign for psychological mobilization of the American people in behalf of the war effort was an outstanding success. A vast army was raised. A polyglot population showed few signs of disloyalty or disaffection. Liberty Loan drives were all oversubscribed and campaigns in behalf of food and fuel conservation, Red Cross contributions, and a dozen other war-support causes were successful. But at the same time, however, it compromised the high moral tone of Wilson's war message. Whereas Wilson had drawn fine distinctions between the evil of the German government and the fundamental decency of the German people, themes of hatred and demonization infected even the rhetorically dispassionate language of the nation's scholars and historians. Moreover, Wilson's projections for the creation of a bold new world order called for a strong and democratic Germany, but Four-Minute speeches and Ford Division pamphlets alike tended to cast the German people and culture, and not just the current German government, as monstrous and irremediable.

The president had said in his war message, "It is a fearful thing to lead this great peaceful people into war." He might as well have said "this fractious, decentralized, class-and-ethnicity riven people," or this "commercial, individualistic, parochial people." The exercise of war leadership in these circumstances called for a unique combination of organizational know-how, patriotic fervor, and psychological manipulation, along with an ultimate willingness to exercise the vast, if normally latent, powers belonging to the national government. America's remoteness from the battlefields and the merciful shortness of the period of its belligerency permitted the country to work through a range of essentially voluntaristic and decentralized approaches to mobilizing itself for what Wilson called "the most terrible and disastrous of all wars." By and large, in creating a huge new military machine, the administration was able to leave fundamental interests and institutions in place. But as slacker raids, repressive legislation, and militant sloganeering indicated, the shotgun was never far from hand, even as the government cultivated the consent of the people.

FOUR

Over There
1917–1918

The U.S. military effort in the Great War reflected both the strengths and the weaknesses of American society in general. The raising, training, and dispatching of more than two million men to France was an impressive achievement, one without which the bloody stalemate on the Western Front would no doubt have continued at least into 1919. The insistence of the U.S. military leaders, most notably commander of the American Expeditionary Force (AEF), General John J. "Black Jack" Pershing, on building a distinct American army and refusing to permit his troops to be dispersed among more experienced Allied formations reflected both political reality and the fact that America was not party to the alliance or treaty systems of America's wartime partners. But humiliating dependence on Britain and France for virtually all of the AEF's heavy weaponry and much of its transport served as a ready reminder of the limited scope of the U.S. war effort.

In the field, the doughboys acquitted themselves well, making up in vigor and energy what they initially lacked in experience, logistical efficiency, and large-unit leadership. The declarations of America's political leaders and moral spokesmen that the AEF represented a new democratic and egalitarian presence amid the jaded and benumbed combatants, however, fell short of reality. Although it was true that the army served as a kind of melting pot, bringing together Euro-Americans of diverse ethnic and religious backgrounds, its treatment of native-born African Americans compromised America's democratic pretensions. For all its limitations, however, the U.S. military effort was a decisive factor in the abrupt end of the war, less because of the AEF's prowess on the field of battle than because the sheer numbers of fresh American soldiers convinced exhausted German troops and their leaders that the war was no longer winnable.

Raising an Army

Reflecting the uncertainty as to the actual role an American army would play in the war, the initial draft quotas were modest. In June 1917, the army called for 687,000 men to be added to the existing force of around 220,000. In reality, by the end of the year, it became clear that the army could accommodate only about 500,000. Through the summer of 1917, more than 200,000 construction workers toiled to build some thirty-two "cantonments," housing and training facilities scattered around the country. By September 1, spurred by guaranteed-profit contracts, privileged access to building materials, and high wages, workers had erected facilities capable of housing 400,000 new soldiers, and by the end of the year, they had completed the massive construction project, one of the most extensive (and expensive) ever undertaken within the United States. Even though wooden barracks were built only for the new recruits into the "National Army" (mobilized National Guard units had to be content with canvas tents), the builders used 30 tons of materials a day and overall pounded 2 billion nails and installed 12 million square feet of window glass. Despite the enormous cost, perhaps as high as $270 million, and the evidence of hasty and even careless construction, the rapid completion of these military bases was a remarkable achievement, a testament to what American know-how, fertilized by governmental largess, patriotic fervor, and good wages could accomplish.

What of the men pouring into these camps? The unspoken national self-image depicted U.S. citizen-soldiers as sturdy individualists, rangy and resourceful descendants of the pioneers. Underlying official U.S. Army tactical doctrine was the notion that the typical American male was somehow a born rifleman, eager to practice his marksmanship against the enemy. Army planners acknowledged that the machine gun had assumed a major role in modern warfare, but officers believed that the sturdy rifleman was the backbone of America's military effort. Hardened by the frontier, eagle-eyed and rugged, army doctrine held, he would soon seize the initiative and restore movement to the trench-ridden European battlefields.

In reality, the draftees who flooded into the camps of the new National Army and the volunteers who joined the existing National Guard and Regular Army units did not fit these stereotypes. For starters, few were familiar with firearms. For every turkey-shooting mountaineer, there were hundreds of city boys who had never even seen a rifle or shotgun. And owing to the shortages of weapons, thousands were not issued a rifle until the eve of their departure for France. Those fortunate enough to participate in stateside target practice failed to impress their more experienced comrades: "They missed everything but the sky," recalled one rural Tennessee soldier of his urban mates.[1]

Nor did the mass of recruits live up to the prevailing image of the bold and hardy offspring of pioneer stock. Almost a fifth of those inducted, for example, were foreign-born. Army officers charged with censoring the mail of American troops in France had to deal with letters written in some forty-nine languages. Nor were the recruits as prepossessing physically and mentally as the national mythology would have it. The typical soldier was just over 5 feet 7 inches tall and weighed about 142 pounds. A staggering 31 percent of all U.S. Army inductees—men who had passed the preliminary screening administered by local draft boards—were found to be illiterate. The reported results of newly designed and administered tests of mental and psychological ability were even more unsettling, for the psychologists who designed and interpreted them reported that fully 47 percent of whites and almost 90 percent of blacks were below the mental age of 13.[2]

Veteran army officers did not in fact believe the psychologists, and for good reason. Biased tests, ill-trained test administrators, and grossly inadequate and uneven testing facilities ensured that the intelligence tests at the least would reveal more about the state of psychological testing than about the actual capabilities of the troops. Indeed, when it turned out that northern-born black soldiers scored higher than whites from Anglo-American Appalachia, psychological and mental testing fell into rapid disrepute, because such a finding conflicted with dearly held racial stereotypes. Even so, however, the profile that emerged of the new American fighting man—a slight urban dweller of medium height and ordinary intelligence, from a polyglot ethnic background who was more familiar with a subway strap than with a Kentucky rifle—suggested that the army's image of itself and the tactical doctrines that rested on that image were questionable.

Who would train these men and lead them into battle? The army turned to its existing officer corps, its more promising regular noncommissioned officers (NCOs), and civilians, especially college men and students, to find the answer. Thus, even as tens of thousands of young men climbed aboard trains, often clad in their best Sunday suits, to make their way to the raw new cantonments, the army was building a massive new makeshift officer corps. The prewar Regular Army already had 18,000 officers and quickly promoted another 16,000 from among its NCOs and private soldiers. Civilians with special skills, such as doctors, were given commissions outright. But of the projected 200,000 officers the army required, it would have to train almost half from scratch, and to this end, it hastily established officer training sites at army posts around the country. By the middle of May 1917, more than 30,000 new prospective officers, mostly drawn from among Spanish-American War veterans and college students and recent graduates, were receiving instruction from officers who were culled from existing Regular Army officers. At best, the military education provided these new cadres was rudimentary. Weapons were in short supply and days were spent mostly drilling and exercising. "My duties are many; my ignorance beyond plumbing. I am quite lost," lamented a young artillery officer-in-training. Regardless of these less-than-ideal conditions, at the end of the ninety-day training period, these new officers, mostly second lieutenants, were sent off to train the first waves of conscripts. "It was a case of the blind leading the blind," admitted a twenty-two-year-old second lieutenant.[3]

The troops themselves often received little strictly military training. In France, the Germans were perfecting new small-unit infantry tactics, closely coordinated with carefully targeted artillery bombardments. The British and the Australians were beginning to understand that the integration of the tank with small-unit infantry assaults could achieve remarkable results. Allied pilots were learning to coordinate air–infantry attacks with devastating results. But American recruits learned nothing of these developments. With orders for khaki cloth and army boots running months behind schedule, many wore civilian clothes through their basic training. Recalled a Wisconsin soldier, "It was about two months before I looked really like a soldier." Many drilled with broomsticks rather than the standard-issue rifle. In France later on, one observer discovered that more than 40 percent of the infantrymen about to go into one battle had never fired their recently issued weapons, much less learned to conduct complex operations. The U.S. Army's air arm consisted of a handful of antiquated reconnaissance planes; stateside artillery was obsolete and tanks were practically nonexistent.

Thus, training for the vast majority of recruits consisted largely of physical conditioning, endless marching, and above all, learning to follow orders, however arbitrary or incoherent. And conditions in some of the cantonments did test the new soldiers' endurance, especially in southern camps outfitted with tents rather than wooden barracks. Recruits sometimes had to fell trees or clear stumps from fields before workmen could complete construction. "Everything is frozen up," recorded a young lieutenant in December 1917 from a camp in supposedly weather-friendly South Carolina. "My feet are frostbitten, and they are bothering me a good deal." Spring brought different miseries, as ungraded camp roads turned into sticky goo, stalling motor vehicles and introducing the new soldiers to that fabled humbler of men, the army mule.[4]

For all the hardship and confusion, most men seemed to thrive. Many received adequate dental and medical care for the first time in their lives.

Food was plentiful and surprisingly varied and nutritious: a typical day's fare at Fort Riley, Kansas, included cantaloupe, fried liver, corn flakes, creamed cauliflower, chili, pudding, stewed peaches, and iced tea. Stateside soldiers at training camps consumed an average of 4,761 calories a day to provide the energy for the strenuous physical conditioning, marching, and work details that were their daily lot. Though veteran officers lamented the lack of sophisticated training in weaponry and maneuvers, the forced reliance on conditioning, morale building, and health probably prepared the troops as well as any system might have for the role they were about to play in what continued to be a grim war of attrition.

Nor were military and civilian authorities concerned only about the physical health and strength of this new conscript army. Those in charge of mobilization felt a powerful sense of responsibility to see to the moral, spiritual, and educational well-being of the recruits. Military service was notoriously associated with dissolute behavior. Soldiers were legendary fornicators, drinkers, blasphemers, and general hell raisers. Communities adjacent to military posts were almost by definition sites of saloons, gambling dens, and brothels. Reports from Europe indicated that venereal disease was rife in all the armies, suggesting that U.S. authorities would soon face problems of both military efficiency and moral behavior. During the Mexican campaign of 1916, observed Secretary of War Newton D. Baker, "our young soldiers had a good deal of time hanging rather heavily on their hands" and were too frequently lured "into unwholesome diversions and recreations." Left to their own devices, Baker lamented, they patronized "cheap picture shows, saloons, dance halls, and houses of prostitution." The conscripting of a mass army raised serious issues to men such as Baker, a quintessential Progressive reformer. This was to be a virtuous, democratic army, different in recruitment, composition, and most importantly, moral stature from any previous army. Thus, even before the declaration of war, Baker vowed to establish a "comprehensive program" for "the regular provision of wholesome recreation" for America's warriors.[5]

To this end, only eleven days after the declaration of hostilities, the War Department established the Commission on Training Camp Activities (CTCA), an essentially private organization, funded largely by participating religious and uplift organizations but armed with the official sanction of U.S. military authorities. Baker named Raymond B. Fostick, another veteran Progressive with a background in social investigation, to head it. Over the course of American belligerency, the CTCA operated largely through such civilian groups as the War Camp Community Service, the American Library Association, and five religious organizations, the most active of which was the Young

Men's Christian Association (YMCA). Raising more than $200 million, these organizations conducted programs designed to bolster troop morale, inculcate wholesome values, and look after the mental and physical health of the recruits. An army of social workers, ministers, educators, and moral guardians arranged recreational, educational, and moral uplift programs of all descriptions. Baseball and basketball tournaments, religious services, heavily chaperoned social affairs involving local citizens, and motion pictures entertained and edified the new soldiers. Libraries and recreation centers were erected, usually under the auspices of the YMCA or other religious sponsorship. CTCA counselors gave advice, encouraged soldiers to write home, conducted mass sing-alongs, and provided both practical and admonitory information about the dangers of drink, loose women, and gambling.

The CTCA also cooperated closely with the War Department and the army in a war against vice in communities near military posts. The May 1917 legislation establishing the draft also banned the sale of alcohol to servicemen and established a prostitution-free zone around all military bases. In cooperation with the army's Military Intelligence branch, other federal agencies, and zealous local religious social purity organizations, CTCA investigators carefully documented the extent of dissolution in a given war-impacted community and turned its findings over to law enforcement and military police authorities. In community after community, this combination of moral outrage, patriotic sentiment, and federal power closed down saloons, scattered prostitutes, and created a cordon of vicelessness around army posts. Although the CTCA and the military authorities enjoyed much local support, however, their efforts also met with resistance on the part of interests dependent on these long-established local services. In notorious New Orleans, for example, local officials initially resisted the efforts of the vice crusaders, and in Louisville, the *Courier Journal* reported that neighborhood denizens, including the beat cops, greeted the closing of the tenderloin district "with sadness and gloom." Undaunted, CTCA officials and military authorities compiled a remarkable record of driving vice underground in dozens of communities. "Even that Gibraltar of commercialized vice," New Orleans, had succumbed, declared a CTCA activist. "Twenty-four solid blocks given over to human degradation and lust and housing six- to eight-hundred women, has gone down with the rest," he boasted.[6]

To social reformers, medical professionals, educators, and would-be guardians of the nation's moral virtue, the four million men inducted into the armed forces represented more than merely a fighting force. They provided a living opportunity for testing and perfecting methods of improving the quality and character of American life. Although many progressive reformers were troubled by, or even opposed to, the U.S. declaration of war, others viewed belligerency as an opportunity to forge a new sense of national identity among the country's polyglot and/or parochial citizens while exposing a whole generation of young men to wholesome, patriotic, and progressive influences. In the educational programs that the army itself ran, as well as in the activities of the CTCA, the effort was always to reinforce the American soldier's sense of distinctiveness and his good fortune in being a representative of the great American republic. Other soldiers, including those of America's friendly co-belligerents, might be fighting to preserve ancient privileges or to promote national aggrandizement at the expense of others. American warriors, however, were to carry with them a distinctive American ideology, a world view that combined moral superiority, unquenchable optimism, and pride in their nation's limitless pursuit of material and social progress.

Even as new recruits were getting their first taste of military life, advance units of the AEF began arriving in France. On July 4, 1917, a battalion of regulars from the 16th Regiment paraded in Paris amid expressions of undying Franco-American solidarity. Other units trickled in, and by October, the First Division was holding down a quiet sector of the Front in northern France and suffering the first U.S. combat deaths on the night of November 2–3. In the fall, more regulars and some National Guardsmen and U.S. Marines came across. By the end of January 1918 about 175,000 U.S. soldiers were training under French and British instructors. In March 1917, Acting Chief of Staff General Tasker Bliss had declared that it would take nearly two years for even a half-million American soldiers to be sufficiently trained and equipped to be able to make the American presence felt in France. But as Allied losses continued to mount and thousands of battle-tested German troops from the Eastern Front began arriving in Belgium and France, it clearly would not be long before, ready or not, the new American conscript army would be joining this advance guard.

Initially, the army showed few signs of being able to train and transport large numbers of soldiers to Europe. But during the winter of 1917–18, Secretary of War Baker realized that its supply and transport systems were in profound crisis and that without major overhaul, the army could not supply the troops that the deteriorating war situation required. In March 1918 he appointed Major General Peyton C. March chief of staff. In effect, March, a much-decorated veteran of the Spanish-American War and the Philippine campaigns, functioned as the chief executive in the army's far-flung and hitherto-chaotic supply, procurement, and transport operations. March centralized supply and procurement, bypassing the entrenched bureau chiefs and imposing a rational system of priorities on them. He recruited leading business executives, gave them military rank, and rapidly began streamlining the army's purchasing, logistical, and transportation arms. Although these actions drew him into bitter controversy with traditionalist fellow officers, including AEF commander General Pershing, March's organizational abilities and his ruthless insistence on efficiency and performance quickly paid off: during March's eight months as chief of staff, the army sent almost 1.8 million men to France, a remarkable record. And they began arriving just in time, for the spring of 1918 brought a series of ferocious German attacks on the Western Front, designed to achieve victory before the doughboys could arrive in sufficient numbers to make a difference.

An American Army?

As the army and the government sorted out these problems of recruitment, transport, training, and logistics, questions about the actual role American troops in Europe would play moved to the forefront. From the start, Pershing, along with virtually the entire military establishment, insisted that U.S. forces would constitute a separate command occupying a distinct sector of the Western Front. European representatives on the Supreme Allied War Council, created in November 1917 to coordinate military operations, called instead for rapid dispersal of American troops into British- and French-commanded bodies. In a series of spirited showdowns with his French and British counterparts, the AEF commander stubbornly held his ground on this key issue. Pershing insisted on avoiding amalgamation of American troops into Allied armies and on creating as rapidly as possible an autonomous and distinct American military presence. He thus voiced both his own inner convictions and reflected the general policies of the administration in Washington. Both President Woodrow Wilson and Secretary of War Baker believed that only such a policy could ensure that American forces would augment, rather than merely replace, British and French troops. Moreover, they understood that the American people expected that American soldiers would fight under American command as a distinct and coherent body. Perhaps most importantly, Wilson, Baker, and Pershing realized that America's distinctive war aims made a strong role in any postwar peace conference dependent on the creation of an autonomous American army. Declared Baker, "The whole theory of our Army differed from the theories of the French and British" and so "It was necessary at all times to preserve the independence and identity of the American forces."[7] With little interest in purely military affairs and convinced that America's economic power and its moral leadership were the keys to advancing U.S. war aims at a postwar peace conference, the president gave Pershing a free hand in implementing these general policies. Having chosen the hard-bitten Missouri cavalryman for the command, Wilson and Baker considered matters of troop disposition and training strictly military matters. Both consistently rejected appeals by Allied leaders to countermand Pershing's determination to create an autonomous U.S. military presence, whatever the risks or obstacles.

In fact, the issue was a tricky one. British commander Sir Douglas Haig and his French counterparts argued strenuously that America should provide basic training to hundreds of thousands of riflemen and machine gunners and send them to France to be integrated into existing Allied units. Building full U.S. divisions wasted time and resources, especially since America did not yet produce the artillery or much of the other equipment a fully armed division would need. Indeed, Pershing himself subsequently admitted, "We were literally beggars as to every important weapon, except the rifle."[8]

Nor, Allied military leaders tellingly observed, did the United States have the trained and experienced officers needed to guide a vast military undertaking. Campaigns on the Western Front typically involved dozens of divisions in coordinated actions, yet when America entered the war, no serving U.S. officer had ever commanded a body of troops as large as a single division in more than fifty years. Modern warfare called for detailed planning, managerial expertise, and the ability to coordinate the movements of hundreds of thousands of men. It was ludicrous to believe that an American army that had stumbled all over itself in trying to locate Pancho Villa could now produce officers necessary to operate even one of its oversized infantry divisions, much less to lead the kind of massive fighting force common on the Western Front. Haig made the point bluntly: If America truly was to play a significant military role, it had to send as many fighting men as quickly as possible to replenish the decimated Allied ranks. The Allies had no need for American divisions, only for American men.

U.S. leaders, however, believed that this was a recipe for dead Americans. Even as the first doughboys arrived in France, Allied generals once again were hurling their own men in futile, costly frontal assaults against the German lines. Indeed, the horrendous losses suffered in the poorly planned French offensive in April 1917 triggered mutinies, as thousands of *poilus* protested the wanton expenditure of men and the miserable conditions under which they fought. And later that year, the British launched an equally bloody and ineffectual assault in Belgium, turning the fields around Passchendaele into a mud-clogged killing field. Piecemeal dispatch of poorly trained men, U.S commanders believed, would simply encourage their haughty co-belligerents to treat the Americans as just another colonial tributary.

Complicating the goal of building an autonomous and fully operational U.S. army in France, however, were the logistical realities of the war situation in 1917 and 1918. After arriving in France in June 1917, Pershing quickly upped his estimates of how many U.S. troops the defeat of Germany would require. By the end of the summer, he was urging an AEF of one hundred divisions, or more than four million men. He was convinced that for such an American army to be successful, months of training, both in the United States and in rear areas and quiet sectors of the front in France, were necessary. Such an American army would consume vast quantities of supplies of every description and would require an elaborate network of depots, bases, railroads, and port facilities. A single American division of 28,000 men would consume at least 20 tons of food, ammunition, and other supplies daily, much of it—along with the men themselves—transported from abroad. But Great Britain held the key to American troops crossing the Atlantic to Europe; as late as the middle of 1918, frantic U.S. efforts to build and otherwise acquire merchant shipping were only slowly bearing fruit.

Dependence on British shipping permeated the running debate between American and Allied military authorities over the role of the American army. The British insisted that its hard-pressed merchant ships and naval escorts be used only to transport front-line infantry units; but without division-level artillery, engineering, and logistical complements, these units could never form the basis for a separate American army. Like poker players, Pershing and Allied military and political leaders anted, bluffed, and gambled, trading the promise of so many ships for this or that mixture of American men. In June 1918, at one particularly tense meeting of the Supreme Allied War Council, the U.S. commander bluntly parried Anglo-French appeals that the creation of an American army be deferred in favor of piecemeal dispatch of infantry units. With German attacks threatening Paris, Supreme Allied Commander Ferdinand Foch pressed Pershing hard. As in the past, Pershing, whose troops had just been sent to strengthen the reeling French forces along the River Marne at Chateau-Thierry and Belleau Wood, remained stubborn on the larger issue. Incredulous at Pershing's apparent lack of concern about the scope of recent German advances, Foch confronted the AEF commander: "You are willing to risk our being driven back to the Loire?"—100 miles south and west of Paris. "Yes," Pershing responded, "I am willing to take the risk." Declared French Premier Georges Clemenceau, "Then we can practically expect nothing from the United States" beyond the current stop-gap help. "That is a great disappointment."[9]

In a sense, Pershing and the Allied leaders were working on different timetables. U.S. political and military leaders were convinced that there could be no decisive offensive action on the Western Front until at least 1919. So evenly matched were the two sides that with the failure of Allied assaults in 1917, there seemed little hope of restoring movement to the Front. However, Pershing believed that in time, American manpower would prove decisive. He was convinced, as he told Theodore Roosevelt, that "The burden of the war from now on is practically upon our shoulders."[10]

But for Foch, Haig, and their political counterparts, the crisis was already at hand. On March 21, 1918, German commander Erich Ludendorff launched the first in a series of powerful blows at the weary Allied lines. Reinforced by three-quarters of a million troops freed up by peace with Bolshevik Russia, Ludendorff devastated British positions along the old Somme battlefield, sent the British Fifth Army reeling back, and seemed about to split the French and British forces and pin the latter against the English Channel. Then Ludendorff's storm troopers fell on the demoralized French farther to the south, rolling up huge gains and threatening Paris itself. Further German assaults in June and early July, employed effective small-unit tactics and close infantry–artillery coordination. German attacks repeatedly mauled Allied forces, with Americans fighting under French and British command engaged for the first time in large-scale action. Shocked by Germany's ability to press such aggressive and costly attacks, pushed back upon their transportation hubs and depots, Allied commanders pleaded with Pershing for the massive infusion of half-trained U.S. infantry units and the shelving of his plans for a vast, cohesive U.S. army.

Pershing, however, believed that these German advances actually buttressed his case. Convinced that even the most powerful German blows would not succeed in routing the Allies, the American general foresaw only more stalemate along the Western Front throughout 1918. Too exhausted to push onward, the Germans nonetheless could still smother the kinds of Allied offensives that had failed so dismally in 1917. But by the summer of 1919, American industry would be producing cannon and munitions in vast quantities. Fresh, well-trained American troops, which Pershing believed to be "far and away superior to the tired Europeans," would spearhead the decisive assault on the German lines. He believed that America "had developed a type of manhood superior in initiative to that existing abroad" and would soon produce "a superior soldier." He was confident that this huge, powerful American army would bring victory and was equally confident that the British and French troops were too war-weary and battered to carry the fight to the enemy. Thus, Allied victory depended utterly on the creation of a distinctly

American army, even if in the meantime the Allies had to run the risk of losing significant ground to the Germans.[11]

In reality, however, Pershing and the Americans misunderstood the military dynamics of the Western Front. The German attacks were powerful and in a tactical sense, successful. But Germany was nearing the end of its manpower reserves. These spring offensives consumed scarce supplies of food and munitions and produced prodigious numbers of casualties. Even as he called for American troops to stem the German attack, Commander Foch became convinced of Germany's underlying weakness and planned powerful counterstrokes. It is true that Allied lines had been pushed back, that the Germans were within a day's march of Paris, and that British troops along the Somme had been routed. But as in 1914, advanced penetration outran supply lines.

Foch reasoned that such a "victory" had to leave his opponents vulnerable to counterattack. Thus, even as the Germans renewed their assaults in mid-July, he began attacking salients and weak points. Sensing that victory might be possible now, in 1918, he pressed Pershing to commit U.S. units rather than hold them back to form the nucleus of the vast American army being formed to lead the 1919 campaigns. It seemed to Pershing, whether in the face of defeat or in the sudden new hope of decisive victory, his European associates sought to thwart the creation of an autonomous American military presence. The May 1917 words of then-acting army chief of staff, General Tasker Bliss, seemed prescient: "When the war is over," he had written, "it may be a literal fact that the American flag may not have appeared anywhere on the line because our organizations will simply be parts of battalions and regiments of the Entente Allies. We might have a million men there and yet no American army."[12]

In the end, Pershing got his way, but Foch's bold strategy soon proved brilliantly successful. Even as Foch launched his first counterattacks, the AEF commander extracted the commitment to assign a separate sector of the Front to the United States. In July he was able to announce the formation of the American First Army, the first of three American armies eventually formed. With the British holding down the northern flank of the Allied lines and French armies now concentrating on the northeastern approaches to the Paris region, Pershing's doughboys would take over some 80 miles of trenches, anchoring the right flank and facing German forces defending the iron mines of the Briey basin and the key rail and supply center of Metz, in Lorraine. Assuming direct command of this First Army himself, Pershing immediately began molding newly arriving troops, now pouring into France at the rate of more than 300,000 a month, into a Second Army, and then a Third Army. By mid-August 1918, though still dependent on French artillery, Allied tanks

and planes, and British steel helmets, beset by shortages of trucks and locomotives, and struggling to construct and operate vast new port and supply
facilities, the AEF had nonetheless taken its place as a full partner in the war.
It now stood poised, in Pershing's estimation if not necessarily that of his
European colleagues, for major offensive action.

Americans in Action

For all the brevity of the duration of active U.S. military operations, American troops were involved in several decisive battles. Between the onset of the
German offensives in March 1918 and the end of the war in November 1918,
more than a million American soldiers served in combat areas. During this
time, discrete bodies of American troops fought in four major engagements: at
Cantigny, Chateau-Thierry, and Belleau Wood in May and June; at the
Aisne-Marne offensive of mid-July; at the St. Mihiel salient in September;
and in the Meuse-Argonne campaign of September–November. In August,
significant elements of U.S. infantry divisions also fought with British and
Empire units in a key offensive that forced the Germans back across the old
Somme battlefield.

At Cantigny, Chateau-Thierry, and Belleau Wood, beginning at the end of
May, U.S. Army and Marine units helped the hard-pressed French to blunt
the second great German stroke. American troops thus played a critical role
in repulsing the southernmost German advance, only 30 miles from Paris.
Three weeks of savage fighting along the River Marne and at Belleau Wood,
a rugged forest preserve, cost 4,500 American casualties, in actions that some
observers regarded as decisive in stopping the furthest German advance since
1914. "You Americans are our hope, our strength, our life," a French staff officer declared in mid-June, as exhausted Marines launched still another bloody
assault on entrenched German positions in Belleau Wood.[13]

In mid-July, at the Aisne-Marne, as many as 310,000 Americans, serving
under French sector command, provided the bulk of the forces in Field
Marshal Foch's first—and some said, most critical—counterstroke, putting
German forces permanently on the defensive. In this vast battle, which grew
out of the successful effort to thwart the German threat to Paris, Foch disrupted German plans to renew its assaults north and east of the French capital. Beginning on July 18, troops of the U.S. First and Second Divisions,
along with a Moroccan division, pushed veteran German units back while

their comrades in the Third Division held off repeated enemy attacks along the Marne River. For its stubborn resistance to German advance, the Third Division became known as the "Rock of the Marne," while advancing men from the First and Second Divisions gained a reputation for recklessness and courage. Declared a veteran French stretcher bearer, "they're first-rate troops, fighting in intense *individual* passion." Wounded Americans, he reported, resisted removal to the rear. His only criticism was "that they don't take sufficient care; they're too apt to get themselves killed."[14]

The chief contribution of these fresh American troops in what turned out to be a decisive campaign was their sheer numbers. As one French general declared, "Without the presence in the attack of your troops the attack would have been an utter impossibility—it would never have taken place. Your presence was absolutely essential." Earlier Allied advances, even when initially successful, had quickly stalled, "but," remarks historian Edward Coffman, "in July 1918 the flood of American reinforcements made the crucial difference." This action actually was the beginning of the end for the German war effort. In mid-July, Chancellor Georg von Hertling later recalled, German leaders were confident that they would soon be dictating peace terms from occupied Paris, so successful had been the offensives of the spring and early summer. "That was on the 15th," Hertling recalled. But "On the 18th even the most optimistic among us knew that all was lost. The history of the world was played out in three days." By now, more than 30,000 American soldiers, most of them in infantry and machine gun battalions, were debarking daily at the French ports, sowing defeatism among the enemy as much by their sheer numbers as by the battlefield prowess they might display.[15]

The two remaining distinctly American campaigns were, in contrast to the Aisne-Marne action, somewhat anticlimactic. The St. Mihiel assault, launched on September 12, was the first major U.S.-commanded action, as 500,000 Americans, along with 100,000 French troops, pushed retreating German forces back about 15 miles in the war-devastated area south of Verdun. General Pershing trained his troops relentlessly, regarding the effort to drive the Germans out of this westward-pointing bulge in the front as a critical test for this first major American-planned and American-conducted action. Indeed, Pershing argued, fresh, well-trained American troops, free of the debilitating effects of long-term trench warfare, should be permitted to push on after reducing the Salient. He was confident that they could achieve a major breakthrough, restoring the kind of "open warfare" American military doctrine emphasized. Aggressive Americans would capture critical railroad lines and coal and iron fields and drive a powerful wedge into the German battle front.

Alas for Pershing's grandiose project, by the time American troops were ready to assault St. Mihiel, Marshal Foch was sniffing decisive victory elsewhere. Spirited British attacks in Belgium and along the Somme were driving the Germans back and bagging thousands of prisoners. Indeed, the Germans themselves, needing now to shorten their defensive lines, had begun a methodical pullback from the St. Mihiel salient even before the American-led assault. Foch scotched Pershing's proposal for a major offensive, once again urging the AEF commander to release his divisions to the French and British, who, he believed, were on the verge of decisive victory elsewhere.

At St. Mihiel, U.S. troops disrupted the planned German pullback and captured German positions ahead of schedule. U.S. commanders, however, felt frustrated, sensing that the speed and power of the American advance had created disorder among the Germans. They were convinced that renewed assaults would achieve a critical breakthrough before the enemy could solidify its defensive positions. To Pershing, the St. Mihiel action demonstrated conclusively the fighting ability of American troops and the U.S. Army's mastery of the logistical, planning, and training problems involved in large-scale action. Certainly, the reduction of this bulge in the front—against which repeated French assaults earlier in the war had been bloodily repulsed—boosted Allied morale, although some critics scoffed that as the Germans were preparing to abandon the salient in any event little justified the American boasts of a great victory.

The final, and most extensive action for U.S. troops was in the Meuse-Argonne campaign, lasting from late September until the end of the war on November 11. With American forces now organized into three separate armies and occupying the southernmost quarter of the entire front, Pershing and his planners believed the time was ripe for a demonstration of American might. In July, Foch had approved a major U.S. offensive west and slightly north of Verdun, but this was before the increasingly desperate condition of the German forces had become apparent. At that time, a U.S.-led offensive in this heavily wooded and broken country seemed a good way to keep the Germans off balance by continuing the pressure that Foch believed would wear down enemy forces and achieve eventual victory. As planning proceeded for the massive American action, however, British attacks farther west and in Belgium were proving surprisingly successful. By September, Foch had concluded that the Germans could be defeated there and then and that the projected Meuse-Argonne assault, which would involve more than a million U.S. troops and huge quantities of munitions and supplies, should be abandoned. Repeatedly he urged Pershing to send fresh American divisions from this well-defended and difficult sector for use by the rapidly advancing Allies in other areas.

Having argued so long for a separate U.S. military presence and having spent weeks planning this campaign, however, Pershing refused to yield. Thus, early on the morning of September 26, 2,700 guns opened up on the German lines, immediately after which troops of the U.S. First Army moved forward, confident of their ability to breach the well-positioned and heavily armed German defense. Despite daunting logistical problems, made worse by severe shortages of locomotives and motor vehicles and grossly under-manned transport and supply services, the great Meuse-Argonne offensive was underway.

Although Pershing and his commanders believed that fresh and vigorous American troops could drive back even well-entrenched German veterans, the Meuse-Argonne battlefield soon proved otherwise. The Germans con-trolled the high ground. They used the difficult terrain to good advantage, sit-ing machine gun nests and artillery to dominate the approaches to the main fortifications. Of all the sectors on the Western Front in which heavy fight-ing occurred during the final phase of the war, this was among the toughest. Despite repeated frontal assaults, the troops of the First Army were soon stalled well short of their objectives. As early as September 29, a situation report revealed that "troops do not seem to be making an organized attack, or to be making an advance." Inadequately supplied with food, water, and ammunition, the First Army, in the words of historian Donald Smythe, "was dead in its tracks." French General Maxime Weygand reported that the American assault "was paralyzed."[16]

Behind the fighting front, the situation was even worse. Shortages of vehicles and transport troops, American inexperience with the conduct of large-scale operations, and the sheer magnitude of effort need to supply huge numbers of troops created a logistical nightmare. Huge traffic jams cre-ated chaos. The wounded could not be evacuated to base hospitals, reserves could not reach the battlefront, and delivery of supplies ground to a halt. As many as 100,000 stragglers clogged the rear areas, unable or unwilling to locate their units. Indeed, the First Army was in dire condition, its battal-ions exhausted, ravaged with influenza, and pinned down by the tenacious German defense. Impatiently, Pershing blamed his divisional commanders and their subordinates for lack of initiative. At one point, he climbed into his car, determined to exhort the troops to greater efforts, only to find that roadblocks, traffic jams, and deteriorating roads made it impossible for him to reach his battered brigades. By the first week in October, far from restor-ing "open warfare" to the Western Front, it seemed rather that (again in Smythe's words) the First Army "would soon be like a giant turtle tipped over on its back, floundering helplessly, unable to move."[17]

After stabilizing his lines, bringing up fresh troops, and dealing with logistical problems, Pershing renewed the advance on October 4 and again on October 14. Smythe's vivid account again: "As with earlier attacks, the U.S. infantry charged bravely, even foolishly, compelling the admiration of enemy soldiers, who nevertheless mowed them down with gusto."[18] But still the going was tough. Slowly the Americans learned the bitter lessons of modern warfare. Flanking movements and coordinated small-unit assaults against machine gun nests and heavily fortified German positions replaced mass frontal attacks. One by one, German machine guns were knocked out, pill boxes seized, strongholds eliminated. Even so, the German defenses, bristling with artillery and machine guns, blunted the American advance. These fresh assaults, like their earlier counterparts, came to a fitful halt short of their objectives, their gains measured in yards. Each day's battle claimed an average of more than 550 American dead.

The final phase of the offensive, beginning November 1, was more successful. By now, French and British troops north and west of the Meuse-Argonne were breaking through once-impregnable German defenses. German military and political leaders had begun to sound out the Allies regarding terms of armistice. Although the still-formidable German army never broke or capitulated, unprecedented numbers of German soldiers, many of them young boys and old men, were surrendering. Even so, the casualties continued to mount as veteran German units, tough and resilient, inflicted heavy losses on the advancing Americans as they pushed past German fortifications. By now, however, American units were advancing several miles a day, part of the general thrust that drove retreating Germans, who paused only to prepare booby traps and destroy farms, factories, and rail lines, back toward the Fatherland.

Several common features characterized these operations. In all cases, American troops were heavily dependent on Allied—usually French—artillery and support services. Both German and Allied witnesses remarked at the doughboys' aggressiveness, bravery, and willingness to take casualties. At the same time, equally notable was the laxness of rear-echelon discipline and the huge numbers of unattached, even perhaps duty-shirking, soldiers who typically accumulated in the wake of battle. French and British observers criticized the poor logistics of the American effort, pointing to the enormous traffic jams, shortages of rations, water, and ammunition, and poor coordination of supply functions near the battlefields. On the tactical side, few contemporary observers or subsequent students could find much brilliance or innovation on the part of American commanders. Despite the criticisms by Pershing and his officers of wasteful Allied tactics, U.S. commanders rarely came up with anything more imaginative than man-killing straight-ahead assaults on entrenched positions. Nor were they able to achieve what they had vowed, namely vault clear of the trenches and restore movement and mobility to the Western Front, at least not until the exhausted Germans were on the verge of defeat.

Dependence on the French, reflecting as it did the lack of American-made equipment, contributed to the Americans' lack of tactical imagination. The stunning German assaults of the spring and the successful British counter-strokes exhibited the effectiveness of close coordination between field artillery and infantry assault, tactics dependent upon much trial-and-error experimentation and close cooperation between the two arms born of long experience. In a typical American battle, on the other hand, French gunners provided at least half of the artillery support, while U.S. artillerymen were just learning their trade as the Great War ground to an abrupt halt, rarely achiev-ing the sort of integration increasingly associated with success. Only in the later stages of the Meuse-Argonne campaign were U.S. commanders begin-ning to master the art of small-unit advance and rolling artillery barrage.

Another problem area for American troops lay in the role of the tank. Typ-ical American assaults, unlike those of the British and especially the Aus-tralians, enjoyed little armored support. At the opening of the Aisne-Marne offensive, for example, only a handful of light French tanks, most of them quickly knocked out, participated. French commanders frequently pulled away tanks earmarked for American actions. For their part, although Pershing and his unit commanders frequently complained about the quality and character of French artillery support, they rarely raised questions about the paucity or allocation of tanks. With the exception of a handful of U.S. officers, notably Lieutenant Colonel George S. Patton, American commanders paid little heed to the offensive potential of the tank. Pershing, an old cavalryman himself, was more interested in building up his mounted reserve in hopes of a break-through into open country than he was in developing tank–infantry tactics. Ironically, in view of American doctrines of "open warfare," the only U.S. troops actually to experience anything like it were those fighting with the British, Canadians, and Australians in the Somme offensive, in which hun-dreds of tanks operating in relatively flat and unwooded country were able to make impressive gains.

Even if the war ended too suddenly for Pershing and his generals to realize their hopes for a decisive tactical and strategic role for American troops, they could find much to be proud of in the AEF's performance. Allies and foes alike attested to the verve, bravery, and enthusiasm of the soldiers and Marines who fought in France. Theirs was a democratic army, bringing the energy and ide-alism of the American republic to the tired battlefields of Europe. Officers had worked hard to transform diverse citizens into a mass army, stressing always the need to abandon Old World ethnic identities and to embrace 100 percent Americanism. But one element in the AEF fit awkwardly at best into this conception of the character and mentalité of a truly *American* military force. Neither the army nor the government nor the American people in general included the 400,000 African Americans who served with the U.S Army during the Great War in their definitions of common citizenship. In the war to make the world safe for democracy, the nation awarded black soldiers a consistent pattern of exclusion, denigration, and disdain.

When the United States entered the war, about 10,000 black soldiers were serving in four segregated regiments. In addition, another 10,000 were enrolled in National Guard units, most of them on a segregated basis. Of the nearly four million men inducted into the armed forces during the Great War, just over 13 percent were African American, nearly all of them serving in the army (since the Marines barred blacks entirely and the navy enrolled only 5,000, using them exclusively as stewards and messboys). The overwhelming majority of blacks serving in the AEF were assigned to labor, stevedore, transport, and engineering units and spent their overseas time unloading ships, building roads and encampments, digging fortifications, and retrieving and burying the dead. Virtually all officers were white. General Pershing himself had acquired his nickname, Black Jack, in the Spanish-American War by leading troopers of the fabled all-black 10th U.S. Cavalry. Since the end of slavery, only three men had overcome the physical and psychological abuse inflicted on African Americans at West Point to earn commissions. The prewar Plattsburg training camps had barred black participants on the grounds, declared the army's chief sponsor of this project, General Leonard Wood, that it must remain unavailable to men "with whom our descendants cannot intermarry without producing a breed of mongrels; they must at least be white."[19]

Although black soldiers had fought well in the Civil War, Indian wars, Spanish-American War, and Philippine Insurrection, white officers held them unsuited for technologically sophisticated modern warfare. Only after considerable pressure on the part of African Americans did the army establish a training camp to produce black officers and agree to organize two black combat divisions. The officer training center at Fort Des Moines in Iowa mixed together virtually illiterate veteran NCOs from regular army units with college and professional men recruited from civilian life in a hastily devised and often demeaningly conducted course. In October 1917, it graduated its only class of black officers, granting junior grade commissions to 639 men, who constituted 0.03 percent of the army's 200,000 Great War officers. The army leadership considered Fort Des Moines a risky, even doomed, experiment. Even Pershing, who had praised the combat performance of his cavalrymen in

Cuba, believed that the experiment with black officers in the Great War was a mistake: "It would have been much wiser," he later reflected, "to have followed the long experience of our Regular Army and provided . . . colored units with selected white officers."[20] White officers balked at serving with black units, barred black colleagues from recreational facilities and social functions, and acquiesced in or encouraged white private soldiers' refusal to accord black officers respect and obedience.

Black units were rigidly segregated. In southern camps, black soldiers were in effect prisoners, restricted from off-base recreational facilities and subjected to the segregationist practices of the host communities. The arming and training of large numbers of African Americans aroused fear and resentment among white southerners, many of whom initially sought to prevent the army from assigning blacks to encampments in southern states. And the encounter of proud black soldiers with racist white citizens and law enforcement officers did produce violent episodes. Blacks and whites remembered vividly—if differently—the Brownsville Affair of 1906 in which a clash between black veterans of the 25th Infantry and local authorities in the Texas town led to the summary dishonorable discharge of three entire companies. And on August 23, 1917, violence erupted again in Texas, this time in Houston. After the beating of a black soldier by local police, soldiers of the 24th Infantry marched on the city. An exchange of gunfire killed twenty people, including five policemen and four black soldiers. Hasty court-martials convicted scores of black soldiers. Twenty-eight eventually received death sentences and fifty-three life imprisonment. Soon after, eighteen men were in fact hanged.

Partly because of fears of such racial violence, the army never brought the two black divisions, the 92nd and 93rd, together as units in the United States, thus denying them critical training and coordinating experience. Neither of these outfits ever functioned as a complete unit. Elements of both saw action on the Western Front, with the men of the 93rd, notably the 369th Infantry Regiment, compiling a distinguished record and receiving many individual and unit citations from the French, including a dozen Croix de Guerre. Although French officers had their share of racial prejudice and they treated the men recruited from their African colonies with condescension, African Americans serving with the French generally reported a degree of acceptance and cooperation lacking in the American army. Even so, French military and civilian authorities did implement an AEF directive that called upon the French "'qu'elles ne gatent pas les negres'—not to spoil the Negroes," which meant that in most areas, black troops serving with the French were denied recreational facilities. Moreover, French officers were not to shake hands with or break bread with black officers, and French civilians were to avoid any semblance of intimacy or hospitality. Historians Arthur Barbeau and Florette Henri observe that the 369th was in combat 191 days, "longer than any other regiment in the AEF, after the shortest combat training of any regiment." The three other regiments of the 93rd that fought with the French also compiled excellent records. These four regiments lost 584 men killed and 2,582 wounded, a number equaling 32 percent of the division's strength.[21]

On the other hand, the 92nd Division gained a reputation for failure. From its inception, this unit endured mishandling and shoddy treatment. On the troopship to France, for example, only its white officers were assigned first-class accommodations. In France, black officers stayed in partially completed barracks while the white officers lived in hotels. None of the 92nd's units had received much training in the United States. The Division suffered a drastic lack of equipment. It underwent frequent and abrupt changes in command. Instead of training in France, its engineering battalions were put to work doing manual labor. Probably most damaging were the attitudes of its white officers from the company level on up to the Army's Third Corps commander, General Robert Bullard. An Alabaman, Bullard once wrote in his diary, "Poor negroes! They are hopelessly inferior." The general commanding the 92nd, Charles Ballou, shared in this contempt for his men, referring casually to the 92nd as the "Rapist Division." At the war's end, he refused to permit photographers to record the awarding of Distinguished Service Crosses to his men.[22]

Despite such leadership, on the whole, the 92nd fought creditably. One regiment, the 368th, however, gained a reputation for cowardice and dereliction of duty when it failed to carry out a particularly difficult liaison maneuver at the outset of the Meuse-Argonne offensive. Given a complex and dangerous assignment, the half-trained 368th became lost and confused. It retreated under heavy German fire. Many of its black officers were cashiered without appeal or hearings. After the war, an official army report on the Argonne offensive exonerated white troops of the 35th Division who had fled in the face of the enemy while concluding that the similar behavior of the men of the 368th Regiment revealed the true character of black combat troops. More objective investigators, however, attributed their actions largely to inadequate training, poor regimental command, and the inherent difficulties of the operation. Army officials considered the formation of black combat units and the commissioning of black officers to be an experiment and proved themselves only too eager to cite the performance of the 368th as evidence of black military inferiority. Ignoring the many contrary examples of effective leadership by black officers, regimental commander Colonel Fred Brown later published a paper titled "The Inefficiency of Negro Officers."[23] Despite the record of the

93rd Division and of units of the 92nd, no African American troops were permitted to march in the Allied victory parade in Paris.

Despite heavy military censorship, stories of the exploits of American soldiers and Marines became a staple of the newspapers back home. Both during and after the war, tales of individual heroism and boldness abounded. African American newspapers publicized the exploits of the "Buffaloes," the men of the 369th Regiment, and even the white *Milwaukee Sentinel* acknowledged that "colored regiments fought well," although its editorial writer could not refrain from a racist addendum to his words of praise, suggesting that the black heroes be sent "a cargo of watermelons." The exploits of white soldiers, in contrast, were never trivialized. Americans thrilled to the story of Marine Sergeant Dan Daly, for example. On June 6, at Belleau Wood, Daly, already a two-time Medal of Honor recipient, ensured his place in the history books. Leading his platoon across a wheat field stippled with red poppies, Daly exhorted his men in the face of relentless German machine gun fire. "Come on, you sons of bitches," he was heard to roar. "Do you want to live forever?"[24]

The poignant story of the "Lost Battalion," a mixed force of about 550 men of the 77th Division that found itself surrounded by the enemy during the Meuse-Argonne campaign, captured public attention. With supplies of food, water, medicine, and ammunition running out, Major Charles W. Whittlesey and his men fought off repeated German attacks. Rejecting demands for surrender, the Americans held out for five days until relieved by advancing units. The heroic stand of the "battalion" came at a high price: of its original 550 men, only 194 marched out, leaving 110 dead comrades behind. Legends about the "Lost Battalion" soon sprang up. It was not true, for example, though widely believed, that the major had greeted the demand for surrender by snarling, "Go to Hell." Another legend, though, was true. At one point, as a misdirected American artillery barrage began to blast his position, Whittlesey dispatched his last carrier pigeon, named "Cher Ami," which miraculously found its way to American lines with a message to halt the errant barrage.[25]

Then there were the exploits of Captain Eddie Rickenbacker, America's first flying ace. Already famous in America as a racing car driver, Rickenbacker commanded Flight One of the "Hat-in-the-Ring" Squadron, leading his flyers in spectacular aerial duels against the fabled Flying Circus of the Red Baron, Manfred von Richthofen. In September 1918, Rickenbacker attacked seven German planes, downed two of them, and won the Medal of Honor.

The greatest individual hero of all was Alvin York, a native of Pall Mall, Tennessee, an infantryman in the 82nd Division. On October 8, PFC York, a religious pacifist who initially sought conscientious objector status, single-handedly silenced an entire German machine gun battalion, killing at least 20 enemy soldiers and taking 132 prisoners as he led the men in his unit out of a German encirclement. When asked by the general commanding his division to estimate the number of Germans he had killed, York replied, "General, I would hate to think I missed any of them shots; they were all at pretty close range—50 or 60 yards."[26]

Yet, finally, the Great War was not a war of heroes or individual heroism. It was mass, industrial warfare, a war of attrition. Although the public might thrill to tales of individual exploits and heroic gestures, few soldiers survived their ordeal by fire with notions of valor and glory intact. In eight days of vicious fighting in the July Aisne-Marne offensive, the U.S. Rainbow Division, composed of National Guard units from all over the country, suffered more than 2,500 casualties, including 566 killed, in its successful attacks. As the exhausted men, at last relieved by fresh troops, pulled back, reported their chaplain, "They marched in wearied silence until they came to the slopes around Meurcy Farm," scene of an earlier assault. "Then from end to end of the line came the sound of dry, suppressed sobs. They were marching among the bodies of their unburied dead."[27]

If nothing else, the smells and sights of the battlefield were enough to destroy illusions of nobility and glory. Poison gas saturated the puddles of putrid water of the combat zone. The bloated corpses of men and animals drew clouds of black flies. Body parts poked out of shell holes and newly dug trenches. The ubiquitous lice, impossible to kill or escape, were everywhere, torturing even the most stoical soldier. In the disorder of front-line life, men relieved themselves everywhere, and the stench of human excrement competed with the smell of poison gas and decaying bodies. "At the battlefront," recalled a private of the 32nd Division, "there was no such thing as sanitation."[28]

American soldiers suffered much from the poor supply and logistics performance of the AEF. Throughout the 1918 combat operations, soldiers were short of food and water. Many veterans reported constantly being hungry. Marines at Belleau Wood dug into the ground to find moist clay to lick, and in the Meuse-Argonne, German machine gunners kept their weapons trained on streams and rivulets in frequently realized hopes of killing desperate Americans seeking water. At supply depots, huge mountains of goods accumulated but owing in part to Allied-imposed shortages of trucks and locomotives and to the relative paucity of supply, transport, and engineering units, getting them into the hands of men at the front often proved beyond the capacity of inexperienced U.S. officers.

Nothing in the experience of even the most rough-hewn soldier prepared him for what he encountered on the battlefield. Field commander Douglas

MacArthur never forgot an image from his first combat action: dying German soldiers entangled a few feet from the American trench, their bloody bodies twitching and writhing on the barbed wire. Lieutenant Joseph D. Lawrence recalled surviving a near-miss artillery shell only to discover as he moved out the "bloody mess of flesh and scraps of an American uniform" that had once been a fellow soldier. Soldiers saw men without legs attempting to run away from danger. Distant muffled sounds of comrades buried alive by artillery fire; burial parties shoveling mangled body parts into hastily dug graves; an American airman, now a "blackened egg-shaped mass," encountered suddenly amid the wreckage of his plane—these images and worse haunted the memories and dreams of thousands of doughboys.[29]

Modern war was literally terrifying. Frontal assaults against well-entrenched machine guns took a ghastly toll. Observers and survivors were both appalled and transfixed at the sight of neat rows of corpses, crumpled forms of what had once been comrades, dotting the wheat fields near Belleau Wood. Of all the horrors, though, it was artillery bombardment, with unseen enemy guns hurling high explosives at men crouched in dugouts and trembling in trenches, that many soldiers described as the worst ordeal of all. The victim, after all, was not only defenseless—his survival was purely a matter of chance. A direct hit several yards away turned comrades instantly from men into pulverized chunks of flesh. Brave men shook uncontrollably. "I want to scream and run and throw myself," recorded Corporal Harold W. Pierce. "When I hear the whistle of an approaching shell I dig my toes into the ground and push on the walls of the dugout." "To be shelled is the worst thing in the world," declared a young lieutenant.[30]

American troops suffered heavy casualties. In the five-and-a-half months of active combat operations, about 60,000 died in battle and 206,000 suffered wounds. Between the end of May and the Armistice—the only period of sustained American military action—an average of 300 Americans were killed each day. The six-week Meuse-Argonne campaign claimed 26,000 of the dead. Although these numbers paled in comparison with the huge numbers of dead and wounded of other armies that fought for more than four years, they were large enough. In addition, another 60,000 military personnel died of disease, half of them in the United States, many of them victims of the influenza pandemic that claimed at least 20 million lives worldwide in 1918 and 1919.[31]

The American wounded were more fortunate than their European counterparts. Throughout the war, French medical services were grossly inadequate, with almost a third of France's 1.3 million fatalities dying from wounds, a far larger proportion than either the British or the Germans. Ignoring lessons that other belligerents learned relatively quickly about the importance of antiseptic conditions and failing to devote sufficient resources to providing adequate facilities or skilled medical care, French authorities acquired a well-deserved reputation for callousness and inefficiency. The primitiveness of conditions in French military hospitals appalled Pershing on his visits to wounded doughboys who had fought under French command. Throughout the period of active U.S. military operations, American units serving under French direction suffered higher casualties and experienced decidedly worse postwound treatment than their American-led counterparts.

British military medicine, however, did eventually achieve high standards of care and treatment. Well before U.S. troops were actively engaged, the AEF posted 1,200 military doctors to the British to gain firsthand experience and benefit from what the British had been learning about the treatment of wounds on the modern battlefield. In addition, even before U.S. belligerency, scores of American doctors and nurses had served as volunteers on the Western Front. Thus, the wounded Americans benefited from the learning curve of the war's first three years. Initially, British doctors were astonished at the deadliness of modern weapons and European battlefield conditions, with the heavily fertilized killing fields of the Western Front taking a ghastly toll as wounds quickly became infected and soldiers died by the hundreds of gangrene and tetanus. Countermeasures, however, were effective, and by 1917 the British had reduced the proportion of deaths-to-wounds by more than 70 percent.

The lethal influenza pandemic of the fall of 1918 rivaled battlefield action as a killer or incapacitator of soldiers. During the period of September–November 1918, almost 100,000 members of the AEF in France were afflicted. About 10 percent of these men died. During its five weeks of training and transport in France, the 88th Army Division, for example, lost about a third of its 18,000 men to influenza and related pneumonia, 444 of whom died of these diseases. It went into combat on October 24, fighting the retreating Germans until the November 11 Armistice, losing a total of ninety killed, wounded, and captured. The unanticipated deluge of flu cases, the severity and lethalness of the disease and its companion pneumonia, and the highly contagious nature of this affliction nearly overwhelmed the army's medical facilities and personnel. "Everything is overflowing with patients," recorded one army surgeon in mid-October. "Our divisions are being shot up; the wards are full of machine-gun wounds. There is rain, mud, 'flu' and pneumonia. . . . In one night I had 60 deaths." In comparison with the flu, wounds, not requiring isolation, were relatively easily treated. In the absence of effective drugs or antibiotics, flu victims however, required labor-intensive treatment, protracted bed rest, and close supervision.

AEF medical authorities warned front-line doctors and nurses not to take these flu and pneumonia cases lightly: "Absolute rest is as vital to them while they are meeting and overcoming the infections as operation is for penetrating wounds of the abdomen."[32]

Despite horrific conditions that some American wounded experienced as supply and transport nearly broke down during the early stages of the Meuse-Argonne campaign, well-equipped and well-trained American doctors and nurses compiled an enviable record. The portable x-ray and improved methods of blood transfusion and intravenous medication that British doctors introduced to military medicine, after all, were initially American innovations. American military surgeons, combining the advanced techniques pioneered in the United States with the trial-and-error experience of their British counterparts, reduced sharply the frequency of amputation characteristic of past wars. Even so, Army doctors cut off 700 hands or feet, 600 arms, and 1,700 legs and treated more than 2,000 facial and jaw wounds. Attesting to the inexperience of U.S. troops and their commanders was the fact that 31 percent of the wounded treated by the U.S. Army were gas victims, many of them suffering—temporarily in most cases—from blindness.[33]

One type of wound—variously known as "shell shock" and "war neurosis"—proved particularly perplexing and frightening. Soldiers who had performed their duties conscientiously and perhaps even heroically might suddenly break. Some began suddenly to twitch or lose the use of their legs. Some turned mute and appeared catatonic. "One of our best sergeants," reported a young lieutenant, after his unit had endured four days of shelling, began "whimpering like a baby . . . his nervous system shattered." Horrific nightmares haunted some, and agonizing bouts of insomnia tormented others. A soldier might perform bravely in combat but lapse into apathy or hysteria hours or even days afterward in rear-echelon training exercises.

At the beginning of the war, British officers and medical men, locked in a mind-set that stressed individual volition and sharp distinctions between honor and disgrace, treated men so afflicted as malingerers and cowards. Hundreds were disciplined, dozens suffering the death penalty. Those "treated" by doctors often endured grisly "cures," which included cold-water immersion, electroshock applications, and brutal applications of physical and psychological pressure. By the time of U.S. belligerency, however, the limitations—to say nothing of the inhumanity—of such "cures" had become apparent. American psychiatrists and other medical officers largely avoided the "treatments" that some British counterparts continued to inflict. Rather, they prescribed a period of rest, good food, and pleasant surroundings, all, however, within a decidedly military environment stressing obedience to orders and the soldier's obligations to his mates back at the front. The goal was to treat the afflicted soldier as close to the battlefront and as quickly as possible, with the aim of convincing him that only by resuming his duties and rejoining his mates could he regain his health.

Those who failed to respond to these methods, although not brutalized physically, were abruptly separated from more tractable comrades. They were subjected to rigid military discipline and assigned demeaning tasks, such as digging latrines, in the hopes that the pain of being so isolated would stimulate feelings of shame, which in turn would overcome their illness and impel them to respond to more positive treatment. Doctors, always fearful that soldiers might claim psychological affliction to escape combat, discouraged use of the term "shell shock," not because it was misleading and imprecise, though it was, but rather because it seemed to lend legitimacy to a soldier's shirking of duty by connecting it to a tangible cause, the terrifying effects of artillery fire.

The AEF kept only sketchy statistics of the numbers of soldiers suffering mental or emotional breakdown, classifying many who showed up at dressing stations in obviously deranged condition as "Not yet diagnosed." During the course of American belligerency, almost 100,000 men were admitted to army hospitals with psychological or nervous ailments, and 42,000 gained disability discharges on the basis of these complaints. By no means were all of these combat related, however, since the training camps in the United States and in France produced thousands of cases of neurological and psychoneurological discharges. In France, the AEF created a separate base hospital for treatment of severe cases of combat-related disorders. This facility eventually treated more than 2,500 men. About 7,500 others received various levels of treatment at other AEF clearing stations and hospitals. No doubt many afflicted soldiers were otherwise wounded or were killed in action before receiving treatment for psychological disorders, and others found ways to disguise their condition.

For thousands of soldiers, the true psychological effects of wartime experience did not become manifest until months or even years later. Three years after the end of the war, veterans' hospitals in the United States housed more than 9,000 neuropsychiatric cases that dated from service in the Great War, and in subsequent years this figure increased. By the middle of 1940, for example, 81 percent of the 11,501 hospitalized AEF veterans were in care for neuropsychological reasons. Many thousands of others struggled on, privately coping—or not coping—with the psychological scars of combat. One of these men was Major Charles Whittlesey. In 1921, haunted by the responsibility he felt for the deaths of so many of his men, this much-decorated hero of the Lost Battalion committed suicide.[34]

After the Armistice the remains of about 70 percent of the men who died in Europe with the AEF were returned to the United States for individual burial. The rest were interred in military cemeteries, mostly in France. At Suresnes, just outside Paris, there are 1,541 graves, with soldiers and Marines buried without regard to rank or race. Stevedores and laborers killed in accidents and victimized by influenza lie next to National Guardsmen and Marines from lily-white units, thus constituting an anomalous breach in the otherwise rigidly segregated Great War military order. Eventually, the government honored a pledge it had made just after the war in an effort to encourage families to leave the bodies of the dead in France. In 1930, Congress provided funds to permit mothers and wives to travel to France to see the gravesites where their loved ones were interred. Now, however, the standard racial order reasserted itself: Black Gold Star mothers were to be sent on a separate ship and were provided with segregated transport and facilities. Several dozen reluctantly accepted the terms of the government's offer, although some mothers rejected them, declaring it preferable "to remain at home and retain our honor and self-respect."[35]

The U.S. Contribution

What was the American military contribution to Allied victory? The optimum case for the decisiveness of U.S. military efforts runs along these lines: Had the Second Division not arrived at Chateau-Thierry at the end of May, German advance units, driving demoralized French and colonial troops before them, would have had a clear pathway to Paris. In stopping the deepest thrust of the powerful German spring offensive, U.S. infantry and Marines there and at nearby Belleau Wood saved the day for the beleaguered French and thus for the Allied cause. In the crucial Aisne-Marne offensive, Americans constituted the bulk of the French-led forces that turned the tide in the latter part of July. And although it was true that British and French troops made the largest gains in the offensives of August–November that ended the war, their success was only possible because of the massive U.S. operation in the Meuse-Argonne, which pinned down large numbers of German troops trying to protect critical military bases, railroad lines, and industrial facilities in that sector. The day after the Germans had capitulated, Pershing hailed "the officers and soldiers of the American Expeditionary Forces who . . . have made possible this glorious result."[36]

Americans too pointed to the contributions of the U.S. Navy. Although prewar ship construction had emphasized battleships and cruisers, it was the U.S. destroyer squadrons, along with scores of smaller sub chasers, many of them refitted yachts, that helped to turn the tide. Destroyers were small, swift, unglamorous craft. With cramped quarters and subject to vertiginous rolling in the Atlantic's heavy seas, they tried the stamina and seamanship of their crews on every voyage. But with a speed of up to 40 knots (as compared with a submerged submarine's 8 knots) and with a shallow draft that made torpedo attack difficult, destroyers, along with smaller antisubmarine vessels, made life increasingly difficult for Germany's U-boat commanders. Operating primarily out of Ireland and the west coast of France, U.S. destroyer squadrons compiled an outstanding record in antisubmarine warfare and troopship protection. And the U.S. Navy, with Admiral William E. Sims serving as commander in Europe, enthusiastically agreed to integrate American squadrons into British command structures.

The first six of an eventual seventy-nine U.S. destroyers arrived in Queenstown, Ireland, on May 4, 1917, followed soon after by additional squadrons. And the Americans arrived just in time. In the spring of 1917, the German gamble—that unrestricted submarine warfare would force the Allies to yield before significant U.S. ground forces arrived in France—seemed on the verge of success. Sinkings mounted month by month: In February, 540,000 tons of shipping; in March, 600,000 tons; in April, 900,000 tons. In all, in 1917, U-boats destroyed more than 6 million tons of shipping, almost half of the tonnage lost in the entire war. Immediately after the U.S. declaration of war, Britain's Grand Fleet Commander, Sir John Jellicoe, told a shocked Sims, "It is impossible for us to go on with the war if losses like this continue. . . . They will win, unless we can stop these losses . . . soon."[37]

In the end, a variety of factors defeated the German naval offensive. Probably most important was the adoption by the British, with full U.S. support, of a convoy system, made possible in part by the appearance of U.S. destroyers in the war zones. Improved depth charges began taking a heavy toll of German submarines. Beefed-up patrols, extensive mining of the North Sea, and the limited ability of the Germans to replace, refit, and augment their U-boat forces steadily reduced the number of sinkings. In the final analysis, the Germans did not sufficiently support their U-boat campaign, continuing to deflect scarce resources to their immobile surface fleet and failing to exploit opportunities to expand drastically the number of submarines they produced.

British naval experts were generous in their assessment of the U.S. contribution to the winning of the crucial war at sea. Holding that adoption of the convoy system was the crucial factor in turning back the U-boat challenge,

Jellicoe declared, "this was only made possible at the date adopted, by the entry of the United States into the war." Historian Robert Ferrell concurs, stating flatly, "The U.S. Navy made the crucial difference, without which the Allies would have lost the war in 1917–1918 for lack of American troops and supplies."[38]

The case for the decisiveness of American arms, whether in France or on the seas, however, has remained unsettled. In France and Belgium, after all, it was British, Empire, and French troops who made the greatest headway, to say nothing of their sacrifices over the preceding four years that eventually wore down the German military machine. And although it was true that U.S. destroyer squadrons arrived just in time to facilitate eventually effective responses to the U-boat onslaught, it was the Royal Navy that still bore the overwhelming brunt of the effort: For every U.S. combat ship serving in the Atlantic, the British had thirteen at sea. It is likely that, as most experts expected, had the war dragged on into 1919, the vast industrial might of America, along with Pershing's vaunted three million trained and equipped troops, would have dominated the Allied effort. Even as the war ended, U.S. shipyards and munitions works were just beginning to produce vessels and weapons in abundance. But in the war that in fact ended on November 11, 1918, it was more the prospect of these seemingly unlimited quantities of men and supplies, rather than the actual performance of American industry and arms, that crushed German hopes. Pershing and his fellow officers, of course, would have preferred the role of clear-cut victors in open combat to that of serving as a vast manpower reserve in the still-attritional combat of the Western Front. Nonetheless, in the end it was America that provided the key to ending the bloody, stalemated conflict and thus helping critically to limit Europe's seemingly interminable slide into ever greater barbarity and chaos. Declares historian David Kennedy in a generally cautious assessment of the American effort, "the AEF's exertions in 1918 undoubtedly helped shorten the war by perhaps as much as a year."[39] Everything considered, this was a splendid achievement.

FIVE

~

Class, Race, Gender

Even as American soldiers took their place on the European battlefields, back home the Great War was bringing to a head critical issues involving class, race, and gender. In 1902, President Theodore Roosevelt had declared that "the two great fundamental internal problems with which we have to deal . . . are the negro [sic] problem in the South, and the relations of capital and labor."[1] During the Great War, many social commentators and public figures would have modified this judgment. If anything, in the intervening decade the "labor problem" had intensified. Widespread racial friction, however, was no longer a mainly southern phenomenon, as the trickle of black migrants northward and westward became a powerful tide, bringing the vibrant culture of southern African Americans, along with sometimes explosive racial tensions, with it. Meanwhile, mounting agitation for full female citizenship was challenging the male-dominated social and political order in ways that even ten years earlier, men of Roosevelt's perspective could only dimly have anticipated. American belligerency required that public authorities and opinion-leading elites confront these racial, class, and gender dilemmas as they sought to enlist ordinary citizens in the great crusade abroad.

Initially, it appeared that the need to mobilize and perhaps appease working people, African Americans, and activist women in the service of national ambitions might generate innovative public policies and even shifts in national consciousness. In the end, however, the brevity of U.S. belligerency, along with the tenacious hold of long-standing class, racial, and gender identities, ensured that wartime efforts to deal with social conflict would remain partial, incomplete, and even abortive. Even so, however, the efforts of government and opinion-setting elites to address the country's festering labor problems, its rapidly changing racial dynamics, and the challenge that an emerging women's movement posed were alive with possibilities even if they remained unfulfilled by the time of the unexpected Armistice of November 1918.

The Working Classes

For millions of ordinary workers, the period of the Great War, most definitely including the years before U.S. entry, accelerated demographic, economic, and social trends that were underway before 1914. In particular, the war reinforced three central developments in the refashioning of the American working class in the first third of the twentieth century. First, it accelerated changes in the ethnic composition of the working class and in the geographic distribution of African Americans. Second, it sharply advanced the electrification of industry and the restructuring of work process that new machinery made increasingly possible. And third, it stimulated workers' demands for greater access to both the fruits of consumer capitalism and greater security and representation in the work place. The federal government responded haltingly, but also innovatively, to the new labor dynamics that the war brought, and nowhere more so than in the area of industrial relations.

All belligerent countries quickly discovered that the economic and manpower demands of the Great War made labor a central concern. The presence of large industrial proletariats and vigorous trade unions forced governments to confront problems of manpower allocation, income distribution, and industrial conflict. Potent socialist and other radical movements, all predicated on the primacy of the working class in industrial society, challenged official versions of the war's origins and purposes. By the war's third year, labor and socialist protest was compelling governments to devise new forms of worker appeasement, representation, and containment. In Britain, militant unionists launched a wave of strikes in protest over wages, working conditions, and "dilution," the hiring of women and other unskilled workers in the place of established craftsmen in the shipbuilding and munitions sectors. In Germany, strikes and demonstrations challenged the government's economic policies, and in July 1917 socialist deputies in the Reichstag were instrumental in forcing through a resolution urging a negotiated end to the war. In France also, workers' representatives bitterly condemned the conduct of the war as strikes in the munitions factories shook Paris and other cities. It was in Russia, however, that the greatest threat to the established order erupted. There, in October 1917, Bolsheviks—Marxist socialists demanding a prompt end to the war and the creation of a workers' state—seized power and immediately called upon workers everywhere to follow their example and repudiate their governments' continuation of the war.

America was far from immune to labor activism and radical challenge. By the eve of U.S. belligerency, the primary national labor organization, the American Federation of Labor (AFL), counted more than two million members, and another 650,000 workers belonged to unions not affiliated with the AFL. An energetic and articulate Socialist Party attracted working-class support, especially in the immigrant and urban centers of the Northeast and Middle West. The radical Industrial Workers of the World (IWW) called for the overthrow of the capitalist political and economic order and its replacement with a workers' republic; it gained wide support especially among midwestern harvest hands, lumberjacks in the South and Northwest, and Mountain State metal miners.

In the years of the Great War, confrontations between workers and employers in the United States peaked. Between 1914 and 1920, an average of more than 3,000 significant strikes erupted annually. In the years 1916–18 more than four million workers conducted work stoppages, and in 1919 alone, the figure reached 4,160,000. Violence marked many of these contests. Employers, determined to assert and maintain unilateral control over the workplace, resisted union demands for recognition. They fired labor activists, hired private police to smash picket lines, and expelled the families of striking workers from company-owned housing. Policemen, federal soldiers, militiamen, and other agents of the state frequently intervened in labor disputes, usually to crush strikes and wreck labor unions. Workers responded in kind, attacking replacement workers—"scabs," in union parlance—and sometimes resorting to sabotage. Observes historian David Montgomery, this was indeed "a decade of strikes of unprecedented scale and continuity," and in the words of another historian, truly "An Age of Industrial Violence."[2]

Thus, the "labor problem" posed a serious challenge to the Wilson administration. As it launched its tentative preparedness program in 1916 and more so as it mobilized for war, the administration had to devise policies and programs designed to enlist workers positively in the war effort and at the same time to silence dissidents. In this effort, the administration was aided by the fact that since 1912, the AFL had been a political ally of President Woodrow Wilson. Disturbed by the savagery of labor violence and by the apparent growing disparity between wealth and poverty, Wilson found in AFL President Samuel Gompers a willing supporter of legislation aimed at curbing powerful trusts and outlawing monopolistic business practices. During Wilson's first term, the Democratic Congress passed laws designed to limit child labor, protect unions from restrictive judicial orders, improve conditions for merchant seamen, and establish an 8-hour workday for operating railroad employees. Gompers and most other AFL leaders also proved loyal supporters of the president's foreign and defense policies, with the AFL president gladly accepting a position on the Council of National Defense. Most union leaders promptly endorsed the declaration of war, and in November 1917, Wilson became the first U.S. president to address a labor convention, telling delegates to the AFL's annual gathering in Buffalo, "while we are fighting for freedom, we must see . . . that labor is free [at home]. . . . I am with you if you are with me," he pledged.[3]

The proadministration stance of Gompers and most other national labor leaders was far from universal, however, even within the AFL. Many laborites viewed war as inherently illiberal, promoted by profit-seeking capitalists but fought and paid for by oppressed workers. Activists in New York, Chicago, Seattle, and other cities criticized Gompers's blanket support for the administration. Thousands of Irish American and German American workers, who constituted the core membership of many of the established labor organizations, bridled at their union leaders' support for the war. In a national referendum conducted in the spring of 1917, the membership of the Socialist Party of America, which claimed the loyalty of thousands of workers, voted opposition to U.S. entry. And although the IWW did not take an official stand on the war, its activists pledged to use the anticipated boom in employment to press aggressive organizing and to force employers to improve wages and working conditions. The Bolshevik Revolution, with its searing indictment of capitalist governments and its stirring appeal for workers of the world to unite against ruling elites everywhere, highlighted the vulnerability of belligerent governments, including that of the United States, to working-class agitation and distrust.

Throughout the period of U.S. belligerency, then, the government attempted to enlist the loyal support of the nation's working class while suppressing dissent. In this attempt, it worked primarily through its friends in the AFL (and the railroad unions, close to the AFL in ideology and political perspective but not affiliated with it), elevating Gompers to the untitled position of its chief labor adviser. With the advice and support of Gompers and labor-relations professionals recruited from private business, academia, and personnel management, Wilson and other federal officials created new agencies designed to mediate labor disputes, allocate manpower, and monitor the economic impact of the war on working people and their families. Older agencies such as the U.S. Department of Labor and its Conciliation Service gained expanded resources and greater visibility. Federal officials profited from knowledge of how the British were attempting to deal with labor problems in their munitions industry. They responded to the demands of workers and union leaders in the construction of the army cantonments, in the suddenly expanding shipyards, and after December 1917, on the railroads by creating boards of adjustment, consultation, and mediation that had strong union representation.

Of greater concern than the labor problems in government arsenals, shipyards, and other facilities, however, were those erupting with increasing frequency in private industry, which produced most of the weapons and munitions. In September 1917, responding to a particularly troubling conflict involving copper miners in Arizona, Wilson created the President's Mediation Commission (PMC) and appointed a brilliant young Harvard University law professor, Felix Frankfurter, to head it. This commission was charged with investigating the events that had culminated in Bisbee, Arizona, that summer as well as other recent episodes of labor conflict occurring in strategic industries. The PMC was also to recommend general policies to enable the government to promote labor peace in crucial sectors of the economy. Long a critic of the authoritarian behavior of American industrialists, Frankfurter found much to confirm his views in the cases that the PMC probed. "Failure to equalize the parties in the adjustment of inevitable industrial contests is the central cause of our [labor] difficulties," the law professor reported. As a remedy, he urged that the administration promote "some form of collective relationship" between employers and workers.[4]

Although Frankfurter generally supported the cause of trade unionism, he stopped short of urging that the government endorse union recognition per se. He feared that in view of employers' hostility toward organized labor, frank advocacy of unionism would impede the war effort. He proposed rather that the government support the formation of shop committees or works councils. In these bodies, worker-chosen representatives would consult with employers about wages, working conditions, and grievances. Where strong unions already existed, of course, collective bargaining would continue to operate, but in an economy in which only a minority of workers belonged to unions— especially the case in the great metalworking sectors that were critical to the war effort—works councils would bring democratic representation to the shop floor while avoiding the contentious matter of union recognition.

Frankfurter's recommendations made sense to Wilson, Secretary of War Newton D. Baker, and other officials primarily responsible for the economic aspects of the war effort. Shop committees were a way of involving workers directly, thus advancing industrial democracy, which many progressives believed long overdue in the autocratic world of corporate America. Employers, however, held correctly that where shop committees appeared, unions would not be far behind. Union activists, they feared, would soon dominate these bodies and thus bring labor organization into the plant through the back door.

Most labor unionists were willing to accept the idea of shop committees. To be sure, IWW activists and the "militant minority" of trade unionists who hoped to use the war for aggressive organizing and for challenging the capitalist order disdained this halfway step. But most AFL leaders, who shared with employers the expectation that unionists would soon come to control shop committees, regarded the government's program as an important step toward expansion of union membership and power. Moreover, at the very outbreak of the war, Gompers had in effect given the government his pledge that the AFL and its constituent unions would not try to exploit the national emergency to force union recognition nor would the AFL countenance strikes during the war emergency. Some potent union leaders demurred from this pledge, but once it had been given, they could hardly refuse to honor it. Overall, government endorsement of shop committees, bringing with it the principle of worker representation and the limiting of managerial authority in the workplace, seemed to many laborites a promising step.

In its labor policy, as in most aspects of war mobilization, the Wilson administration did not settle upon definitive arrangements until the spring of 1918. Through the fall of 1917 and into early 1918, the boom in employment, along with rising prices, triggered a mounting number of work stoppages. Faced with growing criticism of his management of the economy, the president called upon his secretary of labor, William B. Wilson (no relation), to devise a permanent government agency charged with ameliorating labor unrest, resolving disputes between workers and employers, and consolidating the administration's hitherto disparate and overlapping labor initiatives. Eventually, after consultation with AFL leaders and employers' representatives, the labor secretary submitted a report calling for a twelve-member board to consist of five labor representatives, five employer representatives, and two co-chairs, one nominated by each group. On April 8, 1918, President Wilson issued an executive order creating this body, the National War Labor Board (NWLB), with labor advocate Frank P. Walsh and former U.S. President William Howard Taft as co-chairs. Although other arms of the government continued to be involved in labor matters, it was the NWLB that embodied the administration's definitive labor policy for the duration of the war.

The NWLB was an unusually vigorous and controversial body. The continuing militancy of workers in the metalworking, munitions, and transportation sectors of the economy, along with employers' refusal to acknowledge workers' right to a voice in workplace matters, forced it repeatedly to tackle difficult issues relating to wages, hours of employment, and worker representation. Reflecting the administration's overall effort to manage the wartime economy without resort to direct coercion, the board stressed the principle of voluntarism. Lacking congressional mandate, it could, in theory, only investigate disputes, publicize its findings, make recommendations, and seek agreement between disputants. As the government's primary instrument for handling labor issues, however, the NWLB carried great prestige and could recommend that the president take drastic action under war powers legislation if employers or workers rejected its recommendations.

Under normal circumstances, the composition of the board, with its five die-hard union advocates, its five equally adamant employer representatives, and the co-chairs chosen by these groups, might well have rendered it ineffectual. But Walsh, a Kansas City lawyer with strong prounion convictions and rich experience in labor problems, proved an unusually persuasive and effective chair. At the same time, Taft, nominally the employers' mouthpiece, moderated his long-standing hostility toward organized labor, seeing in the war emergency the need for compromise and accommodation. Most important, however, was the administration's strong support for the board's often-controversial rulings. The president and his advisers, concerned about ensuring labor loyalty and sensitive to the damage that unresolved worker grievances could do, consistently upheld decisions that largely supported worker advocates' views on wage increases, hours of labor, and perhaps most crucially, worker representation. In the summer of 1918, the president ordered a government takeover of the telegraph lines because of the refusal of the Western Union Company to honor NWLB recommendations concerning union recognition; he sent a clear message that, in the words of historian Joseph McCartin, "the NWLB was a new power to be reckoned with."[5]

Not all important NWLB rulings favored organized labor. In Bridgeport, Connecticut, in the heart of the weapons and munitions industry, striking machinists rejected the board's efforts to resolve a long-term dispute with the Remington Arms Company and other employers, staging a series of walkouts through the summer of 1918. The limits of voluntarism quickly became apparent when the president threatened to remove draft exemptions, thereby forcing these skilled workers, primarily concerned with retaining the wage and status differentials that their skills had won for them, back on the job. In general, however, NWLB investigations, reports, and rulings strengthened the hand of workers seeking higher wages and representation in dealings with management. Union activists in the coal mines, urban transit systems, and electrical industry were particularly skillful in using board intervention to discredit high-handed employers, recruit new members, and establish union footholds. So emboldened did local militants become that even national leaders of labor organizations grew concerned. By invoking the NWLB and securing its support for their demands, local activists often bypassed their national organizations. They ignored bureaucratic procedures and, by virtue of the waves of new members now surging into unions such as the International Association of Machinists and the International Brotherhood of Electrical Workers, threatened the positions of established leaders.

The abrupt end of the war also brought an abrupt end to important NWLB activities. Bethlehem Steel and other employers could now with impunity ignore orders to recognize independent worker-chosen shop committees, claiming that the end of hostilities canceled any obligation to abide by government rulings. In March 1919, the board itself ceased operations. While it functioned, however, it seemed to spearhead a dramatic breakthrough in U.S. industrial relations. Labor history up to 1917 was not wanting in episodes of militant unionism, grass roots organizing, and widespread worker mobilization. In virtually all cases, however, employers had defeated union drives, often with the aid of public authorities. But the wartime board, with its contingent of union representatives and the administration's clear interest in sustaining worker loyalty in a world suddenly exploding with radical challenges, presided over a sharp, if brief, reversal of the normal dynamics of labor relations in the United States. Fueled by wartime employment and inflation, as well as the friendly treatment of union goals in Washington, union membership expanded dramatically. Having stabilized at about 2.5 million in 1915, membership in labor organizations vaulted to about 3.4 million in 1918 and topped the 4 million mark early in 1919. In July 1918, in the middle of the board's most hectic and productive period, an enthusiastic Walsh had posited that the NWLB would "be not only a big thing for the country during the war, but . . . perhaps it will furnish a basis for a real industrial regime thereafter."[6] In the aftermath of war, these hopes proved to be misplaced, but memories of the positive role that this innovative agency had played in altering, if not transforming, the conduct of industrial relations remained vivid among union supporters and employers alike.

The government did not confine its wartime activities in labor relations to NWLB action. On the railroads, strongly organized before the war by brotherhoods not affiliated with the AFL, the United States Railroad Administration (USRA) granted significant concessions in wages and work rules, incorporating union representatives in adjustment boards created to deal with grievances and disputes. Contractors doing government work in the shipyards, building housing for workers in areas of heavy military production, and

1. Thomas Woodrow Wilson, 1856–1924. (National Archives)

2. Women played a critical role in the Great War–era peace movement. Here social reformer Jane Addams (second from left, front row) leads an American delegation bound for the International Peace Conference in The Hague, Netherlands, April 1915. (National Archives)

3

4

3. Women demonstrate in behalf of greater military strength during a monster Preparedness parade in New York City, May 1916. (National Archives)

4. Wilson termed conscription a "selection from a nation which has volunteered in mass." Here Secretary of War Newton D. Baker selects the first capsule in the second draft lottery, June 1918. (National Archives)

5

6

5. Conscription, while generally accepted by the American people, triggered sharp opposition in some quarters. These New York City women battle police in an effort to present an antidraft petition to Mayor John Mitchel, June 1917. (National Archives)

6. As casualties mounted in 1918, the government conducted "slacker" raids, rounding up men suspected of draft evasion. Soldiers are preparing to cart these New York City men to an armory for interrogation. (National Archives)

7

8

7. Throughout the summer of 1917, workers labored furiously to build cantonments for the new mass conscript army. These drafted men are reporting for service at Camp Travis, near San Antonio, Texas. (National Archives)

8. A soldier of the Great War: Verne Andrew Jackson Pitman (1896–1961), a private in the Salvage Division, Quartermasters Corps, and the author's father-in-law. (Pitman family photo)

9

10

11

9.   Said French Marshal Joffre, "We want men, men, men." These U.S. Army Regulars were among the first American units to embark for France in 1917. (National Archives)

10.   General John J. Pershing, with an aide, during the Mexican campaign of 1916. Stubborn, tough, apolitical, "Black Jack" could be relied upon to build the American Expeditionary Force into a distinctive U.S. military presence in France. (National Archives)

11. An American hero, Private First Class Alvin C. York of the 328th Infantry Regiment, 82nd Division. On October 8, 1918, York killed at least 20 German soldiers and captured another 132 in the Argonne Forest near Cornay, France. (National Archives)

12

13

12. American troops on the Western Front were heavily dependent upon Allied-supplied weapons such as this French rapid-fire gun. (National Archives)

13. Esnes, France, October 1918: The AEF never did solve its combat-area logistical problems, as this chaotic scene during the Meuse-Argonne campaign attests. (National Archives)

14

15

14. Almost 206,000 Americans were wounded during the Great War. A Salvation Army lassie helps a stricken doughboy to let the folks back home know what has happened. (National Archives)

15. About 30 percent of American casualties in France were gas victims, including this soldier being treated at American Evacuation Hospital No. 2, Baccarat, France, in June 1918. (National Archives)

16

17

16. These African American National Guardsmen from New York fought as part of the French Fourth Army. Note the distinctive French-issue ridged helmets. (National Archives)

17. These men from New York's fabled 369th Regiment, 93rd Division, also fought under French command, earning a unit Croix de Guerre. The regiment was in combat for 191 days, longer than any other American outfit, but was not included among the U.S. troops marching in the victory parade in Paris. (National Archives)

18

19

18. By the 1930s, U.S. participation in the Great War had become a subject of fierce political controversy. Antiwar advocates circulated grisly images such as this so as to remind their countrymen of the price paid in 1917–18. (From *The Absolute Truth*, an undated booklet in the author's possession)

19. Men of the U.S. Army's 28th and 82nd Divisions, Hill 223, Ardennes Forest, France, 1918. "Wipe your eyes and dry your tears/ We'll all be back in a few short years," ran the words of a World War I ditty. Twenty-six years later, the bloody Battle of the Bulge was also fought in the Ardennes. (National Archives)

20

21

20. U.S. Army Signal Corps photographers in Northern Russia, June 25, 1919. Conscripts from Michigan and Wisconsin wondered why they had been sent to this exotic land rather than to France. (National Archives)

21. A squad of Yeomanettes, San Francisco, June 1918. The navy, unlike the army, actively recruited women, awarding them formal military rank. (National Archives)

22. The battleship *Arizona* on review in New York harbor, 1918. The navy loved its great battleships but it was the doughty destroyers that helped the Allies to turn the tide in the critical battle against the U-boats in 1918. (National Archives)

23. The vast shipyard at Hog Island, in the Delaware River, employed more than 34,000 workers but didn't begin to turn out ships for the navy until the war was almost over. (National Archives)

24. The war—temporarily, as it turned out—opened unaccustomed employment opportunities for some women. These rivet heaters and passers were taking a break from their work at the Puget Sound, Washington, Navy Yard. (National Archives)

25. These women did men's work on the Great Northern Railway, Great Falls, Montana, 1918. (National Archives)

26. This U.S. Department of Labor poster invoked the spirit of wartime patriotism but did not prevent a record number of strikes during the period of U.S. belligerency. (National Archives)

27

28

27. The Four-Minute Men of Newark, New Jersey. Along with their counterparts around the country, these men and women purveyed patriotism wherever an opportunity arose to promote the war effort with short, snappy speeches. (National Archives)

28. These schoolchildren in Cortland, New York, display their patriotism in behalf of the Second Liberty Loan drive, 1917. (National Archives)

29

30

29. Chinese Day during the Fourth Liberty Loan campaign, October 1, 1918. Even wartime exigencies, however, did not force abandonment of the nation's cruel anti-Chinese legislation, although they did foster a more inclusive notion of citizenship for people of European descent. (National Archives)

30. Iowans enlisted the potato in Herbert Hoover's Food Administration drive to conserve food for the war effort. (National Archives)

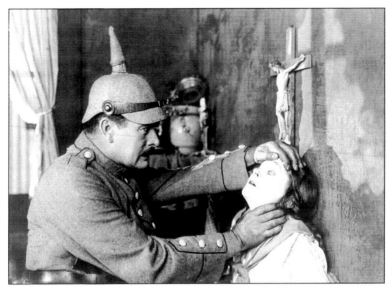

31

32

31. The film: *Stake Uncle Sam to Play Your Hand*; the actors: Mae March as a Belgian damsel and A. C. Gibbons as a rapacious Hun; the goal: to promote a 1918 Liberty Loan drive. (National Archives)

32. The deadly influenza pandemic of 1918–19 killed at least 30,000 American soldiers and ravaged the civilian population as well. (National Archives)

33

34

33. These Philadelphians were active in the American Protective League, a volunteer cit-izens' group sanctioned by the federal government to identify and harass those suspected of disloyalty, even after the end of hostilities. These self-appointed investigators and their supporting staff posed for the camera early in 1919. (National Archives)

34. Men in suits—The Big Four at Versailles: British Prime Minister David Lloyd George, Italian Premier Vittorio Orlando, French Premier Georges Clemenceau, and American President Woodrow Wilson. (National Archives)

making clothing for the armed forces found that compliance officers and gov-ernment investigators were quick to impose union-generated standards and conditions.

Laborite critics warned that what the government granted, it could take away. Unions might grow during wartime and workers might see improve-ments in wages and conditions, but the wartime state would brook no resist-ance or opposition. Where conciliation and compromise proved ineffective, repression would soon follow, as the treatment of the Bridgeport strikers demonstrated. Militant lumber and timber workers also found this out in the fall of 1917. When the IWW attracted a following among loggers and timber workers, the U.S. Army responded quickly, for certain kinds of lumber were crucial in the building of Great War–era airplanes. The army created a special Spruce Production Division under the command of Colonel Brice P. Disque and sent 10,000 soldiers to work in the camps. Disque also created a govern-ment-controlled organization, the Loyal Legion of Loggers and Lumbermen, to force employers to grant concessions to workers and to preempt the IWW. A "union" in name only, the 4Ls, as it was called, represented a bold instance of direct government intervention in economic life and industrial relations and a troubling challenge to independent unionism.

Even more ominously, the government resorted to outright repression in its efforts to secure labor loyalty. Agents from the Department of Justice's Bureau of Investigation and from the army's newly created Military Intelligence Divi-sion monitored the labor scene closely. Federal agents tapped telephones, opened mail, and harassed dissident unionists. Even investigators employed by the NWLB were not immune from this treatment, with investigators shad-owing co-chairman Walsh himself. Reports from Military Intelligence charged that the board was honeycombed with subversives and antiwar zealots, with one such brief indicating that "most of the men on the NWLB are ex-dynamiters."[7]

These absurd charges did nothing to impede the board's operations, but more vulnerable organizations suffered from government surveillance and repression. A particular target was the IWW, long an object of loathing and fear on the part of mainstream politicians and business persons. Even though the IWW did not officially oppose the war, its militant organizing, its harsh criticisms of the mainstream labor movement, and its revolutionary rhetoric left it friendless and vulnerable to extreme repression. The crackdown on the Wobblies, as IWW members were popularly known, was swift and decisive. Even before federal agents could begin a campaign of legal harassment, local vigilantes, usually aided by public officials and policemen, had launched phys-ical attacks on IWW offices and leaders. In June 1917, businessmen and city authorities rounded up hundreds of copper workers conducting an IWW strike in Bisbee, Arizona. They herded the men into railroad cars, took them to the desert, and stranded them without water or provisions. Six weeks later, a mob in Butte, Montana, lynched IWW organizer Frank Little. On September 5, federal officials, uneasy with this vigilantism, began a concerted attack on the IWW with a series of raids, and later that month, they secured indictments of 166 officials and organizers by a federal grand jury under the terms of the Espionage Act, passed in May. The ensuing trials led to dozens of convictions and crippled the IWW by embroiling it in lengthy legal proceedings.

Although NWLB co-chairman Walsh and other progressives decried these attacks on the Wobblies, AFL leaders were slow to defend the rights of dissidents. After years of being denounced by swaggering IWW militants as labor fakirs and government stooges, AFL leaders saw in the wrecking of the radical union a validation of their own progovernment policy as well as the hamstringing of an annoying and sometimes dangerous rival. Indeed, Gompers and other labor leaders collaborated closely with the government in suppressing dissident elements within even the mainstream labor movement. Alarmed by antiwar sentiment among his membership, the hard-boiled Gompers worked with the Committee on Public Information to attack those in the labor movement who voiced less than complete support for the government's war program. In August 1917, for example, the AFL provided the public front for a largely CPI-funded organization, the American Alliance for Labor and Democracy. This primarily paper organization conducted a savage campaign of innuendo and misrepresentation against a rival organization, the People's Council of America for Democracy and Peace (PCADP). This group was formed by progressive unionists, socialists, and others critical of the Wilsonian agenda and supported labor-backed initiatives launched in several belligerent countries, including Germany, calling for "peace without victory." Gompers and his allies labeled supporters of the PCADP as "conscious or unconscious agents of the Kaiser" who jeopardized the AFL's new status as a privileged and protected organization.[8] After the Bolshevik Revolution of October 1917, Gompers traveled to Europe under government auspices to help stiffen support for the Allied war effort among working people and labor leaders, all too susceptible, American war directors felt, to the blandishments of peace-without-victory advocates. Civil libertarians and independent-minded laborites cautioned that, in the event of a change in the political climate, government sponsorship could boomerang. The stern hand of repression could well turn against the "loyal" labor movement. But flushed with the success of their policies and reaping the rewards of cooperation, Gompers and his associates paid no attention to such warnings.

The impact of the Great War on working people, of course, was not con-fined to its role in reshaping industrial relations. Even in the months of great-est labor turbulence, the vast majority of workers stayed on the job and had little contact with the emerging system of government-influenced industrial relations. The post-1915 economic boom stimulated further the shift of pop-ulation from rural to urban areas. The curtailment of European immigration helped to encourage the migration of men and women of both races out of the South, as centers of industry in the Midwest such as Detroit and Akron asso-ciated with the vast expansion of automobile production and increasing elec-trification of home and industry mushroomed. Wartime inflation fueled work-ers' demands for higher wages.

Meanwhile, U.S. entry into the war, combined with the tendency of war production to concentrate in the Northeast, created a massive crisis in working-class housing in that part of the country. Cities such as Chester, Pennsylvania; Bridgeport, Connecticut; Gary, Indiana; and scores of others underwent a population explosion. For example, in Chester, a shipbuilding, locomotive, and arms-producing center, one report observed that "over-crowding and congestion of people in small houses has absolutely reached the limit."[9] Munitions factories could not fill orders because the lack of housing impeded efforts to recruit workers. Crowded and unsanitary condi-tions bred epidemics, accompanied sharp increases in infant mortality, and left people vulnerable to the deadly influenza pandemic that killed thou-sands of Americans in 1918 and 1919.

Here too the federal government responded with innovative, if abortive, programs. Most notable was the creation in May 1918 of the United States Housing Corporation (USHC), with funds eventually reaching $100 million to permit the government to build and operate workers' housing in war-impacted areas. Even before Congress established the USHC, the Emergency Fleet Corporation, an arm of the United States Shipping Board, had begun to build emergency housing for the thousands of new war workers employed in places such as Hog Island, near Philadelphia, as the nation worked furiously to overcome its maritime and naval deficits. Innovative federal programs in public health and child welfare, reflecting both the characteristic Progressive era concern with social efficiency and alarm over the high proportion of con-scripts deemed medically unfit for service, also flowered briefly during the final year of the war.

As with the NWLB, these new agencies and programs were short lived. Although progressive reformers viewed the war-created emergencies as an opportunity to involve the federal government permanently in such areas as housing, social welfare, and medical care, popular forces in support of a modern welfare state were too weak to sustain these experiments in public action. In the wake of war, the government began liquidating its housing properties, reducing funding for health and child care, and generally withdrawing from the provision of direct support for working people and lower-income citizens. As with innovations in industrial-relations policy, however, memories of these innovations lingered, keeping alive Progressive era beliefs that purposeful federal action, should another national crisis arise, could ameliorate or even prevent social pathologies.

On the whole, the Wilson administration could claim success in its handling of the "labor problem" during the Great War. Its policies had helped to keep labor unrest within manageable bounds, and it had secured the enthusiastic support of the country's largest and most influential labor organizations for its wartime policies. On the whole, the country's multiethnic working class lent at least tacit support to the war effort, eagerly snapping up war-created jobs and submitting to conscription and military service with little class-specific resistance. Wilson's progressive supporters welcomed the positive interventions of the wartime state, regarding such bodies as the NWLB and the USHC as harbingers of a more dynamic and responsive federal presence in industrial and social affairs. Still, many were troubled by the harsh attacks on dissidents, whether those in the pariah IWW or in the more moderate PCADP. In its zeal to promote Wilson's particular vision of the U.S. war effort, critics believed, the administration had repeatedly violated basic civil liberties. Having declared domestic war on labor liberals who sought the kind of "peace without victory" that Wilson, before April 1917, had so passionately championed, the administration had left itself dangerously dependent on conservative hard liners.

African Americans

There was not one "Negro problem" during the years of the Great War but several. As the only citizens subject to systematic racial segregation, African Americans posed significant logistical, legal, political, and public relations dilemmas for the war administration simply by virtue of their existence. Matters of recruitment and training, the conduct of racially prejudiced local draft boards, white southern resistance to the presence of black troops in the South, and the uses to which African American troops would be put were constant sources of concern to Secretary of War Baker and military leaders. In addition to these military issues, however, the rapidly changing role of African Americans in the broader economy and social order posed unprecedented challenges. In the 1910s, large-scale migration into northern industrial centers, an increasingly vocal and influential civil rights movement, and growing militancy and dissatisfaction on the part of African American masses brought racial matters more forcefully into public arenas than at any time since the end of Reconstruction.

Moreover, in critical ways, the "Negro problem" intersected with the "labor problem," as the new federal labor-relations bodies came up against the irrationalities and injustices of workplace segregation and discrimination. Whether workplaces bred conflict between white and black workers, or more rarely, interracial unionism, racial matters profoundly affected wartime labor relations. Meanwhile, struggles over jobs, housing, and public space pitted people of both races against each other in bloody outbreaks that rocked war-impacted communities such as East St. Louis, Chicago, and Omaha. Less overtly but pregnant with future implications, the latent issue of colonialism, although only vaguely and imprecisely acknowledged by President Wilson and other official U.S. spokesmen, threw the domestic problem of "the color line" into vivid and troubling international context.

President Wilson, however, never quite grasped the complexities of America's Great War–era "Negro problem." Born in Virginia and raised in Georgia, the president had absorbed unreflectively the color prejudice common to men of his class and background. Although in his 1912 presidential campaign Wilson had pledged "absolute fair dealing" to African Americans, in fact he turned racial matters over to southern cabinet members and to the Democratic Party's largely white southern congressional leadership. During Wilson's first term, government bureaus began rigid segregation among federal employees. Postmaster General Albert Burleson even ordered segregation of customer windows at post offices. African Americans were demoted, virtually barred from presidential appointments to government offices, and generally subject to humiliation and disadvantage within the federal government. When frustrated African American leaders protested, Wilson insisted that the government's new segregationist personnel policies were race-neutral and accused black leaders who urged him to honor his 1912 campaign promises of personal effrontery.[10]

Nor did the president or any of his top advisers acknowledge or speak out forcefully against the violence that southern blacks especially endured at the hands of lynch mobs, local government officials, and private citizens. During the thirty-year period, 1890 to 1920, violent attacks directed against African Americans reached epic proportions, especially, but not exclusively, in the

South. In the period 1889 to 1909, for example, vigilantes, local officials, and frenzied white citizens lynched an average of eighty-five blacks each year in the southern states. During Wilson's presidency the numbers remained high: eighty in 1915, fifty-four in 1916, thirty-eight in 1917, fifty-eight in 1918, and seventy in 1919.[11] In addition, gang attacks, house and church burnings, and ritualized subordination and humiliation added to the pogrom-like atmosphere that African Americans endured. Beyond vague criticisms of extralegal violence, Wilson never exerted his vaunted moral leadership to condemn or even acknowledge this frightening crisis in law enforcement. To be sure, he conceded in 1918, "lynching is unpatriotic," but in his one public statement on the subject, he avoided all reference to race, and civil rights advocates were told that "the Federal Government has absolutely no jurisdiction over matters of this kind."[12] Throughout his public career, in both official statements and private conversations, Wilson demonstrated virtually no understanding of the character or implications of American racism, a profound limitation for a man determined to lead in the creation of a new democratic order in a world in which racially defined colonialism played such a crucial role.

The vast social and economic changes of the 1910s, however, thrust racial issues onto the national agenda. The combination of expanding munitions production and the virtual curtailment of European immigration after 1914 created a large-scale demand for workers in northern industry. In response, attracted by the promise of good wages, repelled by the white South's racial subordination, and determined to establish themselves as full participants in American life, African Americans surged into northern cities. Between 1914 and 1920, an estimated half-million southern blacks found their way to these centers, boosting the African American populations of Chicago, Pittsburgh, Detroit, Cleveland, and dozens of smaller communities by hundreds of thousands. Whereas in the period 1870 to 1910, black migration from the South to the North had averaged 67,000 people per decade, in the 1910s the black population in the North and West grew by 750,000.[13]

Social and economic problems accompanied this great migration. Although the prejudice and hostility of white workers and employers deprived these migrants of the full range of job opportunities, by the war's end, thousands were working in the slaughterhouses of Chicago and Omaha, the steel mills of Gary and Pittsburgh, and munitions and armaments plants throughout the Midwest and Northeast. The crisis in urban housing was particularly hard on African Americans, as discrimination funneled blacks into overcrowded and inferior dwellings. The African American neighborhoods in Chicago's meatpacking district, according to one report, were "a festering slum," and in booming southeastern Pennsylvania, blacks were forced to occupy houses "that had no water and no toilets, whose roofs leaked and whose cellars were [routinely] flooded." Most trade unions rejected blacks as potential members and collaborated with employers to restrict African Americans to insecure, unsanitary, and ill-paid work. Employers recruited black strikebreakers, exacerbating racial tensions and contributing to the atmosphere of incipient violence that pervaded industrial centers such as Gary, Chicago, and Philadelphia. An outbreak in East St. Louis on July 2, 1917, exemplified these conditions. In this Illinois city, rumors of a mass influx of blacks allegedly recruited to work in its sprawling munitions, chemical, and metalworking plants, combined with exaggerated concerns about black incursions into white neighborhoods, triggered a savage outburst that left at least forty-seven people dead, thirty-nine of them African Americans.[14]

Government officials, editorialists, and southern agriculturalists faced suddenly with labor shortages responded by blaming the victims. The *New York Times* decried the "Harmful Rush of Negro Workers to the North," and the governor of Minnesota urged federal authorities to "stop the movement of Negros [sic] to this section at once."[15] Southern planters railed against greedy and unpatriotic laborers, who forsook the fields for military service or newly available industrial jobs. The president could relate to tales of avaricious black workers: he responded sympathetically when one of his friends reported that her black laundress was taking advantage of the wartime labor shortage to demand higher prices for her services.

Others feared that gullible African Americans would prove easy targets for enemy propaganda. In a widely reported incident, one black citizen was heard to declare, "The Germans ain't done nothin' to me, and if they have, I forgive 'em." Rumors circulated of German agents stirring up black field hands and industrial workers, fomenting strikes and sabotage. In June 1918, CPI Director Creel reported to Wilson that "the colored population . . . has been torn by rumor and ugly whispering ever since we entered the war." Secretary of War Baker was disturbed by news of "more unrest among . . . [blacks] than has existed . . . for years."[16]

The war did stimulate unprecedented activism within black communities, both North and South. Movements arose that rejected mainstream values and sought to align African Americans with international crusades of an anticolonial, socialist, and antiwar character. In the expanding urban black ghettoes, organizations such as the Universal Negro Improvement Association, led by West Indian immigrant Marcus Garvey, and the African Blood Brotherhood took root. Both rejected the goal of integration into white society, issuing instead militant calls for black nationalism. The radical IWW's recruitment of workers without reference to race also attracted black activists frustrated by the racism of the AFL and the railroad brotherhoods. In New York and other cities, organizations such as the Friends of Negro Freedom published such magazines as *The Messenger*, combining antiwar views with calls for race-blind socialist transformation.

Despite the fears of government agents and superpatriots, however, none of these movements attracted mass support, at least during the Great War. The CPI, along with state, local, and private governments and organizations, bombarded African Americans with propaganda, combining appeals to patriotism with veiled warnings about the evils of disloyalty and unauthorized activism. Newspapers and CPI reports trumpeted the enthusiastic support of black citizens for conscription, war loan subscriptions, and the policies of the administration. In fact, however, much of this "support" was artificial, generated by official and informal pressure. Thoughtful observers reported that apathy and indifference to official propaganda were widespread, as was draft delinquency. If only a small minority of blacks specifically opposed the war, another 40 percent were steadfastly immune to the most eloquent patriotic appeals.[17]

For most civil rights organizations, however, the war seemed to offer opportunities for racial advance. The National Association for the Advancement of Colored People (NAACP, founded in 1909), the National Urban League (1910), and other religious and civic organizations, along with major black newspapers such as the *Chicago Defender*, at once affirmed the loyalty of black citizens and sought to use the war emergency to press their claims for racial justice. In May 1917, for example, the NAACP sponsored a national meeting of its members and representatives of other African American groups to discuss black participation in the war effort. Conference resolutions both pledged support for the war and demanded racial progress. The delegates urged "colored fellow citizens to join heartily in this fight for eventual world liberty . . . to enlist in the army," and to back the war effort with faithful labor and patriotic enthusiasm. In addition, however, the conference called attention to "the reasonable and deep-seated feeling of revolt among Negroes at the persistent insult and discrimination to which they are subject."[18]

Throughout the war, African American leaders remained divided over the balance that representatives of their race should strike between the two poles of loyal support and insistence on justice. In July 1918, for example, W. E. B. Du Bois, the brilliant African American editor of the NAACP's magazine, *The Crisis*, and one of the most respected and militant race leaders of the Great War era, startled his readers with a stridently prowar editorial, which he titled "Close Ranks." "Let us not hesitate," he urged. "Let us, while this war lasts, forget our special grievances and close our ranks shoulder to shoulder with our white fellow citizens. . . . We make no ordinary sacrifice," he pledged, "but we make it gladly and willingly with our eyes lifted to the hills."[19] This effusive pledge of black loyalty, contrasting as it did with his trenchant earlier criticism of the administration and his keen insights into the international racial dimensions of the Great War itself, aroused protest among black activists. Du Bois's critics believed that support for the war should be specifically contingent on the administration's favorable response to the demands of black Americans for equality and fair consideration. Those who accepted the army's offer of a segregated officers' training camp rather than engage in futile efforts to force integration likewise drew criticism from some impatient black leaders. During the 1910s, whatever the contributions of black farmers, soldiers, and workers to the war, African Americans operated in an atmosphere of official and public disapproval and suspicion. With disfranchisement robbing them of political influence and with religious, academic, and journalistic organs, North and South, widely sharing assumptions of racial inferiority, black reformers and intellectuals had to steer a narrow course between militant advocacy and pledges of cooperation and loyalty.

Despite the president's personal limitations and the general climate of racial antagonism, however, the logic of the U.S. war effort forced members of government to respond, however grudgingly, to some of the racial facts of life. As one reform leader, temporarily working with Military Intelligence, argued, "The co-operation of this large element of our population in all civilian and military activities is of vital importance."[20] Troubled by bitter black protest over the army's handling of the August 1917 Houston riot, Secretary of War Baker convened a meeting of prominent black editors, educators, and public figures. Out of this gathering grew Baker's agreement to the formation of black combat divisions and his appointment of Emmett J. Scott, formerly the private secretary to black leader Booker T. Washington, as his special assistant. Scott was to serve as a confidential adviser in "matters affecting the interests of the 10,000,000 Negroes of the United States, and the part they are to play in connection with the present war."[21] Scott visited training camps, criticized inadequate provision of recreational and training facilities for black recruits, drew to Baker's attention the racially biased actions of local draft boards in the South, and served generally as an intermediary between the black soldiery and the army. He found in Secretary Baker one of the few members of the administration with a relatively liberal outlook on racial matters.

The administration also responded to the problems faced by black workers and their families and to the racial dimensions of industrial conflict. In May 1918, the U.S. Department of Labor created a Division of Negro Economics (DNE) and named as its director Dr. George E. Haynes, a Fisk University professor. Haynes, along with African Americans whom he recruited into the

DNE, worked to expand employment opportunities for blacks, foster interracial cooperation in industry, and highlight the distinctive concerns of black workers and their families. He strove to make the services of other federal agencies, as well as state employment agencies, more responsive to the problems of black workers. Haynes also reached out to private employers in an effort to improve conditions for African Americans but often ran into blatant racial prejudice. For example, the president of the National Lumber Manufacturers' Association declared, "when it comes to sitting in council with Dr. Haynes, a negro, you will have to excuse me: In the South, we do not sit in conference with them."[22]

Other government bodies such as the Food Administration and the CPI employed black journalists, publicists, and field workers to bring African American citizens into the networks of conservation and propaganda that buttressed the U.S. war effort. Although African Americans derived some satisfaction from having their importance as fighters, producers, and consumers officially acknowledged, men such as Scott and Haynes were recruited exclusively from the moderate ranks of black leaders. Although genuinely seeking to better the conditions of black workers and soldiers, they saw as their primary role the furthering of the war effort; pressing for equality took a back seat to the deflecting of African American resentment over discrimination. Thus, in July 1918, Haynes told the country's African Americans in a widely circulated speech, "any person . . . who does not work hard, who lags in any way . . . is against his country and is, therefore, our bitter enemy."[23]

Of potentially greater importance to black workers than the largely exhortative efforts of men such as Haynes and Scott were the operations of the administration's labor relations policies. The key role that black labor played in the war effort ensured that federal agencies such as the United States Employment Service (USES), the USRA, and the NWLB would have to confront race matters. African Americans sometimes found these bodies supportive of claims to fair treatment. For example, when southern planters complained that military service and industrial employment were siphoning off black field hands who constituted their traditional labor supply, the U.S. Department of Labor and its subsidiary, the USES, urged higher wages and expanded labor mobility as a solution.

The new USRA, created in December 1917 when the government took over operation of the railroads, also initially seemed to offer hope for black railroaders. From the inception of the railroads in the nineteenth century, African Americans had been employed in a variety of capacities, especially in the South. However, employer policies, trade union rules, and white workers' hostility had ensured that they could work only in certain trades, could never advance to well-paid and responsible positions, and would remain forever vulnerable to white incursions on the jobs they did perform. As a character in Lloyd Brown's novel about black working-class life observed: "just remember this as long as you're black and live in Mississippi: there's three main things Cap'n Charlie won't 'low you to do, and that's mess with his women, vote in the elections, or drive a railroad train." Indeed, in the decade before the Great War, white workers on southern railroads had waged a concerted campaign to drive blacks out of occupations such as locomotive fireman that they had held for several generations.[24]

The critical importance of the railroads, however, along with federal takeover, seemed for a time to slow this trend. The USRA's investigators and field representatives were not particularly progressive on matters of race, and the director general himself, Secretary of the Treasury William G. McAdoo, was a Georgia politician and a firm advocate of white supremacy. But often the sheer need to keep the trains running impelled USRA agents to side with black workers in disagreements with white employers and co-workers. Sleeping car porters, for example, received wage increases in the summer of 1918 after presenting their case to USRA officials. "For the first time in all their existence as Pullman porters," declared an organizer, "they could speak their honest opinion. . . . For once their constitutional rights . . . were not invaded." When white workers sought to drive African Americans from the railroads' operating and repair sectors, black railroad workers turned to the USRA for redress, occasionally with success. The appeal of a black brakeman in Texas was eloquent: all he sought, he petitioned USRA officials, was "the protection that is guaranteed by the U.S. government." And indeed government bodies sometimes did recognize the effects of discrimination in hiring and job advancement. For example, in 1918, a federal investigating commission acknowledged that unions and employers had colluded to "limit the proportion of colored workers." USRA rulings voided some union contracts that ignored black workers' seniority rights and in effect protected the job rights of African Americans in the face of the claims of less-qualified white workers.[25]

The NWLB also proved at least partially responsive to the appeals of black workers. Field investigators found it hard to square the announced democratic and egalitarian rhetoric of the war effort with blatant inequality in the workplace. Some NWLB field agents were aggressive champions of equal rights. Florida's racist governor, Sidney Catts, labeled federal labor investigators "white carpet bag officers" whose flouting of southern racial "customs" "inflamed . . . the minds of the negroes."[26] For the most part, however, NWLB administrators and agents were not racial crusaders; rather, they found the naked racial injustice of southern workplaces so blatant and irrational as to impede the war effort. Often rulings in behalf of black workers seemed but commonsensical to such men and women. Thus, the board intervened in a case involving a large commercial laundry in Little Rock, Arkansas, to gain equal pay for the same work performed by black and white women in servicing a large nearby military post. Backed by highly publicized NWLB investigations, interracial unionism began to emerge in the coalfields, iron mines, and steel mills of Alabama. In New Orleans, the board at first ruled in favor of black workers' claims for equal pay on the city transit system, although eventually it bowed to local pressure from white workers, transit officials, and politicians to scale back the awards granted to African American workers.

Modestly favorable treatment by new federal agencies—even though these bodies soon proved unreliable vehicles for black workers' aspirations—helped to fuel an unprecedented degree of interracial labor organization. Although the black middle and professional classes, with good reason, continued to regard the railroad unions and the AFL as impediments to black progress, African American workers in the coal mines, metal factories, slaughterhouses, lumber mills, and other work sites were now often willing to join in a labor movement that on occasion proved responsive to the logic of solidarity across lines of race and ethnicity. The United Mine Workers, which since its inception in 1890 had been a biracial union, led the way, but even AFL unions in lumbering, meatpacking, and metalworking made gestures toward cross-race organizing. Fiercely resisted by employers and economic and social elites, as well as by white working-class elements determined to preserve the "wage of whiteness," biracial unionizing efforts found some support among NWLB personnel during the federal agency's brief period of existence.

In the last analysis, however, the federal presence proved too brief, too sporadic, and too responsive to white employers, workers, and political leaders to bring about sustained changes in workplace race relations. In the agricultural South, by mid-1918, planters' insistence on keeping wages low and restricting rural black mobility had sabotaged the relatively liberal initiatives of the USES and Department of Labor. Southern states and communities, with the encouragement of another federal agency, the United States Department of Agriculture, adopted draconian "work or fight" measures. These directives, modeled after an order issued in May 1918 by Selective Service Director General Enoch Crowder, sought to force black men and women to work for whatever wages agricultural and domestic employers offered. Southern sheriffs and policemen operated as enforcers for planters, compelling blacks who attempted to switch jobs in quest of higher wages to remain with the initial employer. In a typical incident, in Lake County, Florida, the sheriff rounded up eight black men who deserted one orange grower for work at a higher-paying nearby grove, ordering the men "to go back to work at the former place, [go] to war, or [go] to jail."[27] Although it sponsored tentative initiatives that would have improved the miserable conditions for black field workers in the South and raised wages in an effort to keep a steady labor supply on the farms, the federal government quickly became part of a repressive apparatus that reinforced traditional patterns of subordination and exploitation. These policies were actually counterproductive, because they further spurred the northward migration of African Americans seeking better conditions. Southern determination to keep blacks powerless and subordinate, however, outweighed calculations of economic rationality and manpower allocation.

Nor did the USRA prove a long-term friend of black railroaders. Immediately after the war, union pressure and white worker militancy, along with the domination of the Railroad Administration's adjustment machinery by southern white employers and unionists, launched an increasingly successful effort to drive blacks out of the operating and repair sectors of railroad work. USRA officials approved union contracts that they acknowledged to be blatantly discriminatory, citing southern customs and unwillingness to risk racially motivated work stoppages as justification. Even the NWLB, probably the most positive of the wartime agencies in appreciation of racial injustice, backed off from support of black workers' rights and its own rulings in favor of equal pay. Though co-chairman Frank Walsh continued to hope that the work of the NWLB would encourage biracial unionism in the South, in the end the board followed the logic of racial division. "I am in favor of equality of opportunity," declared co-chairman Taft. At the same time, however, he endorsed the basic premise of inequality, holding that "the cost of living of a negro in a southern city . . . is less than that of a white man, as we would wish it to be."[28]

Insofar as African Americans were concerned, the Great War did not last long enough. In previous wars, notably the American Revolution and the Civil War, the key importance of the African American population had forced progressive change in their status and opportunities. During the Great War, this process seemed initially to be in operation once again, as democratic rhetoric, the realities of military and industrial manpower needs, the growing assertiveness of African Americans, and new federal initiatives briefly promised renegotiation of the country's racial policies and practices. The great migration into the North, with its reconfiguration of the country's urban and industrial contours, the growing strength of civil rights and race conscious movements, and the determination of African American people to escape subordination remained potent forces. However, the rapid retreat of the federal government in race matters after the war left African Americans only poignant memories of what it was like to get a fair shake from their government.

Women and War

The "woman question," as people of the Great War era referred to the bundle of issues relating to the status and role of women in American life, involved concerns even more threatening to and potentially subversive of established structures of power and authority than either the "labor problem" or the "Negro problem." True, controversies over women's rights and roles rarely erupted into violence. Nonetheless, the implications of women's claims to equality challenged social, political, and personal patterns of living and thinking. Women's rights advocates implicitly sought redefinition of the most private matters of sexual and family relations as well as those involving political and economic power. Definitions of masculinity cut across the lines of race and class. Thus, even moderate feminist challenges to male hegemony threatened men already experiencing challenges to their conceptions of manliness associated with the era's accelerated industrial and social change.

During the first two decades of the twentieth century, women's activism revived after a period of relative dormancy during the Gilded Age. For example, just before the onset of the Great War, the campaign for female suffrage, sputtering at the turn of the century, gathered strength and gained important successes. The militant tactics of British feminists, although rarely directly adopted in the United States, created public controversy in the United Kingdom that echoed across the Atlantic. Meanwhile, the advance of women workers into new occupations challenged popular assumptions about "women's place" and called into question gendered understandings of the division of labor. The events leading up to the U.S. entry into the war and then American belligerency itself provided a whole new range of issues through which men and women advanced differing conceptions of female citizenship. During the war, President Wilson, despite his reliance on socially conservative southern congressional and electoral support, became the first president to back female suffrage, and members of his war administration advanced, albeit tentatively, pioneering programs and agencies that recognized the economic and social concerns of women workers and social advocates.

Despite these gestures, federal authorities, editorialists, employers, and other opinion leaders sought to ensure that war-generated new roles for women did not challenge existing patterns of gender domination and subordination. Agencies such as the CPI and the Food Administration joined clergymen, business leaders, and popular writers in appealing to women, whose motherly fear for their sons' safety might otherwise impede military recruitment, to put patriotism ahead of selfish maternal instincts. Women who discouraged enlistment were characterized as veritable traitors, guilty of sissify-ing their sons. In one popular film, a vain, self-absorbed mother dissuades her son from joining the National Guard; thus, the subtitles informed the audi-ence, he was "stripped of his right to aggressive young manhood by an overzealous mother." Posters, films, and written materials hammered home the theme that the war emergency required women to put aside supposedly "female" virtues of nurturing and domesticity and willingly give over their sons and husbands to the nation's service.

For vocal women activists who challenged the war effort or asserted femi-nist demands too strenuously, federal authorities did not hesitate to employ the powerful weapons of repression that the war made available. Dissenters such as anarchist Emma Goldman, socialist Rose Pastor Stokes, and antiwar proponents such as Kate Richards O'Hare and Dr. Marie Equi faced prosecu-tion and imprisonment for their utterances and actions. Invoking women's special responsibility to preserve life and resist the breakup of families— valued in peacetime as quintessential "feminine" virtues—scores of women activists now faced the wrath of authorities who charged them with being "unnatural" and subversive. For example, in June 1917, federal agents arrested O'Hare, accusing her of having made seditious remarks a few days earlier in a speech in a small North Dakota town. A Kansas-born socialist, O'Hare had allegedly charged "that the women of the United States were nothing more than brood sows to raise children to get into the Army and [be] made into fer-tilizer." O'Hare denied these charges, contending that her remarks had avoided direct criticism of the U.S. government and hence were permitted under the terms of the Espionage Act. A federal jury convicted her nonethe-less and she was sentenced to five years in prison, eventually serving thirteen months before Wilson commuted her sentence.[29]

The war experience itself had ambiguous effects upon women's status and circumstances. Women played critical roles in the peace and antipreparedness campaigns, on the one hand, and in organizations supporting military and naval enhancement and vigorous prosecution of the war effort, on the other. Meanwhile, war created unprecedented occupational opportunities for women, although the advent of peace eroded most of these gains. Gaining the vote, in part attributable to the circumstances of war, was a great achieve-ment, but there was little initial evidence that female suffrage greatly affected the distribution of wealth, power, and influence in American life. Nonethe-less, women's wartime activities helped to define the boundaries of debate over the place of female citizens in a rapidly changing republic and, in the words of historian Barbara Steinson, "created a climate for the continuing role of women on the public stage."[30]

Questions of war and peace, antimilitarism, and preparedness provided the framework for sharp debate over the nature of female citizenship. American women participated in both the pre-1917 peace movement and preparedness efforts. Although significant differences characterized leaders in both movements, women who took active parts in resisting the drift toward war as well as those who lined up on the side of military and naval preparedness were asserting, albeit each in her own idiom, claims to expanded female citizenship. Moreover, both camps insisted that women qua women offered unique perspectives on questions of war and peace, preparedness and pacifism, that politicians, statesmen, and military leaders ignored at their and their nation's peril.

In the debates over foreign and military policy in the period 1914 to 1917, those who supported preparedness as well as those who were aligned with the peace and antipreparedness camps shared membership in the country's economic, social, and educational elite. Few working-class or conventional middle-class women added their voices to the controversies over Wilson's diplomatic response to the war and the administration's efforts to bolster the armed forces. Largely deprived of suffrage, subordinated by patriarchal economic and familial circumstances, and unaccustomed to outspoken public activity, the vast majority of American women were silent. The largest female-membership organization, the General Federation of Women's Clubs (GFWC), represented relatively educated and leisured women in a loose national coalition of local organizations. Discouraged, with few exceptions, from participation in the labor movement, working-class women were largely dependent on middle-class and elite spokespersons for the public airing of their concerns about wages, working conditions, and matters of health and hygiene. Organizations such as the Daughters of the American Revolution and religious auxiliaries reflected the social concerns of elite women or relied on male leaders to bring women's presumed priorities into public arenas. Both the leading organizations advocating and opposing women's suffrage were elite-dominated bodies with few direct connections with the great mass of women.

Not surprisingly, these same leaders dominated women's organized response to the crisis of 1914–17. For women such as Jane Addams, founder of the Chicago social settlement Hull House and a veteran crusader in behalf of women's rights and social justice, the European war offered a profound challenge to America and especially to its women. Along with other Progressive-era women activists such as Alice Hamilton, Margaret Sanger, and Florence Kelley, Addams had worked hard to connect the campaigns for suffrage with industrial safety, workers' protections, and other social welfare issues. Many of these "social feminists" had supported Theodore Roosevelt's 1912 presidential bid on the Progressive Party ticket, seeing in the former president's "New Nationalism" program a means of enlisting the federal government in behalf of these reforms. To Addams and other women active in the Progressive movement, war was an affront to women's "nurturing instinct." By virtue of their maternal and life-sustaining biological and cultural functions, women held it in special horror, and progressive women had a special obligation to attempt to stop the "wholesale slaughter of thousands of men a day." [31]

To these social feminists, action against war and against warlike preparations was a logical and necessary extension of their prewar activism. Jane Addams, Lillian Wald, Emily Stanton Balch, Florence Kelley, Crystal Eastman, and scores of other women's rights and social welfare activists played central roles in the American peace organizations that sprang up in response to the European carnage. Addams's activities during the Great War exemplified the transition from advocacy of women's rights and social welfare reform to pacifism. In September 1914, she participated in the establishment of the preeminent antiwar organization, eventually called the American Union Against Militarism (AUAM), and in 1915 helped to found the Woman's Peace Party (WPP), serving as its national chair. She collaborated with European antiwar women advocates, eventually leading an American delegation of forty-seven women to participate in the International Congress of Women in the Netherlands in the spring of 1915, the only international peace conference held during the war. Challenging male-dominated conduct of politics and diplomacy, Addams and her allies and associates asserted the centrality of women in efforts to end the killing. Thus, the International Congress declared that "one of the strongest forces for the prevention of war will be the combined influence of the women of all countries" and linked a call for mediation by neutral powers (most notably the United States) with a demand for full political rights for "the mother half of humanity."[32]

Armed with the International Congress's appeal to President Wilson to lead neutral nations in efforts to mediate between the warring powers, Addams and her American colleagues returned to the United States in the summer of 1915, even as the *Lusitania* crisis whipped up anti-German feeling. With her reputation as a leading progressive, Addams had no fewer than six meetings with Wilson during the latter half of the year. For his part, the president, disturbed at the rise of belligerent interventionism, seemed guardedly receptive to the women's campaign for U.S. leadership in efforts to bring about a negotiated end to the war. In a January 1916 meeting with Addams, for example, he said of the International Congress's resolutions in behalf of neutral mediation, "I consider them by far the best formulation which . . . has been put out by anybody."[33]

Despite the president's Preparedness program, Addams and most other peace advocates supported his reelection in 1916. To be sure, in January of that year, she testified in Congress against expanded military expenditures, stressing women's special concern about the militarization of American life. Moreover, the organization that Addams chaired, the Woman's Peace Party, played a prominent part in antipreparedness parades and demonstrations, often adopting militant slogans and dramatic visual images to ridicule Preparedness. Still, as late as January 1917, Wilson did seem sincere in his efforts to use U.S. influence to end the war and sustained the belief among peace advocates that he shared their pacifist orientation. Although the AUAM brought together both male and female antiwar activists, Addams and her WPP associates believed fervently that women's roles as mothers, nurturers, and healers gave their voices particular authority in the struggle to direct the nation's energies toward peace and away from military intervention. Declares historian Steinson, "It is difficult to believe that there would have been a viable peace movement in the United States after 1914 without the participation of women . . . women imbued it with a new spirit at a time when the male-dominated organizations of the prewar years were rapidly lapsing into inactivity."[34]

But women activists were also integral to the Preparedness movement, often relying as well on notions of female essentialism to advance the cause of military and naval buildup and to promote the Allied cause. Bridling at the claims of feminist pacifists to speak in behalf of American women, these Preparedness advocates refuted assertions that women were somehow "natural" pacifists or that support for a strong military establishment was incompatible with commitment to home and family. Organizations such as the Women's Section of the Navy League, the Women's Department of the National Civic Federation, and a variety of patriotic and veterans auxiliary organizations, and leaders such as Mary Colvorcoresses, Elisabeth Poe, and Mary Simmerson Logan maintained that in the dangerous world of the modern state, it was they who were the effective promoters of peace. Only a strong military and a powerful navy could discourage aggressors and thus defend the American home and family. Only by evincing a willingness to take up arms to defend the nation's honor and interests could America prevent war. Only by preparing young men through military training and equipping them with the finest weapons could the nation avoid sending them, in the words of one Preparedness advocate, "like sheep to the shambles to be slaughtered . . . by the disciplined . . . soldiers of a prepared foe."[35]

These women were typically from the conservative Anglophile families of the Northeast. Campaigns to provide medical care and relief for victims of

German aggression in Belgium initially brought many of them for the first time into public activity. These women vigorously both challenged their antipreparedness counterparts and asserted, more often by their actions than by explicit declarations, their autonomous female role in public discourse on questions of war and peace. Although women active in the Preparedness movement were more likely to function in organizations adjunct to male-dominated parent bodies such as the Navy League, they proved strong and resourceful proponents of women's right to participate in public affairs even when nominally acknowledging women's putatively subordinate political role.

The onset of U.S. belligerency, of course, transformed the role of women on both sides of these issues. Although some peace advocates continued to oppose war, most antipreparedness activists fell silent or gave quiet support to the Wilson administration, now foregrounding the president's calls for a fair peace settlement. Addams, although nominally remaining opposed to U.S. belligerency, lent her name to civilian groups providing amenities and services to American soldiers and in 1918 even spoke at Liberty Loan rallies. Pro-Allied and propreparedness women, of course, faced no such dilemmas. The WDNCF and similar organizations enlisted women in support of the war effort. They rolled surgical dressings, prepared comfort kits for soldiers and sailors, promoted war bond sales, encouraged cooperation with food and fuel conservation, and denounced antiwar and other "subversive" elements. Vindicated, they felt, by the course of events, they embraced the opportunity to display women's patriotism and to give evidence of women's special importance during the war emergency.

For the great majority of American women, however, these countercrusades were secondary. For most, it was the departure of sons, husbands, brothers, lovers, and friends that registered the war's impact. For a relative handful, however, service in a military or quasi-military capacity briefly offered the promise of expanded opportunities, although in the end women were denied full recognition for their service and the chance to carry their experiences over into postwar employment. Naval leaders, almost completely intransigent regarding the recruitment of African Americans, showed surprising enlightenment when it came to opening doors to women. The army, however, remained resistant. Although eventually employing about 30,000 women as nurses, clerks, translators, and switchboard operators, army authorities could not bring themselves to award these women military rank or to consider them fully parts of the AEF, even though thousands went to France and many served with distinction under military command.

Early on, Secretary of the Navy Josephus Daniels, a progressive newspaper editor in civilian life, ordered navy recruiters to accept applications from

women. Because modern warfare demanded thousands of rear-echelon personnel to handle communications, keep records, and process paperwork,
enrolling women would free men for combat duty. During the course of American belligerency, the navy recruited more than 11,000 women (and its subsidiary branch, the U.S. Marines, another 269) for these tasks, according
them equal rank with male personnel, although a parenthetical "f" for female
was attached to their rank designation, indicating that they were not to be
assigned to shipboard service. On completion of their tours, these women
received honorable discharges and were eligible for veterans' benefits,
although the navy offered none the opportunity to continue in the service.
There were no female officers, but several women did attain the rank of chief
petty officer, the highest noncommissioned naval rank.

The army, however, despite its even greater need for clerical and other noncombatant personnel, was slow and inconsistent in recruiting women and in
recognizing their value. True, in 1898, the army had established an Army
Nurse Corps (ANC), and during the Great War more than 21,000 women
served in its ranks, half of them overseas. The army's ambivalence about their
role and status plagued nurses and hindered their effectiveness. Directors of
army hospitals, for example, often treated professional nurses as little more
than orderlies, denying them a direct role in patient care. British and Canadian army nurses were awarded temporary officers' rankings during the war,
but their AEF sisters had no formal authority over patients or enlisted men.
Indeed, military authorities often insisted that male army ward masters, who
typically had no medical training, control nurses' access to hospital supplies
and medicines. Many nurses did not actually know whether they were members of the AEF or of civilian organizations such as the American National
Red Cross (ANRC), which served as a recruiting and placement agent for the
army. Despite these obstacles, army nurses compiled a splendid record. Hundreds volunteered for special surgical units that treated badly wounded men
immediately behind the front line. Overseas, 100 ANRC nurses died, all of
them of influenza and other diseases, along with 134 of their stateside counterparts, and several were wounded by enemy fire. The AEF, along with
British and French armies, awarded 200 decorations to U.S. Army nurses for
bravery under fire. Despite the desperate need for medical personnel, the army
denied employment to more than a thousand Red Cross–registered black
graduate nurses, although eventually a few were permitted to tend ill and
wounded soldiers from black regiments stateside.[36]

In addition to nurses, another 6,000 women served with the AEF under military discipline but without formal military status. Recruited piecemeal
through civilian organizations such as the Red Cross and the YWCA, these

women worked as telephone operators, translators, clerks, typists, and "welfare workers," that is, hostesses and servers at canteens established by the civilian-operated Commission on Training Camp Activities. The telephone operators—dubbed "Hello Girls"—and other clerical and welfare workers wore uniforms and were directly responsible to AEF officers, yet they were not officially part of the AEF or the U.S. Army. Some women serving with the Signal Corps did not learn until after the war that they had not been in the army. About sixty of these women died, mostly from influenza, during their period of service with the military. Despite their uniforms, an official swearing-in ceremony, and being subject to military regulations, these women were considered "civilian contract employees," and as such were not eligible for veterans benefits or postwar medical care necessitated by service-related illness.[37]

Women's experiences in civilian employment during the Great War paralleled those of their sisters serving in or with the armed forces. Necessity opened up occupations formerly closed to women, although resistance and hostility from employers and male co-workers colored working women's wartime experience. In contrast to women serving with the military, however, civilian war workers frequently protested inequality and poor treatment, both individually and collectively. Federal officials took belated and sporadic notice of the special problems and opportunities associated with female employment in munitions and other essential industries, creating temporary agencies to monitor women's performance and their reception by employers and co-workers. In a few cases, federal agencies such as the USRA and the NWLB intervened to uphold women's claims for equal pay, access to promotion ladders, and fair treatment in the workplace. With the Armistice, however, even these tentative steps toward gender equality ended. Peace brought the wholesale displacement of women from occupations briefly available to them during the war emergency, just as it brought the swift termination of the armed services' experiments with recruitment of women.

Even before U.S. belligerency, the Great War opened up jobs to female employment otherwise off limits to them. The war-stimulated economy and the virtual ending of European immigration created labor shortages that women, along with African Americans, exploited. After April 6, 1917, crash programs of munitions and other war-related production, combined with the departure of men into the services, forced employers and government officials to turn to women. In early August 1918, after the government had stepped up conscription, the call for all sorts of women workers intensified. One recruiting poster proclaimed in vivid red lettering, "Stenographers! Washington needs you," and Bridgeport munitions makers hired airplanes to drop leaflets urging women to take up factory work.[38]

Despite such appeals, however, the actual increase in the total numbers of female wage workers was modest. The wartime employment boom did not bring large numbers of new female workers into the paid labor force. What it did do—and did so dramatically—was reconfigure the patterns of employment among women already working for wages. Specifically, the numbers and proportions of women working as domestic servants, seamstresses, laundresses, and in related occupations plummeted while the numbers of women employed as clerks, factory operatives, telephone operators, and transport workers soared. For example, during the decade of the Great War, about 400,000 women joined the ranks of semiskilled manufacturing operatives and common laborers, and more than 750,000 began employment as office clerks, typists, stenographers, cashiers, and telephone operators. Meanwhile, more than a half-million women left domestic service, nonfactory dressmaking and sewing, and personal laundry work. By the end of the war, women were toiling in a wide range of new industrial and commercial occupations. They drove trucks, operated drill presses and automatic lathes, toiled in brickyards and canneries, operated streetcars, inspected shell casings, and operated electric cranes in steel mills. They assembled airplane motors, produced explosives, and built rubber tires. Thousands of women poured into government and corporate offices as filing clerks, stenographers, typists, and bookkeepers.

The government-run railroad system relied heavily on women workers, whose numbers reached a peak of more than 100,000 at the end of the war. Most worked as clerks in railroad offices but women also repaired tracks, cleaned cars, and operated mechanical goods-lifting machinery. In repair shops, dressed in a kind of uniform called a "womanall," they did electric welding, cut metal with oxyacetylene torches, and performed other once male-only tasks.[39]

Wartime employment boosted the economic status of hundreds of thousands of women. Concentrated in the lower-wage and lower-skilled occupations, they benefited particularly by the tendency of wartime wages to rise disproportionately in these categories. As was the case throughout American society in the Great War era, African American women encountered more obstacles and enjoyed fewer opportunities than their white sisters. Few, for example, gained entry into the government's expanding army of clerical workers. In the manufacturing sector, black women were usually relegated to the dirtier and more physically demanding work that white women avoided. Few black women received training in technologically advanced communications, commercial, or manufacturing operations. Even so, black women left agricultural and domestic work for whatever limited opportunities the industrial and commercial world offered, thousands of them joining the Great Migration of

African Americans from the South into the Northeast and Middle West. Declared one former domestic who found a manufacturing job, "I'll never work in nobody's kitchen but my own any more. No, indeed!" Even a physically taxing job as a common laborer beat ill-paid and often personally demeaning domestic work. "We are making more money at this than any work we can get," reported a former domestic who landed a wartime job as a railroad laborer. Moreover, she added, "we do not have to work as hard as at housework."[40]

Women workers encountered all sorts of obstacles. General social and governmental attitudes were contradictory and confused. Although some reformers saw the discipline and sacrifices of war as a wholesome check on allegedly dissolute American youth, in fact fat pay packets and workplace experience contributed to the autonomy of young women. On the one hand, of course, women's labor was crucial for the war effort. Government agencies, patriotic organizations, and private employers bombarded women with propaganda urging them to join the labor force—"For Every Fighter a Woman Worker," read one poster. At the same time, however, moralists feared that new employment opportunities increased women's vulnerability to social and sexual experimentation. Higher incomes meant money for fashionable clothing, cosmetics, and amusements. The free passes that railroad workers were granted allowed impressionable young women dangerously unsupervised travel opportunities, some critics felt.

But if predatory males endangered innocent American girls, wanton women also threatened America's brave soldiers. Churchmen, publicists, and moral guardians worried that pleasure-mad and newly "liberated" working girls would offer dangerous companionship to lonely soldiers and contribute to the spread of dissolution, prostitution, and venereal disease. Newly emboldened working women, feared prominent editor Edward Bok, were a constant menace to America's "clean-blooded and strong-limbed" fighting men. The Florence Crittenton Mission, a private organization dedicated to assisting sexually errant women, announced in June 1917 that it had already "signed up over 1,000 fallen women who have pledged themselves not to go near the [military] camps."[41]

Other concerns centered around the effects of arduous labor on women's reproductive functions. Prevailing medical opinion saw sustained labor as detrimental to women's delicate organs, although most experts stressed the allegedly ruinous effect of employment per se, especially in morally questionable surroundings, rather than discrete physiological dangers. Thus, the federal War Labor Policies Board singled out poolrooms and saloons as places of employment for which women were "clearly unfit." However, few authorities expressing concern about reproductive issues thought to investigate specific industries in which women—and, for that matter, men as well—did face specific health jeopardy. For example, neither employers nor government investigators raised questions about the effects of the element radium, used to paint the faces of glow-in-the-dark wristwatches and instrument panels, on the young girls who were instructed to lick the ends of radium-saturated paintbrushes before applying the chemical to the dial. Nor, despite widespread knowledge of health and safety problems in the British munitions industry, did the dangers posed by close work with the chemicals and powders used in munitions production come under detailed scrutiny. Work itself, rather than specific chemical or organic dangers, was the focus of attention, with the implicit message that the end of the fighting would and should return women to domestic roles and leave the stresses—and the wages—of industrial and commercial work to menfolk. Declared NWLB Secretary W. Jett Lauck, "Women are the mothers of the race . . . and cannot be dealt with on the same terms as men workers."[42]

Working women often faced sharp opposition from male co-workers and from labor unions. To some extent, resentment of new female employees was an economically rational response to any sudden expansion of the labor force, especially at a time when men were facing conscription. But male workers' hostility toward their new co-workers went deeper. For women to don welders' goggles, run lathes and drill presses, and operate heavy equipment was to threaten the bases of blue-collar workers' masculine self-identification. "Dilution" of skilled labor processes by substituting hastily trained women for machinists and electricians struck at the heart of male workers' social identities. In the Pennsylvania Railroad repair shops, plumbers petitioned employers to "get rid of" new female co-workers. Male workers shunned female co-workers, hid their tools, and sabotaged their work. Women in a Baltimore machine shop told a government investigator, "the men had tried to drive them off the job with their [welding] torches." Through their unions, male workers successfully petitioned state legislatures to ban females from a wide range of occupations. In 1919, for example, new legislation in Ohio prohibited women from working as gas meter readers, bellhops, and iron molders as well as declaring mines, quarries, furnaces, bowling alleys, and even shoeshine parlors off limits to women workers.[43]

By no means did all male co-workers attempt to intimidate and discredit female co-workers. Some unions actively recruited women. Although the AFL leadership was often diffident, female union membership expanded dramatically during the Great War. As late as 1920, even after union membership had begun to recede from wartime peaks, almost 400,000 women, about

10 percent of total union members, belonged to labor organizations. The Machinists' union actively sought women members, enrolling more than 12,000 females at the peak of wartime production, although at the same time, many working machinists led the fight against female advance in the shops. Unions in textiles, the needle trades, and leather goods gained thousands of new women members. Small organizations of clerical workers appeared.

Nor were women reluctant to defend their interests. They participated enthusiastically in many of the 6,000 strikes that broke out during the period of U.S. belligerency. The telephone industry, over which the federal government assumed control on August 1, 1918, was a particular arena for women's labor activism. Embryonic unions of telephone operators in New England, the South, and the Pacific Coast areas protested low wages and unfair treatment. In the period from September 1918 through the next summer, thousands of women struck in defiance of the government, although they gained only half-hearted support from their union, the International Brotherhood of Electrical Workers. This organization of skilled male electricians claimed jurisdiction over their jobs but, in effect, limited female members' ability to establish permanent unions. Often they bargained away women's interests in conferences with government representatives and managers. Even so, declares historian Maurine Greenwald, "Thousands of sixteen- and seventeen-year-olds momentarily brought the American Telephone and Telegraph Company . . . to its knees." Throughout the Great War years, women activists, whether in unions or through less formal local organizations, participated enthusiastically in NWLB-shop committee elections, fought for equal pay and fair treatment, and served as energetic organizers, often goading male-dominated unions. "If you don't stand up for the girls," one angry activist told the president of her local union, "you yourself may be in danger."[44]

Whether through unions or less formal methods of collective actions, women activists made ready use of the various boards and agencies that the government established to oversee wartime labor relations. Local activists, trade unionists, and social feminists attached to such agencies as the NWLB and the U.S. Army Ordnance Department's Women's Branch attempted, though with limited success, to commit the government to equity for women workers. The NWLB officially endorsed this concept but intervened only sporadically, and on the whole, ineffectually, to induce employers to implement it. When women on the board's staff attempted to establish women's issues as priority concerns, the predominantly male bureaucracy resisted successfully. Although co-chair Walsh was personally responsive to women's interests, board Secretary Jett Lauck exhibited at most a condescending and paternalist view of women workers. In charge of day-to-day operations, Lauck derailed the efforts of female staff members to create a separate women's investigative arm to monitor and force compliance of equal pay provisions. Although in its brief career the NWLB did issue path-breaking rulings in behalf of equal pay and did occasionally succeed in raising the wages of women, overall, in the words of its historian, Valerie Connor, "it was unable to accept women as responsible partners in the formation and administration of policy because, fundamentally, it rejected the basic equality of women in industrial matters."[45]

During and immediately after the war, various other government agencies also addressed the special problems related to widespread female employment. Shortly after the United States entered the war, the Council of National Defense, the umbrella organization created in 1916 to coordinate military production, established a Women's Committee ostensibly to mobilize women's support for the war effort. Both the Railroad Administration and the army's Ordnance Department established branches to facilitate female employment on the railroads and in the armaments plants. And in July 1918, Congress appropriated money for a Women-in-Industry Service, attached to the U.S. Department of Labor.

The most active of these new bodies during the war were the Ordnance Department's Women's Branch and the USRA's Women's Service Section. Representatives of these agencies were charged with investigating conditions among women workers and encouraging employers and male workers to accept women in the shops. They strove to protect the interests of female workers, calling attention to pay discrepancies and the widespread sexual harassment that prevailed in work sites. At the same time, however, they took with great seriousness their mission of promoting efficiency, raising production standards, and maintaining labor peace. During the brief period of their active efforts to deal with the distinctive problems and opportunities associated with widespread employment of women, these earnest and astute investigators attempted with only limited success to reconcile these divergent goals.

In theory, it only made sense to treat female workers with dignity and respect and to compensate for their inexperience with well-designed training programs and patient on-the-job instruction. In practice, however, both class and gender issues complicated the efforts of investigators. Employers resented the intrusion of any governmental officials, to say nothing of their particular hostility toward educated and articulate females armed with government authority poking into details of plant management. Moreover, many managers suspected that these women, who were in fact often recruited from the social feminist ranks, of harboring prounion sympathies. Observed Women's Branch investigator Mary Anderson of the employers she encountered, "they were distrustful of us . . . they thought of me particularly as what they probably called a 'red-eyed labor leader' who would be destructive rather than helpful."

Meanwhile, on the shop floor male workers focused on the government agents' role as facilitators of dilution. For a generation, machinists, metal workers, and other skilled workers had been resisting employers' efforts to reorganize and mechanize their work so as to lower labor costs and gain greater control over work processes. The sudden influx of female workers to meet the wartime emergency, in their view, was little more than a convenient excuse for further assaults on men's standards and prerogatives. Under the cloak of war emergency, employers would be free to resume their efforts to erode workingmen's wages and self-respect. College-educated women investigators—of the same social and class status as the employers—actively promoted deskilling and thus seemed to be doing the employers' dishonorable work for them. Anderson, who went on to become director of the U.S. Department of Labor's Women's Bureau, later observed that "I do not think that we accomplished as much as we should have." Employers and army officers alike "felt that they had to run the show. As usual, they did not want women to interfere in any way."[46]

Overall, the Great War accelerated some changes in women's roles and status while leaving basic questions of gender relations in a state of flux. The postwar transformation of the Department of Labor's Women-in-Industry Service into a permanent Women's Bureau afforded a kind of recognition of the permanency of women's emerging role in industrial, commercial, and government employment. Even so, most of the inroads made during the war into male-dominated trades and occupations did not survive. Urban streetcars provide a vivid example of the impermanent state of women's wartime employment. Despite the opposition of the transit workers union, by early 1919 hundreds of women were employed as conductors on mass transit vehicles, their entry into this previously male preserve assisted by women's rights groups, NWLB rulings, patriotic appeals, and employers seeking to cut wages. But after the war, male resistance stiffened and public concern faded. By 1930, census takers could only find sixteen women in the entire country employed as streetcar conductors.

The most significant and permanent war-related advance for women was gaining the right to vote on a national basis. The suffrage movement long antedated the war and before 1917 had won some notable victories on the state level. During the war, the largest and most influential suffrage organization, the National American Woman Suffrage Association, combined support for the war effort with pressure in behalf of female voting, stressing the link between the granting of women's political rights and the quest for a just and permanent peace. Beginning in January 1917, the more confrontational National Woman's Party (NWP) had begun picketing the White House, its militants bearing signs that read, "Mr. President, How Long Must Women Wait for Liberty?" After U.S. entry into the war, NWP demonstrators grew more vocal. Their placards now proclaimed the hypocrisy of fighting for democracy while denying women the ballot. Through the summer of 1917, the White House gates became the scene of almost daily scuffles and assaults, as outraged war supporters attacked the suffrage advocates. Police responded by jailing suffragists. Further arrests in August led to gruesome efforts by jailers to force-feed hunger-striking NWP prisoners, and highly publicized protests continued to contrast the democratic pretensions of the war effort with the treatment of nonviolent activists.

Initially evasive and then only grudgingly supportive, President Wilson by 1916 had come to believe that support for passage of a constitutional amendment would both advance his progressive agenda and prove politically expedient for himself and his party. Eventually, in the fall of 1918, with the picketing suspended, he urged adoption of a constitutional amendment as a war measure. Seventeen states had already granted the vote to women, and they might well play a critical role in the November congressional elections. Sharing the view that women were natural allies in his postwar efforts to achieve a nonpunitive peace and convinced that a Democratic congressional majority was crucial to his ability to exercise leadership in treaty-making, the president broke precedent by addressing the Senate during its debate on the suffrage amendment. Both parties, he pointed out, had declared themselves favorable to women's voting; only the question of whether suffrage should be nationally mandated through a constitutional amendment remained unsettled. The conflict raging in Europe, he reminded the senators, "is a people's war," a war for democracy. And if democracy meant anything, it meant that "women shall play their part in affairs alongside men and upon an equal footing with them."

In the event, Congress did not adopt the amendment until the following summer, with the requisite number of states ratifying it only in mid-1920. Even so, women's critical role in the war effort made it difficult for opponents of suffrage to resist the growing public sentiment in behalf of political equality. After all, in 1917, the British House of Commons had adopted suffrage legislation, as had most of the Canadian provinces. "We have made partners of the women in this war. . . . This war could not have been fought . . . if it had not been for the services of the women," Wilson had told the Senate in 1918.[47]

The debate over suffrage within the context of the sacrifices and agonies of war both revealed and obscured some of the latent gender issues of the Great

War era. To suffrage supporters, women's willingness to shoulder new burdens, take up unaccustomed work, and support their sons and brothers had clearly earned for women the right to political equality. But what did this "equality" really mean? By granting suffrage, would men be conceding something truly important? Would women constitute an identifiable segment of the electorate, with its own interests and demands? Would the organizations created to achieve suffrage now become powerful weapons with which to wrest from men significant portions of real power? Were men who fought and faced the terror of battle and had done so, according to the propagandists, to protect virtuous American womanhood, to have as their reward a diminishment of their prerogatives and dilution of their voice and influence at home?

U.S. participation in the Great War raised powerful class, race, and gender issues. It resolved none of them. The postwar federal government retreated from its innovative, if sporadic, wartime efforts to address issues of class relations, racial injustice, and gender arrangements. In proclaiming a democratic crusade, the Wilson administration had been forced to address, however reluctantly and episodically, the claims of disadvantaged and subordinated citizens. The government agencies and the wartime rhetoric soon faded, but the claims of working people, African Americans, and women alike for fuller inclusion in the American polity, economy, and social order did not disappear. Nor did the sense of power and efficacy that thousands of labor unionists, race leaders, and women activists briefly, but excitingly, experienced.

SIX

Making the Peace
1918–1920

It was only when faced with the problems of making peace that the American people truly confronted the question of what they had been fighting for and discovered the divisions among them concerning war aims and their expectations for the postwar settlement. Throughout the period of U.S. belligerency and the peace-making process, President Woodrow Wilson articulated a particular vision of America's war aims and the postwar world order. Reflecting the president's distinctive combination of civic, religious, and ethical imperatives, the Wilsonian vision served ably in mobilizing U.S. forces, fostering cooperation with the nation's co-belligerents, and providing a basis for the Armistice that ended the fighting in November 1918. After the war, however, Wilson's efforts to translate his vision into a peace settlement were more problematic, frequently clashing with the harsh realities of a war-ravaged Europe. Yet when he brought the completed peace treaty back to the United States in the summer of 1919, he did so with pride, believing that the establishment of a League of Nations far transcended in importance the many compromises and concessions he had made in Paris.

The Wilsonian Vision

Wilson believed that historical experience and divine providence destined America to play a special role at this critical juncture in history. The Great War marked the transformation of international relations and the mechanisms by which states conducted them. Industrialized warfare had rendered traditional diplomacy obsolete. The death and destruction of the past four years revealed the bankruptcy of diplomacy based on alliances, military and naval rivalry, and the "balance of power." Believing also that scientific and technological advance was creating the means by which human beings, acting through democratic governments, could decisively ameliorate poverty, insecurity, and prejudice, Wilson saw in the Great War the death throes of the old order. Out of its horror and destruction must come a new, cooperative world system. Guided by God, America and America alone could lead the way to its creation and thereby redeem the Old World and, indeed, humanity itself.

Wilson was by no means alone in believing that his country embodied unique virtues and had a special destiny. Physical separation from Europe, material abundance, and the potent religiosity of American culture fostered widely held assumptions of American exceptionalism. Americans belonged to the "party of the future," in the words of one of its most influential prophets, Ralph Waldo Emerson, and not to the "party of the past." "To the West, to the West / To the land of the free / Where mighty Missouri rolls down to the sea / Where a man is a man if he will toil / And the humble shall gather the fruits of the soil"—so ran the words of a nineteenth-century ballad of the Western movement. This was a "virgin land," which bred a new kind of man, an "American Adam," free of the sins and corruptions of the Old World, embodying the progress, democracy, and virtue of the New. In the words of Wilson's fellow Princetonian and Great War–era novelist, F. Scott Fitzgerald, in the "fresh, green breast of the new world, [man stood] face to face for the last time in history with something commensurate to his capacity for wonder." For Fitzgerald, the dream of a new start and a special redemption was just that, a dream, doomed to tragic failure. But for Wilson, it was the essence of America, its raison d'être, more alive and more needed in the wake of the Great War than ever before.

Nor was Wilson alone in giving this sense of American exceptionalism a providential cast. Throughout their history, Americans had infused their experience with universalistic religious meanings. From the Puritans' "errand into the wilderness" to the Founding Fathers' appeal to Nature's God and Abraham Lincoln's invocation of "Him who has never yet forsaken this favored land," providential assumptions permeated America's public ideology. School primers no less than Sunday sermons constantly reinforced Americans' sense that their country enjoyed a special sort of divine dispensation. This "political millennialism," in historian Gregory Butler's words, was a recurrent theme in American history, conveying "the core experience of being specially elected by God to fulfill His redemptive purposes."[1]

Wilson articulated these themes in a particular time and place and with a distinctive voice. Jefferson might appeal to a benign deity's favor in the launching of the American national project and Lincoln might invoke his blessing in the bloody business of civil war. Wilson's understanding of the relation of Christian precepts to public life, however, was more pervasive and more active. His belief in America's special destiny and in the providential nature of the American project was both intrinsic and operational. "America was born a Christian nation," he asserted in 1911. America had grown rich and confident, but "We do not judge progress by material standards."[2] America's greatness lay in her conformity to biblical strictures and in her ability to use her material success in the service of mankind. Americans now must acknowledge the obligations that being the beneficiaries of divine favor imposed. In his war message to Congress, Wilson had made this point clear: "The day has come," he declared, "when America is privileged to spend her blood and her might. . . . God helping her, she can do no other."

Wilson used this language in virtually all his major public statements in the period surrounding American belligerency. His words were not mere genuflections to vague notions of civil religion but rather expressions of fundamental conviction. "America was born to exemplify that devotion to the elements of righteousness which are derived from the revelations of the Holy Scripture," he insisted. Only conformity to *these* standards, and no mere calculation of political advantage or national interest, could bring success, first in war and then, most crucially, in the establishment of a new, transcendent international order. Modern times had brought blessings of material bounty, medical advance, and technological achievement. But as the events of 1914–18 showed, they also brought unprecedented horror. Any postwar settlement that stopped short of restructuring on a moral and Christian basis the ways in which the world's people's related to each other would be a tragic failure. "The stage is set," he declared in 1919, "the destiny disclosed." Guided by "the hand of God . . . America shall in truth show the way" to a new and sanctified world order.[3]

Wilson was eloquent about the religious bases of American belligerency and peace making and about the duties that had devolved upon him and his countrymen. Other assumptions that he shared with most Americans, however, went unexamined and little articulated. In particular, Wilson hardly bothered to give voice to his implicit belief in the superiority of Western ethical systems and political and cultural institutions. Nor did he explore the problematic ways in which the American economy related to the world order of the Great War era. But themes of necessary Western dominance and American economic expansionism were powerful, if only sporadically acknowledged, components of the Wilsonian worldview. His tacit insistence on the legitimacy of Western superiority and on the intrinsically progressive role of

American enterprise compromised his moral vision and complicated relations with both his wartime partners and the peoples of the non-Western world.

Wilson never doubted the superiority of Western civilization. He shared the racial Darwinism that accompanied Western advances in technology, industry, and social life. America's uniqueness did not mean estrangement from western Europe. As a scholar and as a statesman, Wilson admired British political institutions and held that American democracy rested on Anglo-Saxon and, ironically, Teutonic foundations. In common with his intellectual peers, he embraced the "germ" theory of U.S. political development, holding that representative government, democratic institutions, and the rule of law were unique achievements of the historic peoples of northwestern Europe and formed the basis of America's free government. True, he had come to believe that distinctively American circumstances, notably the presence of a frontier, had purified these European origins and that America now stood as the lineal descendent of what had begun in Europe. And he further believed that militarism, imperialism, and economic rivalry now distorted and compromised Europe's otherwise-superior culture. But whatever his criticisms of European statesmen, he remained steadfastly Eurocentric in his perspective and a partisan of Western civilization.

Indeed, it was precisely because the war threatened to discredit what Europeans had accomplished that America—the purified descendent of Europe—must intervene. Western political institutions, economic practices, and social arrangements represented mankind's highest achievements; their spread throughout the world was necessary and progressive. Wilson feared that this debilitating war would so cripple Europe economically and so discredit it morally as to allow other, intrinsically less worthy, nations and races to assert world influence. In a very real sense, Wilson's insistence that America remain apart from its European associates in both the military and diplomatic aspects of the Great War reflected his determination to carry forth the mission of Western civilization free of the sins and errors of Mother Europe herself. These views, implicit in Wilson's every wartime speech and action, remained largely unarticulated but were nonetheless basic to his approach to war and peace.

Wilson was more vocal with respect to the role of the U.S. economy in the modern world, but here he rarely explored the practical implications of his views. In common with many public men of his generation, he worried about possible stagnation of the American economy. Periodic depressions, sieges of massive unemployment, and evidences of social misery and labor violence punctuated the years of his adult life. The sharp recession of 1913–15, which threatened to derail his administration, was but the latest example of the volatility of the U.S. economy. The frontier that had so beneficially helped to shape America's political institutions had come to a close, shutting off a key source of economic growth and material abundance. Like many of his contemporaries, he saw in foreign markets a solution to the problems of the domestic economy. After initial hesitation, he hailed the territorial acquisitions of the Spanish-American-Philippine war of 1898 to 1902 in part for providing a boost to the U.S. economy. During his first term as president, his tariff, regulatory, and banking policies had been aimed in part at expanding America's international trade.

Desire to ameliorate domestic problems through foreign trade and acquisition of colonies for economic gain were commonplace ideas among Western politicians of the pre–Great War era. British and German statesmen and economists duly noted the increased interest of the United States in international commerce and calculated the competitive impact American goods and capital might have on their own economies. Nationalists in less-developed lands, especially Latin America, viewed with apprehension U.S. economic initiatives and colonial acquisitions, understanding that the dynamic American economy, with its growing financial power, might quickly dominate their vulnerable economies and imperil their fragile political independence.

Wilson, however, explained America's outward thrust in different terms. People in other lands, he believed, should welcome rather than fear U.S. expansion. To be sure, there were examples of high-handed exploitation of underdeveloped countries. As president, he approved a treaty—which Theodore Roosevelt's supporters killed in the Senate—containing an apology to the Colombian government for the arrogant way in which the United States had seized control of the Isthmus of Panama in 1903 to build a canal there. Even so, however, he believed that Latin Americans should rejoice in the expansion of trade and the opportunities for closer association with the American republic that the opening of the canal offered. America's economic achievements, he declared, were really the common property of all mankind, providing the material underpinning for the expansion of democracy and enlightenment. The American businessman operating abroad "comes into . . . competition . . . without any arms, [bringing] only those peaceful influences of intelligence, a desire to serve." Where other nations sent gunboats to gain selfish economic advantage, America used its wealth and enterprise to advance all that was best in Western civilization. Addressing a meeting of salesmen in 1916, he urged them to compete aggressively for markets abroad. "You are Americans and are meant to carry liberty and justice and the principles of humanity wherever you go. . . . Go out and sell goods," he urged, for American enterprise "will make the world more comfortable and more happy, and convert them to the principles of America."[4]

Indeed, America's business system underwrote its providential role in the world. Observes historian N. Gordon Levin Jr., "Like the Puritans, who placed earthly vocations, or callings, in a larger context of service to God and man, Wilson saw the enlargement of foreign commerce in terms of duty in the service of humanity."[5] Whether as scholar or politician, Wilson took little notice of the sordid realities of labor exploitation, corporate domination of colonial economies, and racial subjugation that characterized Western imperialism. In the decade before his presidency, Wilson, unlike many other college presidents and public figures, said nothing about widely publicized revelations of Belgian atrocities committed against the people of the Congo. Nor did he acknowledge the gruesome toll of natives killed—more than 200,000 by some estimates—in the U.S. subjugation of the Philippines.

Wilson was certain that his country alone could guide less-developed people such as the Filipinos to Western forms of liberty "without plundering them or making them our tools for a selfish end." To be sure, he did criticize U.S. corporate and financial interests when he believed them involved in exploitative schemes. He insisted that the expansion of American economic interests must benefit the host peoples and, in common with many progressives on both sides of the Atlantic, believed that wise public policies could harness capitalism to the cause of beneficial economic and political development. As president, he withdrew government support for consortiums of banking interests that he believed were acting selfishly in China and Latin America. He initially voiced doubts about the wisdom of assuming colonial responsibilities, hinting that the country had enough domestic problems to occupy it without undertaking the governance of remote possessions. His secretary of state, William Jennings Bryan, was a leading anticolonialist and reinforced Wilson's distrust of international bankers and would-be imperialists.

But in the final analysis, the penetration of underdeveloped lands by the West was as inevitable as it was progressive. "The East [by which he meant Asia] is to be opened up and transformed . . . the standards of the West are to be imposed upon it." Asia, he insisted, would soon be "made part of the universal world of commerce and of ideas which has so steadily been a-making by the advance of European power." The question was not whether the nondeveloped world would be opened up; it was who would do it. And to this question, Wilson had a ready answer: "I believe that God planted in us visions of liberty," he declared in 1912, adding "that we are chosen . . . to show the way to the nations of the world how they shall walk in the paths of liberty."[6] Wilson and his supporters believed that America could simultaneously stand against the old, exploitative imperialism associated with Europe and use growing American financial and economic influence to create a new and positive relationship between the West and the dark-skinned masses of the nondeveloped world.

Thus, the American president brought to his contemplation of the ending of the war and the shaping of the peace a mixture of ideas and attitudes. His eloquent appeals had helped to mobilize the populace in behalf of high-minded aims against an enemy that posed no physical threat to America. His presence as part of the anti-German coalition had helped to sustain the resolve and loyalty of labor and liberal elements in the Allied countries otherwise susceptible to antiwar appeals. And his public declarations of war aims, most notably as contained in his Fourteen Points statement of January 8, 1918, offered hope to the Germans that they could concede military defeat without facing national humiliation and improved the chances that the German people would embrace democratic values in the wake of the war. Wilson's conviction that he and his countrymen fought for redemption of humanity and not for selfish or exploitative advantage thus proved a powerful advantage in fighting the war to a successful conclusion, but whether it would serve as a basis for making peace remained uncertain.

Armistice

For all its horror and killing, the Great War ended ambiguously. Between March and November 1918, Germany won an overwhelming victory in the east and then suffered decisive defeat in the west. On both the Eastern and Western Fronts, the formal end of hostilities in 1918 left key territorial, military, and political questions unresolved. In the east, in the Treaty of Brest-Litovsk, signed on March 3, the Germans imposed draconian terms on Russia's Bolshevik regime, which was desperate to end the war. Forced to cede almost a third of the prewar czarist empire's European land and population, the revolutionary government also faced violent counterrevolution within its shrunken borders. The fate of Ukraine, Poland, and other regions of central and eastern Europe remained unsettled, with nationalist forces, revolutionary movements, local strongmen, and German-supported puppet governments vying for control even as the war lurched to an end in the west.

There the situation was more clear cut but nonetheless paradoxical. The sudden turning of the tide in the late summer and fall of 1918 had sent German troops into retreat. By the beginning of November, Allied and American forces had liberated most of northern France and parts of Belgium. Even so, the German army remained intact and continued to inflict heavy casualties on advancing forces. When the guns fell silent, the Germans remained in control of three-quarters of Belgium, a slice of northeastern France, and almost all of Alsace-Lorraine. Victorious France and Belgium had suffered enormous damage to farms, mines, transport, buildings, livestock, and public infrastructure, whereas Germany had almost entirely escaped damage. No Allied or U.S. soldier set foot in Germany proper until after the signing of the Armistice.

Why, in view of their decisive victories of the fall of 1918, did Germany's opponents settle for less than unconditional surrender? Some influential figures urged a continuation of the war until German forces had been destroyed and the German people had experienced the bitterness and humiliation of outright military subjugation. General John J. Pershing, for example, urged an invasion of Germany and a relentless campaign to shatter the German army. In ten more days of fighting, he later declared, "we would have rounded up the entire German army, captured it, humiliated it." Former President Theodore Roosevelt was, as usual, particularly vociferous. "Let us dictate peace by the hammering of guns," he demanded, "and not chat about peace to the accompaniment of the clicking of typewriters."[7]

In fact, however, both practical and political circumstances favored an Allied–American policy of armistice rather than surrender. It was all very well for hard-liners to urge an assault on Germany proper, but such a campaign would have been both exhausting and bloody. The German armies might retreat rather than cling to French and Belgian territory, but who could doubt that they would fight ferociously in defense of their homeland? Sir Douglas Haig, the British commander, was among those weighing in on behalf of armistice. His troops, although successful in breaching the Hindenburg Line, had suffered horrendous casualties in the advances of the summer and fall of 1918. The French too were exhausted and had little stomach for fighting their way across Germany and besieging Berlin.

Ironically, German weakness as well as German strength also spoke against the continuation of the war. Since at least the spring of 1917, mass strikes, democratic and socialist agitation, and even evidence of disaffection within military units had troubled Ludendorff and the German Empire's civilian government. Of course, American and Allied leaders welcomed internal division and stoked the fires of dissent with prodemocratic propaganda. But the success of the Bolsheviks in Russia echoed powerfully within the German Empire. In July 1917, militant socialists, impatient with the moderate Social Democratic Party's continued support of the war, called for revolutionary overthrow of the existing order. Later, radicalized workers, organized into "soviets" in emulation of the Russian revolutionaries, defied employers and trade union functionaries alike. Just as in Russia, disaffection spread into the navy and the army. German leaders feared Russian-like revolution in Germany, itself a prime goal of the Bolsheviks. "The central question [now]," declared one cabinet minister early in November, "is not the Kaiser's abdication but whether we shall have Bolshevism or not."[8]

To the Allies, the prospect of Bolshevik revolution in Germany was sobering. Declared U.S. Secretary of State Robert Lansing at the end of October 1918, "We have seen the hideous consequences of Bolshevik rule in Russia, and we know that the doctrine is spreading westward," into Germany itself. Wilson warned that too complete a collapse of the established order there might result in "bolshevikism [sic] worse than in Russia." Western statesmen, determined to crush what they thought of as Prussian militarism, increasingly had to factor into their calculations the specter of red revolution spreading across Europe from defeated Germany. "Bolshevism there rampant," said an upper-level state department official, "will mean the same thing at a later date in France, Italy and England, even in America. . . . Germany cannot safely be annihilated."[9]

Reinforcing these calculations lay Wilson's distinctive understanding of the reasons for American belligerency and of the character of the postwar settlement. The United States fought as an "associated power," not as a formal ally of Britain, France, and Italy. In April 1917, the president had asserted America's disinterested war aims. "We have no selfish ends to serve," he declared. "We seek no indemnities . . . no material compensation." Americans fought "for the rights of nations great and small and the privilege of men everywhere to choose their way of life." Wilson insisted that the postwar settlement must be based on fairness and justice for all peoples, most definitely including the Germans. Although he decried the traditional notion of the "balance of power" as the aim of diplomacy, Wilson feared that too thorough a smashing of Germany would remove her as a makeweight to the victorious Allies and create a political and military vacuum in the heart of Europe.

On January 8, 1918, Wilson outlined his views in an address to Congress. He put forth a series of stipulations, which came to be called the Fourteen Points, that articulated principles he and other internationalist progressives had been advancing since the outbreak of fighting in 1914. Although he could no longer speak of "peace without victory," he sought to direct the attention of his countrymen, as well as that of the peoples of the Allied countries, away from retribution and hatred and toward the building of a democratic and open new world order. Some of the Fourteen Points that he advanced as bases on which the war ought to be ended addressed specific issues of territorial adjustment. Belgium must be "evacuated and restored."

The Germans had to leave French soil and, presumably, return Alsace and Lorraine, taken in the Franco-Prussian War of 1870–71, to France. The many distinctive peoples now ruled by the Austro-Hungarian, Turkish, and German Empires must have the right to national self-determination. A Polish state was to be created and the smaller states of southeastern Europe must be restored and guaranteed their independence and territorial coherence. On the murky and chaotic situation in Russia, Wilson called for the evacuation of Russian territory by hostile (i.e., German) forces. This included the fair adjustment of territorial, economic, and political disagreements with a view to bringing a free Russian state, presumably purged of its Bolshevik aberration, back into regular intercourse with other nations.

Other points dealt with the structure of the postwar economic and diplomatic order. Secret treaties and other clandestine arrangements among the nations were to be eliminated. The high seas must be open to all commerce without interference. Tariffs and other barriers to free international trade must be reduced or eliminated and the production of armaments must be curtailed. Disagreement over colonial matters must be resolved in a "free, openminded, and absolutely impartial" manner, with the interests of subject peoples duly considered. Crowning the Fourteen Points was Wilson's call for a "general association of nations," specifically charged with "affording mutual guarantees of political independence and territorial integrity to great and small states alike." As late as September 27, 1918, Wilson reaffirmed these principles. In a major address calling for decisive victory, the president eloquently renewed his appeal for an association of nations and restated his belief in a nonpunitive settlement and in free and open international commerce and diplomacy.

Neither the Fourteen Points nor this fourth Liberty Loan address said anything specifically about Germany. The speeches advanced no territorial, monetary, or economic claims. Those embracing the Fourteen Points as the basis for peace with Germany "do [not] presume to suggest to her any alteration or modifications of her institutions," nor did they "wish to injure her or to block . . . her legitimate influence or power," although Wilson strongly implied that Germany's enemies could not trust its current autocratic and irresponsible regime. All in all, the Fourteen Points envisaged an impartial peace that would serve as the basis for a new, democratic, and cooperative world order. This was so even though the American president was simultaneously urging his fellow citizens to exert "Force, Force to the utmost, Force without stint or limit" to destroy Prussian autocracy.[10]

Wilson issued the Fourteen Points unilaterally, without official consultation with America's co-belligerents. He did so for several reasons. Most immediately, he was responding to the actions of the Bolsheviks. Upon gaining access to the czarist archives in October 1917, Lenin's regime had begun publishing the contents of the secret treaties that bound the members of the anti-German alliance in what amounted to agreements to grab German territory, divide up its colonial possessions, and impose exploitative economic arrangements on Germany and its allies once the Central Powers had been defeated. The Russian revolutionaries publicized the contents of these treaties to discredit all the warring countries and thereby to strengthen their appeal to workers and soldiers everywhere to demand an immediate end to the fighting. Coming as it did in the winter of 1917–18, a period of Allied military defeat, civilian despair, and eroding morale, the Soviets' action required a prompt and inspiring response.

Then too there was the failure of the Allies, either before or after the onset of American belligerency, to make public an explicit statement of their war aims. The latest effort had been at an Inter-Allied Conference, held in Paris beginning on November 29, 1917. There, Wilson's representative, Edward House, had urged British, French, and Italian leaders to come forth with a frank declaration of what Germany's foes were fighting for. Such a declaration, Wilson believed, would counteract the sordid details of the secret treaties, and it would help to deflect peace proposals floated in the summer by Pope Benedict XV, who had urged an end to the fighting and a return to the prewar status quo. But the Allies could not issue a unified statement of war aims precisely because they were divided from each other, united only by the determination to defeat Germany. Certainly, none of the Allies could renounce territorial ambitions, colonial spoils, or economic advantage, in view of the still-binding terms of the secret treaties that called for exactly these outcomes and held together the Allied coalition.

Wilson, of course, knew of the special interests and divisiveness among America's wartime partners, but before the Bolsheviks' action he could afford, he felt, to ignore them. In the summer of 1917, for example, he had told House quite frankly, "England and France *have not the same views with regard to peace that we have* . . . [but after the war] we can force them to our way of thinking, because by that time they will . . . be financially in our hands."[11] But at the beginning of 1918, with war weariness deepening daily and with the cynicism and greed of the Allies' war aims so dramatically exposed, a bold and idealistic proclamation of what Germany's enemies were fighting for was crucial.

Given the divisions among its enemies and the lack of punitive references in the Fourteen Points, it was natural that when confronted with military defeat, German leaders appealed to the American president for an armistice.

Thus in October 1918, as Allied forces pierced the Hindenburg Line and took thousands of prisoners, Ludendorff informed civilian leaders that only a prompt halt to the fighting could save the army from abject defeat and perhaps disintegration. By now, the German government was headed by Prince Max of Baden, who had long urged a compromise peace and was supported by a loose coalition of socialist and liberal parties in the German Reichstag. On October 3, the new German chancellor cabled Wilson, asking for an armistice, to be based on the terms outlined in the Fourteen Points. For the next month, the two leaders exchanged messages, with Wilson insisting that Germany acknowledge Allied military victory and seeking assurances that the German government's recent adoption of democratic changes was real and substantial.

Throughout the nerve-wracking negotiations over the terms of armistice, German leaders hoped that their appeal to the Fourteen Points would save Germany from harsh treatment. The German army, after all, was still intact and continued to control large chunks of Allied territory. Moreover, even if Germany faced defeat in the west, it had been victorious in the east and remained there a barrier to Bolshevik expansion. In response to internal agitation and in hopes of further softening Wilson's terms, German authorities had agreed to wide-ranging democratic reforms. Indeed, by the time the actual Armistice was signed, Emperor Wilhelm II had abdicated and Germany had become a republic, thus presumably removing the elimination of "German autocracy" as an Allied war aim. With radical revolutionary activity mounting within Germany, Prince Max and his civilian and military cohorts reasoned, the Wilson-led belligerent coalition might be eager to end the war and permit a reformed Germany to resume its role as a bulwark of stability in Europe.

Such reasoning, however, was unduly optimistic. From the issuance of Prince Max's initial telegram, Allied leaders had bridled at Germany's transparent effort to avoid retribution by basing its armistice request on Wilson's Fourteen Points. Had they fought for four long years and suffered such staggering casualties only to have the naive and idealistic American president presume to make peace without them? Wilson might want something like a "peace without victory," but British Prime Minister David Lloyd George, French Premier Georges Clemenceau, and Italian Prime Minister Vittorio Orlando could not go to their long-suffering electorates without attaining tangible evidence of victory. Moreover, what guarantee would there be that the so-called reforms within Germany were not merely camouflaging the military dictatorship of Ludendorff and his nominal superior, Paul von Hindenburg? For that matter, what guarantee was there against the Germans using the respite provided by an armistice to regroup and rearm while still occupying Allied territory?

For his part, Wilson had no intention of attempting to make unilateral peace with Germany. Indeed, it quickly became apparent that the sudden turning of the tide against Germany had actually weakened his hand vis-à-vis his co-belligerents. The longer the war lasted, the greater the need for American troops and resources; conversely, the collapse of Germany would free his associates to impose extreme demands on it, demands that in Wilson's view could only sow the seeds of future bitterness and war. Through his emissary, House, he negotiated with his war partners even as he negotiated with the Germans, stepping up his own demands on German authorities while he sought to moderate the Allies' requirements for an armistice. In a key concession to the Allies, he acquiesced in giving military leaders on the ground wide authority to formulate the precise terms of armistice. Wilson further conceded that British and French views on the freedom of the seas and on monetary reparations to be exacted from Germany would influence the practical application of the Fourteen Points. The crucial point, Wilson believed, was that the basic framework of the Fourteen Points and Allied commitment to the creation of a league of nations must remain intact.

As detailed discussions among military leaders proceeded during the first week of November, Germany's military and internal situation deteriorated. Allied commander Marshal Ferdinand Foch, determined to eliminate the German threat to French security for the foreseeable future and backed by French civilian leaders, imposed rigorous terms. The Germans were to evacuate all occupied territory, including Alsace-Lorraine; to abrogate the Treaty of Brest-Litovsk and evacuate all Russian territory; to withdraw all troops to points at least 20 miles east of the Rhine River; and to accept Allied bridgeheads and zones of occupation in German territory at key junctures on the Rhine and to pay the costs of their maintenance. Additional terms opened German ports to Allied commerce and turned the entire German navy over to Allied control, along with thousands of locomotives, railroad cars, trucks, and airplanes. The Allied blockade of Germany was to continue to guarantee German compliance with these terms.

At 5:00 in the morning of November 11, 1918, representatives of the new German republic signed the Armistice agreement, which became effective at 11:00 A.M. on that day. Shooting continued until the very end, and sometimes even after. "I fired 164 rounds at him [the German enemy] before he quit this morning," Captain Harry S. Truman of Battery D, 129th Field Artillery, wrote to his wife. Shortly before 11 o'clock, across from the British lines, a German machine gunner fired off a belt of ammunition, stood up, doffed his helmet, and bowing to his erstwhile enemies, walked slowly away from the battle line. As the guns fell silent, reported a veteran British infantryman, there came a "curious rippling sound. . . . It was the sound of men cheering from the Vosges [mountains of eastern France] to the sea.[12]

Making Peace

Later that day, President Wilson addressed Congress. "Everything for which America fought has been accomplished," he told the people. But had it? In reality, the president knew that in many respects his most difficult battles lay ahead. In theory, the Armistice had been based on the Fourteen Points, but in actuality the terms of the military agreement ending the fighting, along with the reservations that the Allies insisted upon, had already compromised Wilson's agenda. The final, great battlefield of the war would be the impending peace conference, where the victors would settle on permanent terms to be presented to Germany and its allies. In view of the chaotic conditions still prevailing throughout Russia and eastern Europe, the diverse war aims of the various Western Allies, the uncertain status of Germany's colonies, and the general destruction and disruption that four years of warfare had wrought, the task facing the peacemakers was formidable indeed.

American circumstances further complicated the treaty-writing process. A belligerent for just eighteen months, the United States had played only a secondary role in the Allies' victory, yet its financial, economic, naval, and even military power now outstripped that of any other nation. The defeat of Germany, the destruction of its submarine force, and the replacement of the Hohenzollern monarchy with a democratic republic did indeed justify Wilson's claim that "Everything for which America fought has been accomplished," at least with respect to the specific factors impelling American belligerency. As for Wilson's broader aim to create a new structure of international relations, he now faced the tasks of persuading his erstwhile military associates and his skeptical fellow countrymen of its legitimacy and feasibility.

American's domestic peculiarities added to the already complex postwar kaleidoscope. Wilson's vision of an American-led new world order clashed with the country's long and cherished traditions of aloofness from European diplomatic and military affairs. Could he persuade the American people to accept the kind of continuous international involvement his plans would necessitate? Initial signs were not good, for in the congressional elections held on November 7, 1918, his party had lost control of Congress in a bitter, partisan campaign in which the president had openly appealed for the election of Democrats to strengthen his hand at the impending peace conference. This defeat now posed innumerable problems for him as he prepared to journey to Paris. Indeed, his very decision to lead the U.S. peace delegation in person aroused controversy. No previous chief executive had traveled outside the hemisphere while in office. Secretary of State Lansing and other advisers warned the president that by attending in person, he would squander his great moral prestige and compromise his ability to advance his high-minded goals. Moreover, in the type of parliamentary system prevailing in Britain, France, and Italy, and now in the German republic, a leader whose party had lost the election would have resigned, to be replaced by the leader of the victorious party. A long-term advocate of parliamentary governance, Wilson would nonetheless remain as chief executive, though now burdened by the seeming rejection by his own people. Better, urged Lansing, to act through representatives, retain a certain Olympian detachment, and leave himself free to advance his vision of a new world order without being sullied by the inevitable compromises that hard negotiations would surely entail.

Armed with his transcendent vision of America's solemn obligations and with a profound religious belief in his cause, however, Wilson shook off these doubts. His decision to represent the United States personally, he believed, was right precisely because it broke with precedent. He had sent thousands of young men to their deaths and had involved his country in the horrific destruction of war. He now had the serious duty of justifying Americans' sacrifices. He would, he announced soon after the Armistice was signed, personally represent the United States at the peace conference, scheduled to open in Paris on January 18, 1919. There he could use his passion, his eloquence, and America's vast moral and material strength to shape a peace settlement that would not be a license for retribution and exploitation but rather would promote international understanding and accommodation. Surely the American people would support him in the struggle for peace as he sought to vindicate the sacrifices they had made in the cause of war.

Wilson led an official American delegation, consisting of Edward House, Secretary of State Robert Lansing, General Tasker Bliss, who had served as U.S. Military Representative to the Allied Supreme War Council, and in a feeble gesture of bipartisanship, a retired Republican diplomat, Henry White. Notably absent were any prominent Republican congressional leaders, most conspicuously Massachusetts Senator Henry Cabot Lodge, slated to chair the crucial Senate Committee on Foreign Relations in the newly elected 66th Congress. A small army of clerks, researchers, aides, and experts accompanied them. In the fall of 1917, anticipating that complex territorial, economic, and demographic issues would face the peacemakers, the president had directed House to organize the systematic collection of information on these matters. Eventually known as The Inquiry, the behind-the-scenes body that House created employed more than 150 people, recruiting academic and legal experts mainly from American colleges and universities. Inquiry members eventually prepared more than 3,000 background reports and papers on questions of boundaries, populations, economic affairs, and a wide variety of other matters likely to arise during peace negotiations. And as summarized and conveyed by the body's brilliant young secretary, Walter Lippmann, it was the Inquiry's studies that lay behind the territorial stipulations of the Fourteen Points and their subsequent detailed elaboration in the president's various statements and messages. In Paris, the president relied heavily on Inquiry reports and on several of its participants serving with the U.S. peace delegation, for Wilson was determined that the postwar settlement would be based on objective assessment of economic, territorial, and demographic facts and not on deals that served only selfish interests.

The peace conference began deliberations on January 19. In May, German representatives were called in to receive a draft version, more than 200 pages long and including 440 separate articles. Over the next six weeks, the Germans subjected the draft to detailed criticism. The unwillingness of the Allies to make substantial changes in the terms initially proposed created a crisis within the government of the new German republic. Eventually, however, under the threat of a resumption of the war and the occupation and perhaps dismemberment of Germany at the hands of the Allies and Polish and Czech troops, the German government agreed to sign the treaty. Its representatives did so on June 28, 1919, exactly five years from the day that Archduke Franz Ferdinand was assassinated in Sarajevo. Subsequently, the conference continued without the direct participation of the Allied and Associated Powers' heads of state and produced treaties for Germany's allies, the last of which, the Treaty of Sevres, was signed by representatives of the Ottoman Empire in August 1920.

From the start, controversy and confusion bedeviled the conference. Was it to be a meeting of the victors, who would agree on terms to be negotiated with Germany? Or would the conference simply impose terms on Germany? If the latter—the approach favored by the French—what happened to Wilson's hopes and the Fourteen Points' promises of a peace without retribution? Was the main purpose of the conference to settle accounts between victors and vanquished? Or was it, as Wilson held, to create a new and impartial structure for the future conduct of world affairs?

Nor were the agenda or organization of the conference carefully planned beforehand. All sorts of tricky questions of procedure and organization quickly emerged. Were all states on the winning side to have equal voice in the deliberations? Should the various components of the British Empire—Canada, Australia, South Africa, New Zealand, India—have separate representation? What about the status of Russia? It was a key factor in European diplomacy, but both because of the unsettled character of affairs there and the outlaw nature of the Bolshevik regime, it was unrepresented in Paris. If committees of inquiry were to be established to investigate complex issues of boundaries and economic arrangements—as surely they must be lest the conference become hopelessly backlogged—how were they to be staffed and their reports to be integrated into the main deliberations? Even after the main belligerent powers had assumed a leadership role by creating the Council of Ten, consisting of the chief executives and the foreign secretaries of Britain, France, Italy, Japan, and the United States, uncertainty and confusion persisted. Declared a veteran French diplomat, "No matter how hard you try, you cannot imagine the shambles, the chaos, the incoherence, the ignorance here."[13]

Eventually, even the Council of Ten, each with his experts, advisers, and clerks, proved unwieldy. In March, Wilson, Lloyd George, Clemenceau, and Orlando began meeting separately, attended only by translators and a single secretary. Between March and June 1919, the leaders* met more than 140 times, usually in Wilson's residence in Paris. As reports and recommendations from technical experts and investigating committees trickled in, the Council of Four proceeded to give shape to the treaty to be presented to Germany. Still, the very multiplicity of complex and contentious issues made the deliberations of even this small body anything but systematic and routine. "At this Conference," observed British Foreign Secretary Arthur Balfour, "all important business is transacted in the intervals of other business."[14]

Dwarfing even these problems of procedure, however, were substantive disagreements among the major powers. To be sure, all wanted to punish Germany. The French, for obvious reasons, sought permanent diminishment of their hated rival and hard-and-fast guarantees against any resurgence of German military strength and diplomatic influence. Unlike the others, France had suffered grievous physical damage, made worse by the systematic destruc-

---

*Orlando walked out of the conference on April 21 in protest over Wilson's resistance to Italy's territorial claims and remained away till May 7. Moreover, the Italian prime minister, whose English was limited, took little part in most discussions not relating directly to Italian interests. Nonetheless, the initially informal gathering of Wilson, Lloyd George, Clemenceau, and Orlando was called at the time the Council of Four, and this is the usage I follow in the ensuing discussion.

tion of farms, factories, mines, and transport facilities by the retreating Germans in the last phases of the war. Insofar as Clemenceau was concerned, a settlement that failed to include significant monetary reparations, sharp limits on German military capabilities, privileged French access to German coalfields (to compensate for German exploitation and destruction of French mines during the occupation), and specific provisions for Allied military monitoring of German compliance with the treaty's provisions was simply unacceptable.

The French were not alone in seeking punishment of Germany. Domestic political considerations, skepticism over the depth of Germany's internal reforms, and revulsion over the behavior of Germany's diplomatic emissaries during the treaty-making process also fueled the determination of the British and the Americans to treat Germany sternly. In the first British general election since before the war, held in December 1918, Lloyd George sought to rouse the electorate in behalf of his troubled coalition government with emotional calls for retribution. In private moments the British prime minister might soberly acknowledge the need for a strong Germany as a bulwark against Bolshevism and as a key element in the postwar economy. But during the election campaign he demonized the German people, vowing to squeeze Germany for financial reparations "until the pips squeaked."

For his part, Wilson had come to believe his own wartime anti-German rhetoric. From his perspective, by the fall of 1918, the Germans had repeatedly shown themselves to be power hungry and cynical. In 1916–17 they had talked peace while preparing for the savage campaign of unrestricted submarine warfare. At Brest-Litovsk, they had imposed a merciless peace on the Russians that even the putatively peace-loving Social Democrats had endorsed. By the end of the war, Wilson had concluded reluctantly that his careful distinction, eloquently expressed in his war message, between the good German people and their malevolent leaders was not in fact valid, although, he remarked, "It took me a long time to believe it." Progressive elements within Germany, he now believed, were "too small a minority to have any influence . . . on the people, as a whole." The Allies must continue to encourage democratic change in their former enemy; a stable and prosperous Germany was, in the long run, essential for a peaceful postwar Europe. But, declared Wilson, "disciplining Germany" was a crucial first step in achieving these ends.[15]

Despite the common determination to punish the Germans, however, the three great powers differed sharply as to the character, severity, and duration of that punishment. In a broad sense, both the United States and Great Britain envisioned a treaty that, while stern in its treatment of Germany, left that country economically viable and politically influential. The elimination of the German fleet, the confiscation of Germany's submarines, the abdication of the Kaiser, and the dismantling of Germany's colonial empire removed the main specific grievances of the British and the Americans. True, the British were determined to exact reparations from Germany and to impose other demands, but they and the Americans were anxious not to cripple Germany permanently lest it become a source of instability and turbulence in the heart of Europe.

In the view of the French, however, this concern with German prosperity and stability was misplaced. The problem was not potential German weakness but historic German aggression. The task of the peace conference was not to find a way to bolster the German state but to render it incapable of military adventure. When Wilson and Lloyd George balked at French proposals for absorption of the coal-rich Saar Basin into France and sweeping demilitarization and Allied occupation of wide swathes of western Germany, Clemenceau accused his negotiating partners of ignoring France's critical need for economic reconstruction and military security once their own narrow concerns had been addressed. "You seek to do justice to the Germans," Clemenceau told Wilson early in the deliberations. "Do not believe that they will ever forgive us [for winning the war]; they only seek the opportunity for revenge."[16]

Bitterness between the French and the British over Germany flared repeatedly. On at least one occasion, the seventy-year-old Clemenceau and the diminutive British prime minister nearly came to blows. According to Clemenceau, one argument between the two became "so violent that . . . Wilson had to interpose between us with outstretched arms, saying pleasantly 'Well, well! I have never come across two such unreasonable men!'" Meanwhile, Clemenceau and Wilson conducted a troubled dialogue. The president regarded the French leader as the epitome of the discredited old diplomacy, while "le Tigre" mocked Wilson's idealism. "Talking to Wilson," he remarked, "is something like talking to Jesus Christ." According to Lloyd George, "When Wilson talks of idealism Clemenceau . . . touches his forehead, as much to say, 'A good man, but not quite all there!'"[17]

But U.S.–British relations were also strained. Despite two decades of growing Anglo–American diplomatic cooperation and the pro-British attitudes of influential government officials, academics, and journalists, sharp differences separated American and British naval leaders and diplomats. They clashed directly over the meaning of the Fourteen Points' call for "Absolute freedom of navigation upon the seas," which Wilson privately regarded as crucial for curbing what he called British "navalism," an unsavory counterpart to the hated Prussian militarism. For their part, however, British statesmen would brook no interference with their nation's historic dominance on the high seas, refusing to do more than agree that posttreaty talks to clarify maritime issues. Indeed, the British accused the Americans of hypocrisy, because the wartime naval construction program of the United States threatened to create an American navy larger and more powerful than its Royal counterpart even as Wilson invoked "freedom of the seas" as a sacred doctrine.

Many among the American delegation reserved a special distrust for Great Britain, whose combination of prewar commercial and financial dominance, cultural arrogance, and wily diplomacy made even sophisticated American diplomats and politicians uneasy. The British, they believed, would stop at nothing to advance the Empire and retain the economic and commercial advantages that it brought. Nor did Wilson and his aides forget Britain's high-handed pre-1917 maritime actions, which had included blacklisting American firms, denying Americans access to British ports and trading facilities, and of course, seizing American cargos. Moreover, "twisting the [British] lion's tail" was a staple of domestic American politics, for large blocs of Irish and rural voters had always loathed the erstwhile mother country. Indeed, once the submarine menace had been destroyed and Germany humbled, John Bull once again replaced Kaiser Bill as the main international antagonist to the United States in the eyes of many Americans.

British diplomats, business leaders, and intellectuals reciprocated these feelings. Even before 1914, signs of relative commercial decline had troubled government leaders and businessmen. The enormous cost of the war, amounting to more than 40 percent of Britain's total national wealth, had forced liquidation of vast international holdings, putting Britain heavily into debt to the United States. With British shipping concentrated on the war trade, Americans had built up a large merchant marine and were encroaching steadily on traditionally British markets. Who could doubt that calculating American businessmen would exploit Britain's financial weakness and attempt to supplant their British counterparts in counting houses and trading marts around the world? Clearly, in the financing of utilities and railroads in Latin America, the competition for trade even with dominions of the British Empire, and access to the oil fields of the Middle East, England and America were destined to remain wary rivals. Moreover, American criticism of British colonialism, widespread support in the United States for violent Irish rebels, and British resentment over Wilson's pretensions to world leadership further fueled Anglo–American discord. Personal and temperamental differences also divided Wilson and Lloyd George, whose extramarital dalliances and blunt assertion of Britain's interests combined to alienate the righteous U.S. president. Throughout the conference, despite common resistance to French demands, Lloyd George and Wilson remained wary and suspicious of each other.

Many other issues divided the peacemakers. The British and the French were united in seeking vast monetary exactions from Germany, whereas American policymakers worried about the effect that inflated claims would surely have on the economic viability of the fragile German republic and on the integrity of the treaty itself. The British, Australians, French, Belgians, and Japanese coveted Germany's African and Asian colonies and spheres of influence. Indeed, secret wartime treaties had already stipulated the division of colonial spoils. Wilson, however, believed that such a cynical grab for territory would discredit the entire peace process and make a mockery of the Fourteen Points' call for "absolutely impartial adjustment of all colonial claims," to say nothing of its call for consideration of "the interests of the populations concerned."

Specific territorial disputes also compromised the peace conference. The Japanese, for example, insisted that their wartime role in driving the German navy and merchant marine from the Pacific entitled them to a large share of Germany's Pacific colonial holdings and to assumption of Germany's special economic and political influence in China, especially on the Shantung Peninsula. Meanwhile, Britain's Pacific dominions, Australia and New Zealand, staked claims to some of these same possessions, and the nascent Chinese republic, which had also joined the war against Germany, appealed to the major powers to reject Japan's claims of special status in Shantung, where the Germans had earlier forced a weak Chinese government to grant economic and diplomatic concessions. Japanese insistence that the treaty contain an explicit statement rejecting racial discrimination—which Wilson, despite his segregationist views, personally favored but which would have been anathema to Britain and its dominions—further complicated these territorial issues.

The Italians also put forth territorial demands. Orlando claimed slices of Austrian territory in the southern Alps by virtue of secret clauses in the 1915 Treaty of London that had brought Italy into the war. More provocatively, the Italians also insisted on acquisition of key ports on the Adriatic, which had not been specified in the treaty but which they argued were as necessary for Italy's military security as, say, Gibraltar and Malta were to Britain's.

Both the Japanese and Italian demands were frustrating and nettlesome. The territory that Italy sought contained large German and Slavic populations, in clear contravention of the Fourteen Points' declaration that any "readjustment of the frontiers of Italy should be effected along clearly recognizable lines of nationality." In laying claim to the Adriatic port of Fiume, the

Italians were attempting to take it not from the now-defunct enemy Austro-Hungarian Empire but rather from a new Yugoslavian state centering on Serbia and Montenegro, fellow belligerents in the war against the Central Powers and seemingly protected in the Fourteen Points from such a takeover of Slavic territory.

As for the Japanese claims, acquiescence would mean blatant violation of several of the Fourteen Points and at the expense of a co-belligerent, China, for which Americans felt a special responsibility. Both the Italians and the Japanese threatened to abandon the peace conference if their claims were not honored. Wilson regarded these dilemmas as annoying sideshows to his effort to ground the settlement in high-minded and universal doctrines of equity, impartiality, and self-determination. Sir Maurice Hankey, secretary to the meetings of the Four, however, held a different view. "President Wilson," he told his wife, "with his wretched, hypocritical Fourteen Points, has already alienated the Italians, and is now about to alienate the Japs."[18]

Big power rivalry and suspicion, genuinely conflicting interests regarding national security and retributive justice, the passionate claims of new nations, the demands of victorious co-belligerents at the expense of weaker allies—all these matters made the deliberations of the Four endlessly frustrating and complex. Historian Alan Sharp outlines the agenda of just one day of treaty-writing. On April 22, in no way an atypical day, the statesmen discussed the disposition of Alsace-Lorraine; Orlando's angry departure over Fiume; Middle Eastern problems relating to the break up of the Turkish Empire; the Shantung question; a possible mutual security treaty among the United States, Britain, and France; provisions for a Baltic port for the new Polish state; and the status of Allied and American troops still fighting Bolshevik forces in northern Russia. In addition, they had to decide on arrangements for the impending visit of a German delegation summoned to hear the terms of the as-yet unwritten treaty, deal with provisions for the demilitarization of the German Rhineland, and discuss means by which the treaty would be enforced.

Clinging to his belief in American disinterestedness and determined to transcend these particular issues, Wilson fought to preserve the core of the Fourteen Points while acquiescing in modifications and even de facto reversals of several individual ones. Rigid application of the self-determination strictures of the Points would be self-defeating if it resulted in the refusal of major powers to sign the treaty. At the same time, however, too many concessions and special arrangements would compromise the integrity of the treaty and the new diplomatic structures resting on it. Thus, for example, he acceded to Japanese claims in China, having to content himself with assurances that the Japanese would not take undue advantage of China's weakness.

"They will go home," he told an aide, "unless we give them what they should not have." He was more successful in resisting Italy's Adriatic claims but only at the cost of alienating Orlando and, apparently, most other Italians. Whereas during his preconference visits to Rome and Venice, mass demonstrations had proclaimed him the savior of Europe, now the slogan "Down with Wilson!" greeted Orlando on his return to Rome after he walked out of the conference over Fiume.[19]

For the president, the key to the whole treaty-making process was the idea of an association of nations, the last of the Fourteen Points. A specific constitution, or covenant, laying out the functions and procedures of such an international body must, he believed, be written directly into the treaty. Such a "League of Nations," as the treaty termed it, would provide a forum for the airing of disputes between countries and a mechanism for the prevention of conflict. Resting on the premise that the war that began in 1914 was the product of secret treaties, military and navy rivalry, and suspicion and jealousy among the leading powers of Europe, the idea behind a League of Nations was to institutionalize the Fourteen Points' stipulations against clandestine diplomacy, closed systems of trade, and military build up. Reflecting the democratic changes that were coming in the wake of the war, this League would reflect the will of the *people* of the various countries and their craving for peace. If the nations had to make open to world opinion their diplomatic negotiations with other states, if an authoritative international body existed to monitor armaments, and if procedures for settling disputes were put in place, the tragic events that culminated in 1914 would not be repeated and humanity would at last be free of the scourge of war.

Ideas of an international congress of nations had a long lineage. Most recently, private organizations such as the International Red Cross had had some success in establishing rules for warfare. In 1899 and 1907, representatives of the European powers had gathered in the Dutch city of The Hague to forge rules for dispute resolution, the conduct of war, and maritime rights. British Foreign Secretary Sir Edward Grey and other leading statesmen believed that face-to-face meetings in July 1914 between the major belligerents would have prevented war. In the nineteenth century, they held, an informal Concert of Europe, by which the major powers conferred as crises between states erupted, had kept the continent free of major wars. Establishment of a formal mechanism for big power consultation and perhaps for an obligatory cooling-off period to permit diplomats to resolve disputes could facilitate a lasting peace.

In 1915 prominent publicists, politicians, and international legal experts in the United States had established the League to Enforce Peace (LEP), hoping to encourage establishment of procedures for mediating and arbitrating disputes among nations. President Wilson had spoken at the founding meeting of the LEP, whose agenda was similar to that of Lord Grey and his associates. At the same time, however, Wilson conferred with progressive elements in the United States, men and women of both political parties who shared his belief in the special obligation of their country to break with the practices and forms of traditional diplomacy and to help create a whole new context for international discourse.

The fruits of Wilson's thinking were evident in his widely circulated "Peace without Victory" speech of January 22, 1917. Capping his ultimately unsuccessful effort to bring about an end to the war before the United States was sucked into it, this speech envisaged a "League for Peace" that would bring the moral force of mankind to bear on international affairs. Without a permanent structure through which peace could be maintained, Wilson declared, any settlement ending the current hostilities would constitute merely a pause in the fighting until such time as some other dispute arose. The president did not specify in detail what this "League for Peace" might consist of, but several points were clear. The United States would have to be part of it, the major powers would have to agree to international limitations of armaments, there would have to be an end to secret diplomacy, and the high seas would have to be made safe for use by all.

During the period of U.S. belligerency, Wilson did little to further specify his ideas about an international organization. Even after the Fourteen Points speech of January 1918, he remained purposefully vague about the actual mechanisms by which the warring nations would unite to prevent future wars. Wartime was not the time to raise potentially divisive issues between the United States and its partners; nor was it the time to focus domestic attention on what was bound to be a controversial departure from America's historic international role. Meanwhile, however, Wilson relied heavily for support, first in his reelection campaign in 1916 and then in his efforts to mobilize the American people for the war effort, on the inspiring prospect of U.S. leadership in creating a new international order through such an organization. Just as the Fourteen Points helped to diffuse radical criticisms of the Allied cause, so his advocacy of a tangible progressive alternative to discredited "balance of power" international politics helped to rally liberals, laborites, and would-be critics of the war to his side.

At Paris, Wilson would have to put his general notions for an international body into concrete form. Support for some sort of organization was widespread in Great Britain and among the smaller powers. The French, it is true, were skeptical that they might achieve their most cherished goals—notably firm guarantees against German aggression—through such an untried device as a League of Nations. Even so, however, given Wilson's immense personal prestige and the general war-weariness of the peoples of Europe, a peace conference that did not advance some sort of ongoing mechanism for addressing disputes would have failed an important test.

Wilson's problem was that the combination of his high-minded goals on the one hand and the need for compromise and concession to often sordid realities on the other raised the League of Nations in his mind to overwhelming importance. Although the French and Italians thought of a League as a possibly useful experiment whose exact powers, procedures, and functions could be left to more leisurely postconference discussions, Wilson insisted that the constitution, or covenant, of the body be incorporated directly into the treaty itself. This in turn meant that crucial questions of structure, powers, representation, and purposes had to be decided in the span of three months amid the general confusion of the peace conference. Moreover, the more Wilson came to see the League as the capstone of the peace settlement, the more he left himself hostage to the goals and demands of other statesmen. Even before the conference, Lloyd George had pointed this out, remarking to his cabinet that the League "was the only thing which . . . [Wilson] really cared much about." The president held views on the freedom of the seas, the disposition of German colonies, and other matters that British leaders opposed, but he would have no choice but to "ease [these] other matters" in return for British support for the League. In a similar vein, Clemenceau assured a French confidant that "When the moment comes to claim French rights, I will have leverage that I might not [otherwise] have," because of Wilson's passion for the League.[20]

The actual drafting of the League covenant was the product of close U.S.–British collaboration. Although Lloyd George himself initially took little interest in the League, members of the British delegation were committed to building a new structure of international relations. To be sure, British and Dominion statesmen who worked with Wilson, House, and Hunter Miller, an American expert in international law, to develop the document had a less exalted view of the possibilities of the League to achieve lasting peace than did Wilson. And the chief British participants, Lord Robert Cecil and Jan Christiaan Smuts, a South African general and statesman, were careful to see that the proposed international organization would not disadvantage distinctive interests of the British Empire, notably with reference to maritime rights and colonial matters. Even so, however, Wilson, who personally chaired the League of Nations Commission in which the details of the covenant were hammered out, found broad areas of agreement with the British and their

Dominion partners. Certainly, both British and American participants regarded the League as a crucial feature of the treaty, in contrast to the French, who viewed it as useful, or not, to the extent that it might contribute to the suppression of German power. One of the French representatives on the commission considering the covenant was overheard saying to a colleague during a lengthy debate over the precise functions and procedures of the new League, "Am I at a Peace Conference or in a madhouse?"[21]

Between February 15 and mid-March 1919, Wilson was back in the United States. During this interlude, House served as his emissary, taking on the task of forging a League document at once true to Wilson's vision and acceptable to the Allies. During Wilson's month-long stay in Paris, widespread hostility toward the peace treaty in general and the League specifically on the part of both conservatives and progressives in the United States became evident, weakening House's hand in his talks with British and French representatives after Wilson went back to America. Needing concessions from the Allies on points in the treaty and covenant important to Americans, House conceded that the covenant would contain only a bland reference to free international commerce, thus undermining the Fourteen Points' statement on freedom of the seas and placating the British. To retain French support for the League, House bowed to French demands that the overall treaty provide for at least temporary occupation of the German Rhineland and French access to Germany's coalfields. Wilson's absence also encouraged concessions with respect to reparations to be imposed on Germany. House even agreed to French insistence on U.S. participation in a treaty of mutual defense among the three Western powers to guarantee France against future German aggression. Perhaps because of the mounting hostility toward the proposed League evident in the United States, House even agreed to separating the League covenant from the treaty, at least for purposes of facilitating discussion. Upon returning to Paris, Wilson professed to be appalled at his emissary's concessions. "So," Mrs. Wilson reported his reaction, "he has yielded until there is nothing left."[22]

In fact, events back in the United States forced Wilson to endorse House's concessions, with the exception of separating the covenant from the treaty. On March 2, thirty-nine senators—more than the number necessary to defeat ratification of the treaty—had issued a "Round Robin" statement vowing to oppose the treaty (and thus the League) as then understood. Among the commonly listed objections to the League was the belief that adherence to it would compromise U.S. sovereignty and force abrogation of the Monroe Doctrine, by which the United States claimed special rights in the Western Hemisphere. After his return to Paris, Wilson now realized, he would have to gain modifications of the covenant draft to protect this sacred cow of American foreign policy. And in doing so, of course, he weakened his ability to object to aspects of the League and of the treaty that were of special interest to his counterparts.

Through March and April the final drafts of the League covenant and the treaty proper lurched toward conclusion. Tensions mounted among the Four, with Wilson at one point going so far as to order his ship, the *George Washington*, to prepare for his sudden departure. Laid up with influenza and possibly suffering a mild stroke, the physically fragile president and his equally exhausted counterparts argued, negotiated, wrote, and rewrote, hammering out a document to present to the German delegation that was summoned to Paris during the first week of May.

The Treaty of Versailles, with the covenant of the League of Nations included as the first of its 440 articles, was thus a hybrid document. Punitive provisions were many. Germany was stripped of its overseas colonies and lost 13 percent of its European territory, including Alsace and Lorraine as well as areas to the east and north. The Saar Basin, site of rich coalfields, was to be controlled for fifteen years by the French under League of Nations supervision. The German Rhineland was to be demilitarized and subject to Allied occupation should the Germans fail to adhere to the terms of the treaty. The German army was to be limited to 100,000 men, and other provisions restricted naval and air capabilities.

The most controversial punitive provision was Article 231, which forced the German representatives to acknowledge sole responsibility "for causing all the loss and damage to which the Allied and Associated Governments and their nations have been subjected as a consequence of the war imposed upon them by the aggression of Germany and her allies." The treaty then provided for the establishment of Inter-Allied Reparation Commissions that would calculate the war costs to be attributed to Germany. These were to include not only the specific damage done to French, Belgian, and Luxembourgian property during German occupation and in the final retreat of the German army but also the costs of veterans' and survivors' pensions. The commissions would also devise a schedule of payments. In the meantime, the treaty imposed a transfer of $5 billion to the victors as a down payment on the full reparations debt, which some observers thought might run as high as $100 billion.

Other provisions specified the details of territorial changes. One article prohibited the uniting of Germany with Austria, the shrunken German-speaking core of the old Austro-Hungarian Empire. With Bolshevik Russia excluded from the conference, the treaty made sweeping changes in the political landscape of Eastern Europe. Thus, for example, it created a new Polish state with an outlet to the Baltic Sea that required carving a League-protected corridor through Prussia, in eastern Germany. Germany was made to abrogate the Treaty of Brest-Litovsk and, upon Allied command, remove its troops from areas ceded in 1918 by the Bolsheviks, although in view of the absence of organized government in large parts of Eastern Europe, de facto German occupation continued in some areas for more than a year after signing the treaty. The treaty further confirmed Germany's status as a pariah nation, despite its adoption of a republican government, by excluding it from immediate membership in the League of Nations.

The League covenant itself, which constituted the first twenty-six of the treaty's articles, specified the purposes, structure, procedures, and membership of the new international body. It gave the major powers—Britain, France, Italy, the United States, and Japan—decisive power to shape and carry through the League's most important functions through a council in which they were permanently represented. An assembly, in which all member states had equal representation, was to meet periodically.

At the covenant's heart were its provisions for preventing war through specific procedural requirements. Article 10 was central to this purpose. This short paragraph pledged League members "to respect and preserve as against external aggression the territorial integrity and existing political independence of all Members of the League." It went on to add that in the event of actual or threatened aggression against a League member, the Council would meet to "advise upon the means by which this obligation shall be fulfilled."

The covenant elaborated detailed provisions for the hearing and resolution of disputes between members and between members and nonmembers, all aimed at providing a cooling-off period and at providing peaceful forums at which states could find alternatives to military action. Clearly designed with the purpose of preventing a recurrence of the events of July 1914, Article 10 and the others relating to dispute resolution represented the peacemakers' chief effort to redeem the millions of lives and the terrible destruction of the Great War by creating a workable mechanism through which the nations might prevent a similar catastrophe in the future.

As statesmen debated these provisions, knotty questions continually arose as to how they might be enforced. French delegates urged the creation of a League army that would intervene to confront an aggressor. Others, however, worried that a literal application of Article 10 would violate the sovereignty of member states. For example, by implying a U.S. pledge to abide by the Council's advice on how to deal with an aggressor, would not the covenant contravene the U.S. Constitution's provision that only Congress could declare war? Rather than settle such contested points during the conference,

Wilson and the others who drafted the covenant relied on Article 10's very lack of specificity, hoping and expecting that the practical value of having a dispute resolution mechanism in place would obviate these kinds of "what if" questions.

Also intended to further the goal of promoting peace and cooperation among nations, the covenant pledged member states to work toward the limitation of armaments. Other articles called for cooperation in the establishment of labor standards, the interdiction of drug trafficking, the promotion of public health, and the maintenance of freedom of communications and commerce. A key provision required members to make public any international agreements into which they entered with other states and to register those agreements with the League, declaring void provisions of any agreements that contravened the covenant.

Article 22 introduced the mandate system for administering the former colonies of Germany and parts of the Ottoman Empire. Largely following arrangements made among the Allies before U.S. entry into the war, the League would assign responsibility for such territories in the Middle East, Africa, and Oceania to League members, who would administer them under League supervision, being particularly solicitous of the interests of the subject peoples. "The well-being and development of such peoples form a sacred trust of civilization," declared the covenant. The covenant divided these territories into categories on the basis of their putative fitness for eventual self-government, with Syria and other Middle Eastern areas being considered almost ready for independence and the German colonies of Africa regarded as less immediately so. In actual practice, the assigning of mandates followed earlier agreements among the Allied powers, with the British, French, and South Africans taking over the African colonies, the British and French dividing the Middle Eastern mandates, and the Japanese, New Zealanders, and Australians assuming the mandates for Germany's scattered Pacific island holdings. Wilson rejected the offer of a mandate for the United States for an Armenian state to be carved out of the Ottoman Empire.

To what extent did this treaty and the League covenant fulfill the promise of the Fourteen Points, under whose terms the Germans had initially requested an armistice? Certainly, the Germans were outraged. Responding to the initial presentation of the Treaty of Versailles on May 7, 1920, German Foreign Minister Count Ulrich von Brockdorff-Rantzau drew particular attention to Article 231, the so-called war guilt provision. After being presented with the victors' terms in the glittering conference room of Trianon Palace in Versailles, he shocked the 200 delegates with his unrepentant tone. "It is demanded of us that we shall confess ourselves to be the only ones guilty of the war," he complained in a manner that seemed to many present to embody the arrogance and imperiousness of the unreconstructed German aristocracy, of which he was a member. But, he added, "Such a confession in my mouth will be a lie."[23]

In later statements, the count insisted that to the extent that the treaty modified or conflicted with any of the Fourteen Points, it was invalid on its face. The Fourteen Points had said nothing about reparations or specific cessions of German territory, nor had it mentioned occupation of the Rhineland or French–League control of the Saar region. Conveniently forgetting the disintegrating state of the German army during the final weeks of fighting and the terms of the actual Armistice agreement, which imposed severe conditions on Germany, the count demanded that the Allies go back to their conference and produce a new document consonant with the Fourteen Points. Ignoring the precedent they themselves had at Brest-Litovsk set for inflicting a harsh peace on their enemies, the Germans took the position that the Armistice had been in reality a truce between military forces, not an admission of German defeat.

The German delegation did itself no favor in the attitude Brockdorff-Rantzau projected. After his presentation, Wilson remarked, "The Germans are really a stupid people. They always do the wrong thing." Added British Foreign Secretary Arthur Balfour, "Beasts they were and beasts they are."[24] German crimes against Belgian and French citizens, inflicted through a publicly announced policy of economic exploitation and *schrecklichkeit* ("frightfulness"), along with the indiscriminate wreckage of civilian homes, farms, and businesses wrought by their retreating army, laid the basis for entirely legitimate financial exactions. German exploitation of French coal and iron mines during the occupation likewise bolstered claims for privileged postwar French access to the riches of the Saar. More problematic, but certainly legitimate insofar as Americans were concerned, was the case for damages on the basis of Germany's controversial submarine campaigns, founded as they ultimately were on a policy of indiscriminate sinkings of merchant and passenger ships. Allied spokesmen also pointed out that in 1871, the then-victorious Germans had imposed a staggering indemnity on defeated France, even though in that case, the war was fought entirely on French soil. Moreover, even a brief glance at the territorial and economic exactions that Germany's military and industrial leaders had contemplated in the event of Allied defeat made the provisions of this treaty look moderate in contrast.

In no mood for balanced judgments, however, Germans everywhere echoed Brockdorff-Rantzau's bitterness. In Berlin, a Socialist member of the legislature declared, "This peace is nothing more than a continuation of the war by other means." Wilson, said the president of the newly elected German national assembly, "promised the world a peace of justice" but instead had helped in "framing this project dictated by hate." Brockdorff-Rantzau urged government leaders to reject the treaty, warning, "Those who will sign this treaty will sign the death sentence of many millions of German men, women, and children."[25]

Nor were the Germans alone in attacking the treaty. U.S. Secretary of State Robert Lansing, a marginal figure throughout the deliberations, received a copy of the bulky document just before it was delivered to the Germans. Rarely consulted by Wilson during the conference, Lansing expressed shock at the treaty's departure from the spirit of the Fourteen Points: "The impression made by it is one of disappointment, of regret, and of depression," he recorded in his diary. Liberals and progressives both in Paris and back in the United States were disappointed by a treaty containing the war guilt provision, studded with violations of Wilsonian principles of self-determination, and seemingly strengthening the colonial power of the Allies and legitimating the French thirst for revenge and economic exploitation of prostrate Germany. Several members of the U.S. delegation staff threatened public resignation, believing that (in the words of one of them) America had "bartered away her principles in a series of compromises with interests of imperialism and revenge." Walter Lippmann, the influential young journalist who had done so much to codify the Fourteen Points, turned against the treaty, having concluded that Article 10 in particular would commit the United States to preserving the international status quo rather than playing the role of democratic catalyst. William Bullitt, an idealistic young state department official sent to Russia to attempt to bring the Bolshevik government into the peace process, submitted his resignation, writing Wilson bluntly, "I am sorry you did not fight our fight to the finish" and predicting that the peace settlement made "a new century of war" unavoidable.[26]

Even those involved in the treaty-making process regarded its economic arrangements as disastrous. In October 1919, influential British economist John Maynard Keynes, a disaffected member of the British delegation, published a savage attack on the treaty, titled *The Economic Consequences of the Peace*. In this polemic, he argued that the territorial, financial, and economic exactions upon Germany would cripple European recovery from the war's devastation and sow the seeds of political chaos throughout Europe. Leading figures in Wilson's wartime administration, notably War Industries Board Chair Bernard Baruch, Food Administrator Herbert Hoover, and War Labor Policies Board Chair Felix Frankfurter, shared this assessment of the treaty's economic shortcomings. At the same time, Wilson's partisan critics in and around the Republican Party attacked the League of Nations as a dangerous experiment that violated the U.S. Constitution and compromised American sovereignty.

But perhaps these attacks said more about the unrealistic expectations of the critics than about the treaty or the League. Certainly Wilson was embarrassed about certain provisions of the treaty, notably the war guilt clause and important territorial provisions. The system of mandates was at best a pale version of his hopes for "fair and impartial settlement of colonial claims," and he remained uneasy about French-imposed demilitarization and occupation of German territory. Inability to include a strong statement on freedom of the seas and more concrete provisions for arms limitations troubled him. Despite these weaknesses and omissions, however, the president believed that he and his colleagues had achieved a decisive breakthrough in the annals of diplomacy. If there were injustices in the treaty—and in candid moments he acknowledged that there were—they could be moderated and rectified in the League of Nations.

Soon after his return from France on July 8, he presented the treaty (and of course, the League covenant) to the U.S. Senate, which was bristling with men opposed outright either to the treaty or to key provisions of the League covenant. Wilson took little time to address the specific provisions of the treaty, concentrating his eloquence on defense of the League. It was, he said, the "indispensable instrumentality for the maintenance of the new order." For America to reject it would "break the heart of the world." Americans had not asked for war and were still reluctant to shoulder the international responsibilities that their wealth and power required of them. But a new role for the American people had emerged. In a passionate statement that expressed the intense religious feeling that infused his public philosophy, he declared: "The stage is set, the destiny disclosed. It has come about . . . by the hand of God who led us into this way. We cannot turn back."[27]

The peace-making process had been a long and difficult one. From the first German note on October 4, 1918, requesting an armistice to this speech before the Senate in July had been more than nine months. The ideals of "peace without victory" and the Fourteen Points, so simple and straightforward when expressed as exhortation and inspiration, had proved complicated and often unrealistic in light of the brutal conditions prevailing in war-torn Europe. Wilson was convinced, however, that in making the League an integral part of the treaty and in providing mechanisms for limiting arms, arbitrating disputes, and resolving differences, he and his colleagues had created the basis for enduring peace. He urged his countrymen to "go forward, with lifted eyes and freshened spirit, to follow the vision." American ideals and values had been compromised but not betrayed in Paris. "The light streams upon the path ahead, and nowhere else."[28] As the Republican-controlled Senate now formally undertook to examine and render judgment on the treaty and, with it, on the League of Nations, Wilson prepared for an even tougher fight than his recent joustings with his European counterparts had demanded.

SEVEN

Postwar America

On July 8, 1919, the USS *George Washington*, formerly the German liner *Kaiser Wilhelm*, docked in New York harbor, bringing President Woodrow Wilson, the peace treaty with Germany, and the covenant of the League of Nations to the United States. Two days later, the president formally presented the treaty (and the covenant) to the U.S. Senate, whose approval by at least a two-thirds majority was necessary for it to go into effect. For the next four months, debate raged in the Senate over the treaty and the covenant, and in August Wilson launched an extensive speaking tour to rally public opinion in support of them. At the end of September, however, he became ill in Colorado and returned ahead of schedule to Washington. Then on October 5, just a year after the German request for an armistice, he was felled by a massive stroke; it initially left him partially paralyzed, affected his speech and memory, and kept him in medical seclusion for about five weeks. On November 19, the Senate rejected the treaty in two separate votes, and four months later, on March 19, 1920, failed again to ratify it.*

While Wilson concentrated his flagging energy on the great crusade to bring the United States into the League, his fellow countrymen took up with a vengeance the political, social, and economic conflicts held in partial abeyance during the war. The continued conflict between Bolshevik forces and U.S. troops, dispatched to Russia in the summer of 1918 ostensibly to attempt to reopen the Eastern Front, was a grim reminder of the still-volatile international situation and cause of continued anxiety and dissension at home. Throughout 1919 and into 1920, racial discord, labor activism, and assaults on politically radical (or putatively radical) groups and citizens rocked the country. As divided government in Washington fueled partisan conflict

---

*On July 2, 1921, Congress ended the war with Germany by joint resolution, and on July 18, 1921, the Senate ratified peace treaties, stripped of the articles relating to the League of Nations, with Germany, Austria, and Hungary.

over the treaty and League, the United States rapidly demobilized the armed forces, dismantled wartime agencies, and debated proposals for resumption of normal civilian economic and social life. Wilson hoped that debate over the treaty and the League would consist of high-minded discourse and sober deliberation, but in part because of his inattention to the sources of domestic conflict and postwar readjustment, the conflict over the treaty and League raged among a populace also wracked by internal disputation and violence.

Bolsheviks

The triumph of the Bolsheviks in Russia in October 1917 sent shock waves throughout the West. From the start, the new Russian regime and the established governments of all the other belligerents were in fundamental conflict. Regarding their victory in Russia as the catalyst for world revolution, Bolshevik leader Vladimir Lenin and his fellow revolutionaries wasted little time before appealing to workers, farmers, and soldiers of all the warring countries to turn against their governments and abandon the war. In November, they began releasing the terms of the secret treaties, replete with their sordid territorial and economic provisions. Believing, at least initially, that their revolution would not be secure unless it spread to industrialized nations of the West, they kept up a drumbeat of rhetoric designed to encourage disaffection in the countries at war. At the same time, the Bolsheviks reached out to the subordinated peoples of Europe's many colonies, aligning themselves with movements of national liberation in Asia and Africa. And these denunciations and appeals had an impact, as socialists, labor activists, and progressive-minded citizens in the United States and elsewhere at least initially greeted the Bolshevik victory as the culmination of decades of struggle in behalf of workers, colonial subjects, and other victims of capitalism and imperialist expansion. Moreover, the Soviet call for peace now reverberated powerfully throughout the populations of the fighting countries, seeming to offer hopes for an end to the bloodletting.

Western politicians and statesmen reacted sharply. There could be only one response to an effort to sow disaffection and disloyalty and to encourage the overthrow of established governments: implacable hostility. Moreover, even though in theory the Bolshevik leaders were as hostile to Germany as to the West, in practice their propaganda and policies benefited Germany even as they threatened the West. In real terms, denunciation of the war weakened Russian resistance to German military advance in the East and eventually resulted in the Treaty of Brest-Litovsk on March 3, 1918. With it came the release of thousands of German soldiers for combat in the West while making the rich resources of Eastern Europe more available to the Central Powers. Thus, for Woodrow Wilson, Georges Clemenceau, David Lloyd George, and other military and political leaders of the Allies, the Russian revolution combined threats to their respective domestic orders with dire military consequences. The massive German assaults, beginning just three weeks after the conclusion of the Brest-Litovsk treaty with the Russian regime, gave powerful evidence of the particular menace to the Allied cause that the revolution posed.

In 1917, Wilson had welcomed the first, or February, Russian revolution. Removal of the czar and the establishment of a constitutional government made it possible for him to portray U.S. participation as part of a glorious democratic crusade. "The great, generous Russian people have been added . . . to the forces that are fighting for freedom. . . . Here is a fit partner for a League of Honor," he told Congress in his war message. But the Bolshevik overthrow of the Provisional government in October, the release of the secret treaties, the willingness of the new regime to settle with Germany, and the harsh repression of opposition groups within Russia quickly turned the president against the new regime. In March 1918, shortly after the signing of the Brest-Litovsk treaty, Edgar Sisson, an American journalist, returned from Russia with documents purporting to prove that the Bolsheviks were little more than German puppets, "accredited and financed agents of Germany," in Sisson's words. This "evidence"—which soon turned out to be fabricated—fed Wilson's belief that Bolshevism was an aberration, a passing interlude in the chaotic affairs of Russia, rather than the basis of a stable and long-lived regime.[1]

In any event, the hostility of Wilson and his advisers toward the Soviet government was profound, and understandably so. After all, the Bolsheviks' initial moves strengthened Germany at a time of maximum peril to the Allied cause. Moreover, there could be no mistake that they sought the destruction not only of Western capitalism but of the political and legal systems that were so intimately connected with it. Ruthless suppression of dissidents within Russia, culminating in the forcible abrogating of a democratically elected Constituent Assembly in January 1918, confirmed Western antipathy to the new regime. To be sure, in the period between their seizure of power in October and the Russian treaty with Germany in March, the Bolsheviks did employ Wilsonian rhetoric in their appeals to the peoples of the belligerent countries to stop the fighting. Like Wilson, Soviet leaders urged a peace without victory, a peace without indemnities and territorial seizures. But Wilson rightly

regarded these appeals as thinly disguised efforts to foment dissent and disloyalty among the citizens of belligerent countries and to pave the way for the triumph of Bolshevik-style revolution throughout Europe and even in the
United States. In his annual message to Congress on December 4, 1918, the
president warned against "the voices of humanity" that were now being used,
in effect, to protect the German autocracy. Slogans of "No annexations . . . no
punitive indemnities" did, he conceded, proclaim "the instinctive judgment as
to the right of plain men everywhere." But now these noble sentiments were
being used "by the masters of German intrigue to lead the people of Russia
astray . . . in order that a premature peace might be brought before the [Ger-
man] autocracy has been taught its final and convincing lesson."[2]

The turbulent situation in Russia both during the war and after the
armistice posed insoluble problems for Wilson and the other peacemakers. In
the Fourteen Points, the president had called for "settlement of all questions
affecting Russia as will secure the best and freest cooperation of the other
nations . . . in obtaining for her an unhampered and unembarrassed opportunity for the independent determination of her own political development,"
but these worthy sentiments provided no practical guidance. Wilson also
affirmed that "the treatment accorded Russia by her sister nations . . . will be
the acid test of their good will," but again, no one knew how to apply this
stricture to a Russia ruled by an authoritarian political faction, seething with
domestic conflict and partially occupied by German troops, even after the
armistice. During the spring and summer of 1918, Allied leaders continued to
hope that the Bolshevik regime was only transitory. Allied support for Lenin's
enemies, urged British leaders especially, might result in the overthrow of the
outlaw government and bring Russia back into the war. The British, French,
and Japanese repeatedly pressed Wilson to dispatch U.S. troops to Siberia and
northern Russia as part of a multipower effort to protect Allied supplies previously sent to prerevolutionary Russia. Allied and American troops would
also aid armed units of former prisoners of war from the
Austro-Hungarian Empire in their efforts to join the war against the Central
Powers, and give support to the Bolsheviks' internal enemies with the eventual goal of restoring a pro-Allied government.

Although Wilson believed the worst of the Bolsheviks, he initially resisted
involving the United States in military action in Russia. The Russian people,
he believed, would soon oust the Bolsheviks; in any event, it was not for others to decide what sort of government they should have. Then too his military advisers, desperate to build the AEF in France, counseled against diver-
sion of resources to any peripheral area, be it Italy, the Mediterranean, or
Russia. Thus, the U.S. representative to the Supreme War Council, General

Tasker Bliss, counseled, "if our Allies have any axes to grind in Russia, let them go and do it. I think the war has got to be ended on this Western Front."[3] Wilson also recognized that the Russian revolutionaries enjoyed considerable support among American socialists, progressives, and laborites, men and women who made up an important part of his own constituency. Too crude or overt a campaign against the Bolsheviks could backfire at home, robbing him of needed support for the war effort and for the kind of peace settlement he sought. He did authorize the expenditure of funds by the Committee on Public Information (CPI) to sow anti-Bolshevik and prowar sentiment among the Russian people. And he approved a campaign of clandestine operations designed to encourage the displacement of the revolutionaries with a more moderate regime, first in the hopes of reopening the Eastern Front and then, after the armistice, in hopes of bringing a responsible Russian government into the new world order being forged in Paris.

Throughout the spring of 1918, however, French and British officials urged the president to send American troops to northern Russia and Siberia. In July, Wilson reluctantly acceded, ordering General John J. Pershing to detach units originally bound for France to join Allied contingents in the region of Archangel, a small port on the White Sea 600 miles north of Moscow. The president insisted that the only missions of this American Expeditionary Force, North Russia (AEFNR) were to protect military equipment earlier sent to the Russian government and perhaps to effect liaison with pro-Allied units of armed former Czech prisoners of war, thought to be active in the region. Thus, early in September 1918, the first of an eventual 5,700 Americans, mostly conscripts from Michigan and Wisconsin of the 339th Infantry Regiment, debarked from the British troop transports *Somali*, *Negoya*, and *Tydeus*.

From the start, these men became involved in a seemingly pointless struggle against irregular forces, harsh weather and terrain, and a sullen local population. The Allied commander in the area, British Major General Frederick Poole, ignored the limitations placed on the use of American troops and deployed them aggressively. Determined to save the surrounding area from Bolshevik control, he pitted his troops, including these Americans, against Red irregulars in a series of offensive actions. Throughout the harsh winter of 1918–19, these men fought in savage little encounters in the frozen woods. Both sides murdered prisoners. Influenza was rampant. "The glory of dying in France to lie under a field of poppies," one soldier wrote home, "had come to this drear mystery of dying in Russia under a dread disease in a strange and unlovely place." Especially after the fighting had stopped in France, morale plummeted, discipline suffered, and resentment flared. Antagonism between American and British troops and officers festered. "Good God," one American soldier wrote home, "you can't believe how those English officers are hated around here . . . the God Damned fools are of more harm than good." Declared a surgeon serving with a Wisconsin battalion, "we were fighting a people against whom war had never been declared and we didn't know why we were fighting them." American forces in the Archangel area suffered 144 combat deaths, 78 deaths from disease, and 305 wounded before the units were withdrawn, amid angry congressional inquiries, in June 1919.[4]

U.S. intervention in Siberia also reflected the confusion and ignorance of local conditions that characterized the adventure in northern Russia. In July 1918, again in response to Allied, and especially Japanese, pressure, Wilson authorized the sending of U.S. troops through the far eastern Russian port of Vladivostok. Their announced purpose was to protect supplies earlier deposited in that city and to assist elements of the Czech Legion seeking to leave Russia via the Trans-Siberian Railroad. Unofficially, the 8,000 Americans, commanded by Major General William S. Graves, were also to monitor the activities of Japanese troops, who eventually numbered 70,000, because Wilson and the other Allies rightly suspected that Japan would seek to take advantage of the disorder in Siberia to gain a permanent economic and military foothold there. Throughout the twenty-one months of the American presence, General Graves tried to adhere closely to his sketchy orders from Wilson and Secretary of War Newton D. Baker, with their disavowal of intervention in the then-raging civil war between the Bolsheviks and their "White" adversaries. Even so, however, intensely anti-Bolshevik U.S. Department of State officials in Washington and on the ground in the Russian Far East attempted to commit Graves to support for the counterrevolutionaries.

And indeed, as the Americans' stay in Siberia stretched through 1919 and into 1920, they increasingly provided de facto support to the Bolsheviks' enemies in the savage civil war that raged throughout this period. At one point Graves's men delivered American rifles to White forces, despite Wilson's initial pledge that the United States would not take sides. Making an already chaotic situation even more confusing was the behavior of the Japanese, who threw their weight behind first one, then another, White faction in hopes of using them to expand Japanese influence. Graves's men found themselves guarding remote stretches of the railroad, clashing frequently with both Red and White partisans, some of the latter of whom used arms provided by the Japanese. Graves, while no friend of the Bolsheviks, was disgusted by the behavior of the White forces he encountered, which, he later wrote, were "roaming the country like wild animals, killing and robbing the people."[5] Before their withdrawal in the spring of 1920, American forces had lost 165 men killed or dead of disease.

The distracted president found it increasingly difficult to defend the continuing U.S. presence. Indeed, when CPI Director George Creel sent author Arthur Bullard to Siberia to explain the reason for the U.S. presence to the local people, Bullard could only throw up his hands at the impossibility of his task. "We are rather in the position of advertising something and not knowing what it is. Buy it! Buy it! [we urge, but] We don't know what" we are purveying. Critics on the left understandably accused Wilson of doing precisely what he had disavowed, that is, intervening in the internal affairs of Russia, and this charge, despite the honest efforts of General Graves to keep free of partisan rivalries, was on target. But at the same time, the hesitant and limited nature of the administration's Russian adventures drew the wrath of conservatives, who regarded the object of assisting in the overthrow of an unscrupulous regime pledged to destroy Western values and institutions an entirely legitimate one. Thus former President William Howard Taft sneered at Wilson's announced goals for the Russian intervention. "No matter how the administration tries to masquerade it," he believed, "it is action against the Bolsheviki," and rightly so.[6]

But Wilson was less devious—and more uncertain—than his predecessor assumed. He combined a fundamental hostility to the Bolshevik regime with reluctance to commit substantial U.S. resources to its overthrow. In September 1919 he lashed out at the rulers of the Soviet Union, describing them as men who "represent nobody but themselves." With even less legitimacy than the former autocrats of Germany, "another group of men more cruel than the czar himself is controlling the destinies of that great people," the Russians.[7] Still, however, he refused to extend formal recognition of, or significant material aid to, the White forces in Siberia. He rejected Allied pleas to expand U.S. military intervention into southern Russia, rebuffing his own emissary's advice to dispatch an additional 25,000 American troops. Although he would surely have rejoiced in the replacement of the Bolshevik regime with a more amenable one, he was in the end unwilling to commit the United States to the level of military and material involvement that such a project would have required.

Sharp debates between Wilson and his wartime partners and among factions within his administration characterized the president's Russian policy. Perhaps the keenest division occurred within the president's own mind as he struggled to reconcile distaste for armed intervention with his profound hostility to the Bolsheviks. In the end, his "policy" amounted to a nonpolicy, a circumstance that he himself recognized. Thus, in May 1919, Wilson remarked, "I no longer regret as much as I did several months ago not having a policy in Russia; it seems to me impossible to define one in such circumstances."[8] Yet although the limited character of U.S. intervention ensured that it would not be a significant factor in the struggle for power in Russia, this did not shield Wilson from charges on the left that he had aligned the United States with the forces of reaction in that troubled land and from the right that he had abandoned the struggle for democracy in Russia.

Reds and Reaction

Division over the Russian Revolution in the international arena had its counterpart at home. The victory of the Bolsheviks and the establishment of an ostensible "workers' republic" in Russia emboldened American radicals and militant laborites. The era of the Great War had been a difficult time for Western socialists. The dream of proletarian unity was daily trampled as workers killed each other in the trenches of France and Belgium. Socialist and labor groups in every warring country split over whether to support the war and how aggressively to insist on labor's rights during such a time of national emergency. But the victory of the Bolsheviks in Russia at a stroke provided an inspiring example of socialist principles in action. The Russian revolutionaries, declared the National Executive Committee of the Socialist Party of America early in 1918, "come with a message of proletarian revolution. We glory in their achievement and inevitable triumph." Added Morris Hillquit, a veteran New York socialist, the Bolshevik regime "is today in the vanguard of democracy and social progress," Eugene V. Debs, the very epitome of the democratic socialist movement in the United States, avowed, "From the crown of my head to the soles of my feet I am a Bolshevik, and proud of it."[9] Labor union members, from Industrial Workers of the World (IWW) militants to ordinary trade unionists, hailed the ostensible workers' triumph in Russia. Antiwar activists saw in the Bolshevik peace offensive hope for ending the war. Artistic rebels, reformers, and critics of the corruptions and compromises of bourgeois society hailed the dawning of a new day of cultural freedom, social progress, and egalitarian efficiency.

In the turbulent wake of war, revolutionary energy seemed to pulsate everywhere. Bolshevik-inspired movements took power in Hungary and parts of Germany, and Soviet sympathizers and left-wing militants asserted themselves in the labor movements of victors and vanquished alike. In March 1919, the Soviet government launched the Comintern, charged with promoting worldwide revolutionary activity. In America, enthusiasm for the

Russian Revolution spurred in 1919 and 1920 the founding of an American Communist Party frankly inspired by and linked to the ruling Bolsheviks in Russia. Hundreds of newspapers and broadsheets proclaimed the overthrow of capitalist exploitation and hailed the achievements of Russian comrades. "The American proletariat is restless," proclaimed *The Communist*. "In these most glorious of all glorious days," cried *The Revolutionary Age*, both royal "thrones and capitalism are crumbling."[10]

Events in the late winter and spring of 1919 seemed to bring this radical activism out of the realm of sectarian polemics and into the lives of ordinary people. In February, a general strike erupted in Seattle, shutting down factories and halting most nonemergency services and deliveries as more than 60,000 of the city's unionized workers left their jobs. Although the strike lasted only four days and the workers responded calmly to provocative police harassment, the city's political and business leaders portrayed the walkout as the entering wedge of revolutionary upheaval. Mayor Ole Hanson accused the strikers of wanting "to take possession of our American Government and try to duplicate the anarchy of Russia." A general strike in Winnipeg, Manitoba, later in the spring, along with an unprecedented wave of strike activity throughout the United States,* fed the illusion that radical revolution in the Russian mode posed a profound domestic threat. "Reds Directing Seattle Strike—To Test for Revolution," screamed one West Coast newspaper.[11]

Overreaction to what was in essence a variation on normal trade union strike action might have eventually dissipated had it not been for a series of bombing episodes in the spring of 1919. Since the invention of dynamite in 1867, some extremists had found it relatively easy to practice "revolution of the deed," that is, to carry on their fight against injustice and oppression by blowing up authority figures. In 1881, for example, Russian revolutionaries had murdered Czar Alexander II by hurling a bomb at his carriage, and in 1916 an explosion at a San Francisco Preparedness parade had killed six marchers. Along with the many assassinations by gunfire during this era— including those of President William McKinley in 1901 and Archduke Franz Ferdinand in 1914—bomb threats were frequent and all too often proved legitimate. Thus, in May and June 1919, a series of mysterious bombing episodes, targeting prominent public officials and industrialists, allowed the perfervid rhetoric of antiradical alarmists to gain new credibility. On April 28, Hanson himself was the target, although the crude homemade device mailed to him failed to detonate. More alarmingly, the next day a maid employed by former Senator Thomas W. Hardwick of Georgia was less fortunate, losing

*See pages 208–15.

both hands when she opened an innocuous-looking parcel addressed to him. Shortly after, postal authorities in New York intercepted sixteen similarly wrapped packages, all of them bombs addressed to senators, cabinet members, jurists, and industrialists. The fact that these explosives were obviously intended to detonate on May Day, a day since the nineteenth century earmarked for public protest in behalf of workers' rights, pointed to the responsibility of radical extremists for this aborted wave of terror. Again, newspaper headlines drove home the point: "Reds Planned May Day Murders," asserted the *Atlanta Constitution*. And then a month later, eight more bombs exploded in eight cities, killing two people and causing extensive damage. One blew off the front of the home of the attorney general of the United States, A. Mitchell Palmer. Although authorities never apprehended those responsible for these attacks, at least one of the perpetrators of the Palmer bombing was himself killed in it and was identified as an Italian immigrant anarchist. An anarchist pamphlet was found near his body. "There will have to be bloodshed," it vowed. "We are ready to do anything and everything to suppress the capitalist class." Other strong, though circumstantial evidence, linked the bombings to cells of Italian anarchists operating in the Northeast.[12]

Antiradical activists hardly needed these bombings to launch a campaign of terror against the Left. In towns and cities across the country, business groups, patriotic organizations, and ad hoc bodies of agitated citizens, in most cases willfully ignorant of the distinctions among labor and radical groups, took these episodes as a license to go after all varieties of socialists, labor activists, and dissenters. May Day 1919 served as a focal point for violent attacks. Parades in New York, Boston, Cleveland, and other cities erupted into clashes between marchers and the police, the latter often assisted by ordinary citizens. In New York, 400 soldiers and sailors stormed the offices of a socialist newspaper, breaking up a reception, smashing furniture, and destroying literature. In Cleveland, mobs of outraged citizens, swelled by a Victory Loan rally, silenced radical speakers, assaulted even uniformed soldiers who dared to voice radical views, and ransacked Socialist Party headquarters. Cleveland newspapers awarded special kudos to ex-Marine John Keller, for although he had lost an arm at Chateau-Thierry, he was so effective with his other arm that "five radicals required treatment by ambulance surgeons."[13]

Throughout 1919 and into the next year, similar attacks punctuated public life in America. In November 1919, members of the Centralia, Washington, post of the American Legion, an ultrapatriotic organization established earlier that year by and for Great War veterans, marched on the local hall of the IWW. Fearing for their lives and not inclined in any event to turn the other cheek, the Wobblies opened fire, killing several Legionaries. In the ensuing orgy of revenge, one Wobbly, Wesley Everett, was castrated, hanged from a railroad bridge, cut down while still alive, and hanged again. The Centralia killings triggered violent attacks on IWW members and other labor radicals up and down the West Coast.

Through 1919, most of these violent attacks were the work of private citizens and mobs, though local police and public officials often collaborated with them or ignored their depredations. Neither President Wilson nor any members of his administration acknowledged or criticized this wave of illegal violence, and civil libertarians believed that official wartime propaganda and repression had fostered an atmosphere of intolerance and lawlessness. And they had a good case. Throughout the war and postwar period, the U.S. Army, the attorney general, postmaster general, and other federal officials sustained a vast and unprecedented network of domestic surveillance and control organizations to monitor and silence critics of the war, labor activists, and radicals. The administration-instigated Espionage Act of June 1917 and Sedition Act of May 1918 provided for the arrest of those deemed guilty of utterances or actions that might impede the war effort, including the providing of advice to men subject to the draft. The Espionage Act gave the postmaster general wide authority to ban from the mail publications that opposed the war or criticized its conduct. The Sedition Act went farther than any previous federal legislation in its negation of the essential elements of the Bill of Rights, barring any "disloyal, profane, scurrilous or abusive language about the form of government of the U.S. or the Constitution of the U.S., or the military or naval forces of the U.S. or the flag of the U.S. or the uniform of the army or navy." It also outlawed speech or written expression that might encourage "contempt, scorn, contumely or disrepute" of government and military agencies and authorities. These draconian measures gave legislative substance to the words of Attorney General Thomas Gregory in November 1917, when, referring to critics of the war, he declared, "May God have mercy on them, for they need expect none from an outraged people and an avenging government."[14]

It was under these statutes that prominent socialists Eugene V. Debs and Victor Berger, who had served as a congressman from Milwaukee, were arrested and convicted. In the fall of 1917, the Department of Justice went after the IWW, arresting scores of its leaders for alleged violations of the Espionage Act. In a series of trials held in the spring of 1918, more than one hundred Wobblies were convicted and sent to federal prisons, many under lengthy sentences. Observed a government lawyer involved in the prosecutions, "Our purpose [is] . . . as I understand it, very largely to put the IWW out of business."[15]

Nor were these laws the only weapons the administration could employ against criticism and dissent. A variety of other statutes dealing with immigrants, foreign trade, and government employment gave officials wide discretion in surveillance and jailing of both citizens and alien residents. For example, under the terms of the Alien Enemies Act of 1798 and not applied since the beginning of the nineteenth century, some 2,300 German alien residents were interned, many in overcrowded and unhealthy facilities, where military and police guards often treated them with contempt and inflicted demeaning and often dangerous punishments.[16]

During the war, the administration also created a vast political police force to monitor and arrest those deemed insufficiently enthusiastic about prosecuting the war. The Military Intelligence Division (MID) of the U.S. Army employed more than 1,300 men and women by the end of the war, and the Department of Justice's Bureau of Investigation (precursor to the Federal Bureau of Investigation) expanded rapidly. Virtually every executive agency in the government had some sort of investigative or harassment arm, from the Department of the Treasury's Secret Service to the Office of Naval Intelligence to the Immigration Bureau and the investigative branch of the Post Office Department. In addition, government officials encouraged vigilantism by enlisting private organizations to search for dissenters, radicals, and antiwar speakers. Most active of various private groups that collaborated with government officials for these purposes was the American Protective League (APL), established by a patriotic businessman in March 1917 to finger suspicious or disloyal elements and to foster patriotic sentiment. Eventually enlisting as many as 300,000 members, primarily recruited from businessmen, professional men, and other upper-income citizens, the APL operated aggressively with the open endorsement of the federal Department of Justice to investigate those whose behavior or utterances its members considered suspicious. During the war, the APL's zealous patriots conducted more than three million of these inquiries, turning over its findings to the Department of Justice and Military Intelligence for action.

Liberals and progressives in America decried these actions. Many of Wilson's erstwhile supporters, who regarded him as the champion of progressive social legislation and enlightened public action, wondered how a government presumably elected to promote high-minded ideals could so ruthlessly turn to naked repression of dissent. Wilson, some of his liberal supporters decided, must be so preoccupied with winning the war that he inadvertently gave such eager repressers as wartime Attorney General Thomas Gregory and Postmaster General Albert Burleson too much leeway. And it was true that the president occasionally demurred at the extent and blatancy of federal suppression. In October

1918, partly in response to complaints by liberals, he counseled Burleson, "I think doubt [as to the wisdom of suppressing a publication] ought always be resolved in favor of the utmost freedom of speech." Again, the next year he told Burleson, "it would not be wise to do any more suppressing."[17]

In fact, however, the president's concern with First Amendment freedoms as they pertained to critics of the war and his conducting of it was at best episodic and halfhearted. He was, to be sure, the quintessential "liberal" in the original nineteenth-century use of that term. Although in theory such liberals were suspicious of government power and committed to free inquiry and discussion, in reality this traditional liberalism was limited to those who played by the established rules and kept their dissent within safe boundaries. It did not extend to purveyors of radically challenging ideas nor did it embrace those who called into question the motives or actions of the good men who conducted the affairs of state. Certainly any fundamental criticism of the American form of government or way of life, especially if it showed signs of contempt or disdain for cherished patriotic symbols or emblems such as the flag or the uniform of the nation's soldiers and sailors, was perforce out of bounds.

Wilson did have some tolerance for sharply expressed criticisms of certain aspects of American capitalism, since he too thought that its corporate practitioners often were selfish, shortsighted, and inimical to the public interest. He took a relatively benign view of wartime labor disturbances, on the whole appreciating that strikes grew out of legitimate grievances and that workers' anger was often properly directed at employers. But in the end, Wilson's understanding of civil liberties was a blinkered and instrumental one. If this was a war for the greater good—and in his view there could be no doubt that it was—citizens (and especially alien residents) would have to sacrifice their right to say or do unpatriotic or harmful things so that the war might be prosecuted with the utmost dispatch. Thus, the blatant disregard for civil liberties that characterized the Wilson war administration was no aberration. Men such as Gregory and Burleson might be overzealous in punishing critics, especially if these men and women came from minority groups, and Wilson might occasionally offer cautious counsels of restraint. But these were his appointees and he backed them in every important controversy surrounding their actions. Criticism of the war and of the men who were conducting it in the name of a higher humanity was simply not within the legitimate boundaries of public discourse.

Wartime agencies continued their activities into the postwar period. U.S. troops were fighting Bolsheviks in Russia, and evidence of system-challenging radical activity was everywhere. It was thus an easy matter for

Gregory's successor, A. Mitchell Palmer, along with a still-potent MID and other agencies, to shift their focus from antiwar activities to those of radicals and suspected radicals. The American Legion, for example, announced that it was "ready for action at any time . . . against these extremists who are seeking to overturn [our] . . . government." Other citizen groups, overwhelmingly consisting of business and professional men and other middle- and upper-class elements, included the National Security League, the American Defense Society, and the National Civic Federation. Far from speaking out against depredations by private citizens and vigilantes, federal officials continued their cooperation with informal networks of patriots to identify and harass labor militants, radical groups, and other dissenters. The encouragement and nurturing of citizen vigilantism was the logical extension of the government's reliance on "voluntarism" for so many of its wartime goals. Because the United States did not have a large civil service or a lengthy tradition of government service, and because the American people were unused to the heavy tax burden that expansion of formal government activities would have necessitated, the Wilson administration relied heavily on encouraging private groups to take on quasi-governmental roles. Examples abounded. There was the Food Administration's mass mobilization of housewives, the reliance on voluntary labor–management agreement in workplaces, and the localization of the conscription process through the use of citizens to choose the men who would be inducted. All of these activities had been promoted and carried through with the maximum of publicity and patriotic hoopla while confining the very real (and at times ruthlessly exercised) coercive authority of the government to a secondary role. Thus, when it came to ferreting out subversives, identifying dangerous radicals, and crushing evidences of dissent, it was natural for the Wilson administration to apply the same pattern of reliance on private citizens while keeping the mailed fist of government coercion on the ready.

During the latter months of 1919 and into early 1920, the federal government's attacks on radicals and alleged radicals reached a crescendo. On August 1, 1919, shaken by the bombings of the spring, Attorney General Palmer created a General Intelligence Division (GID) within the Department of Justice, choosing a twenty-four-year-old government lawyer, J. Edgar Hoover, to head it. Along with the department's Bureau of Investigation, the GID launched wide-ranging investigations of radical and allegedly radical publications, groups, and individuals. Hoover compiled a file index that soon included more than 200,000 cards on suspect organizations and leaders. Palmer asked Congress for and received an appropriation of more than $2 million to finance its fight against subversion. "We have every reason to believe," a Palmer aide told congressmen, "that the Russian Bolsheviki are pouring money in here at the rate of that much a month."[18] With critics in the press and the Republican Party urging him on, Palmer laid plans for a series of sweeping roundups of men and women he and his informants suspected of disloyalty.

Because it would be difficult to secure convictions of large numbers of U.S. citizens even under the repressive wartime legislation, Palmer decided to focus his efforts on alien residents. And it was true these noncitizens made up large proportions of several radical organizations, especially in the Northeast. By virtue of recently passed immigration legislation, these men and women were not accorded rights to habeas corpus, jury trials, or legal counsel. They could be arrested, detained, and quickly deported for mere advocacy of "anarchist" doctrines or membership in an organization that espoused such views. Legal proceedings in these deportation cases consisted of hearings before U.S. Immigration Bureau functionaries, without the right of counsel or cross-examination. Gaining the cooperation of officials in the Immigration Bureau (which was housed administratively in the U.S. Department of Labor) and working closely with police in local communities, Department of Justice agents conducted the first in a series of sweeps on November 7, 1919, targeting an obscure organization, the Union of Russian Workers (URW).

Over the next several weeks, federal agents and local police carried out additional raids in northeastern cities. These mass assaults on radical organizations culminated on the night of January 2, 1920, with raids in thirty-three cities in twenty-two states. Authorities took more than 4,000 people into custody and followed up these sweeps three days later with further roundups. Although Secretary of Labor William B. Wilson and some of his assistants were uneasy about the scope and character of these raids, Immigration Bureau officials cooperated fully. Palmer, earlier under fire for his alleged lack of diligence, now became a public hero. The New York Times, for example, hailed the massive January raids. "If some or any of us," an editorial announced, "have ever questioned the alacrity, resolute will, and . . . vigor of the Department of Justice in hunting down those enemies of the United Sates, the questioners and the doubters have now cause to approve and applaud." As for the response of the president and Palmer's cabinet colleagues, Secretary of State Lansing's entry for the cabinet meeting following the January raids read simply, "No real business. All politics."[19]

Although Palmer claimed to be upholding law and order by ridding the nation of subversives, in fact these raids constituted an orgy of repression and violations of due process. During the raid on the URW, for example, federal agents and New York City police indiscriminately rounded up everyone, including passersby, who happened to be at the address at which the URW maintained its modest offices. Though they had warrants for only 27 arrests, authorities took 200 people off, many of them citizens. Local police often took the federally coordinated raids as an invitation to victimize immigrants in general. They ransacked homes and offices, routinely conducted warrantless searches, and confiscated or destroyed tons of literature and organizational records. An Immigration Bureau inspector told a congressional committee that in Boston, federal agents and local police simply "went to various pool rooms, etc., in which foreigners congregated, and they simply sent up in trucks all of them that happened to be there." Those detained were sometimes held for months without legal counsel or notification of family members, often in cold, filthy, and overcrowded detention centers. Unprovoked beatings were common, many of them at the hands of informal citizen auxiliaries hastily recruited by the Department of Justice to augment its forces. "Conditions could not have been worse," reported a Department of Labor official inspecting the hastily prepared facilities in Detroit, but conditions in other centers were at least equally harsh.[20]

In the end, Palmer overstepped himself. Attacks on such organizations as the URW—actually an informal social club for lonely older immigrants and not in any sense a band of violent revolutionaries—did draw criticism, however belated, from editorialists and political opponents. Assistant Secretary of Labor Louis Post, serving as acting secretary during William B. Wilson's illness, scrutinized arrest and deportation orders scrupulously, canceling more than 70 percent of those coming before him and effectively criticizing the excesses associated with the raids when appearing before congressional committees. As evidence of the Department of Justice's violations of citizens' rights and mistreatment of innocent persons mounted, Palmer and his minions came under judicial and congressional criticism. Palmer's prediction that revolutionaries would attempt to launch disruptive demonstrations and perpetrate public outrages on May Day 1920 proved ludicrously wrong. The wholesale attacks on individual rights triggered a spirited response from influential legal authorities and activist groups, notably the National Civil Liberties Bureau, which effectively used the Palmer raids and other outrages to promote an expanded conception of individual rights and due process.

Even so, the antiradical excesses of the wartime and immediate postwar months had significant and lasting negative effects. The creation of a potent federal apparatus for the silencing of dissent and the imposition of conformity was an enduring legacy of the Great War and its aftermath. Conflation of all varieties of radicals into a common stereotype of bomb-throwing fanatics helped to narrow the range of acceptable political discourse. The de facto destruction of the IWW aborted what had been a useful goad to established labor unions and what might have developed into an effective industrial union movement embracing the kinds of unskilled and ethnically suspect Americans largely ignored by the American Federation of Labor (AFL). The persecution and harassment of immigrants and aliens under the guise of national security lent sanction to racist and authoritarian impulses rarely absent in American life. Government-sanctioned hysteria discouraged the kind of cosmopolitan public discourse that Wilson needed if he was to gain acceptance of the expanded international role for the United States that the peace treaty and the League covenant would require. Moreover, the Wilson administration's assaults on ethnic minorities and civil liberties fed the anger and resentment of the president's erstwhile progressive supporters, already dubious about a peace settlement that fell so far short of his promises and their expectations.

Domestic Conflicts

Indeed, apart from conducting its high-profile assault on dissidents, the Wilson administration paid little attention to domestic policy in general. Those who had hailed Wilson's prewar attacks on corporate malpractice, his support for positive labor legislation, and his denunciations of the Republican Old Guard during his reelection campaign in 1916 expected a renewal of progressive initiatives after the war. Prominent progressives such as philosopher John Dewey, journalist Walter Lippmann, and wealthy activist Amos Pinchot had supported the war in part because they believed that the national emergency would foster the use of positive government action to benefit organized labor, improve conditions in public health and economic security, and generally impose order on what they considered chaotic and often destructive capitalist development. In 1917, Dewey, a towering figure among progressive-minded citizens, welcomed the onset of war because he believed that its conduct would require "instrumentalities for enforcing the public interest in all the agencies of production and exchange." With the war won, possibilities for renewed progressive advance seemed great. Reform-minded *Survey* magazine reported on a wide variety of proposals and programs designed to sustain war-generated public programs in labor relations, health care, housing, and regulation of the economy. Organizations from the National Municipal League to the National Catholic War Council urged renewed efforts to moderate and direct the impact of industrial and urban growth. One prominent organization of influential Protestant clergymen warned that unless the government moved to redistribute wealth, eliminate poverty, and bring corporate greed under control, "this war will have become murder on a colossal scale."[21]

And it was true that during the war, the federal government had injected itself directly into the regulation of economic life and even into social provision as never before. Hopeful progressives cited the activities of the War Industries Board, the National War Labor Board, the U.S. Railroad Administration, the Public Health Service, the U.S. Employment Service, and the U.S. Housing Corporation as evidence of the administration's commitment to social justice and equality. If government could play a positive role in furthering the business of killing other human beings, the progressives reasoned, surely it could even more effectively promote the general welfare and ameliorate inequities and social tensions during time of peace. Although there were many visions of the exact shape that a postwar liberal order would take, one thing was sure, according to the iconoclastic economist Thorstein Veblen: "There can be no return to the *status quo ante*" for there had to be a "revision of . . . the present system of vested interests."[22]

But neither Wilson himself nor any prominent member of his administration showed more than marginal concern with the economic and social problems that the abrupt end of the war brought. Far less did they promote ambitious plans for accelerated reform. From Wilson's perspective, wartime experiments in government action were temporary, to be abandoned when the fighting stopped. True to the general policy orientation of the Democratic Party and especially its Southern wing, Wilson had always been chary of assertive federal action in social and economic policy, seeing government power as a needed check to corporate influence but not as a means of building an elaborate structure of social welfare. As early as December 1918, the president served warning that the administration was not about to sustain the wartime experiments in regulation and social provision. Americans, he declared, did not want to be "coached and led" in the adjustment to peacetime life. "They know their own business, are quick and resourceful . . . and self-reliant." He pledged that his administration would do nothing to impede Americans' determination to "go their own way" and would do little to "mediate the process of change."[23] True to his word, Wilson watched with equanimity as the new Republican Congress slashed budgets or eliminated entirely programs in housing, health care, and manpower allocation. Under his direction, the War Industries Board, the National War Labor Board, and a host of other new agencies wrapped up their business and liquidated themselves, in most cases before he returned from Paris in July.

The administration's hands-off attitude toward domestic policy was nowhere more evident than in the realm of race relations. During the war, manpower needs and the influx of African Americans into industrial centers had forced the government at least to acknowledge the existence of racial problems. The Department of Labor had created the Division of Negro Economics to monitor employment among blacks, and Secretary of War Baker had appointed Emmett Scott as his special assistant to advise him on problems relating to the treatment of black troops. After the war, some of the "reconstruction" proposals that circulated so freely among progressives called for explicit inclusion of blacks on an equal basis in government programs and for the passage of a federal antilynching law. Black leaders echoed this view, often in a militant idiom. As W. E. B. Du Bois declared in May 1919, blacks had "fought gladly and to the last drop of blood for America" but America "is yet a shameful land," scarred by discrimination and lynching. African Americans must demand equal rights but they could not depend on benevolent whites to secure them. "We are cowards and jackasses if now that war is over," he challenged, "we do not marshal every ounce of our brain and brawn to fight" for them.[24]

Indeed, wartime rhetoric about equal rights, the exploits of black troops, the economic and geographic mobility of blacks, and a rise in race pride and color consciousness triggered activism around the country. Membership in the National Association for the Advancement of Colored People (NAACP) boomed, drawing in thousands of farmers, workers, and housewives. In Texas, dozens of new NAACP branches emerged during the war. In 1919, membership there tripled. "Send me a copy of the Thirteenth, Fourteenth, Fifteenth amendment[s]" to the Constitution, urged one branch secretary, because "the time has come that the white man and the black man to stand on terms of social equality [sic]." Black labor activists challenged racism and discrimination in the shops and factories as well as in the trade unions, which expanded rapidly during the war and immediate postwar period. Biracial unions emerged in the lumber products, meatpacking, and metalworking sectors. Formerly all-white packinghouse unions in Chicago now recruited black workers, who in turn proved militant and effective trade unionists. Cross-race workplace cooperation even emerged in the South. In Bogalusa, Louisiana, for example, white sawmill and lumber workers battled company guards and police in a futile effort to protect a charismatic black organizer who had been instrumental in building a biracial local union there. Even in Mississippi, notorious for the pervasiveness of its racial oppression, the pride black citizens felt about the deeds of their sons and brothers in uniform translated into efforts on the part of African Americans to redefine their relationship with dominant whites.[25]

But if the war experience fueled black activism, it also triggered violent white reaction. In Texas, for example, the rise of the NAACP and efforts on the part of blacks to exercise political rights met brutal response. White farmers and farm laborers, incensed over the gains blacks had made in landownership and agricultural prosperity, retaliated violently, burning homes, threatening families, and killing blacks who dared resist. In Arkansas, local mobs and law enforcement officers in Phillips County responded to efforts of black sharecroppers to organize a union with terror and mass arrests. The NAACP reported that as many as 250 rural blacks may have been killed, some in officially sanctioned mass murders, during the first week of October 1919. During that year, lynchings, almost all of them in the southern states, killed seventy-eight African Americans, a number that represented an increase over the 1917 (thirty) and 1918 (sixty-three) totals. Several of the victims were war veterans, captured and murdered while wearing the uniform of the U.S. Army.[26]

Although lynchings were overwhelmingly confined to the South, mob outbursts targeting African Americans erupted throughout the country. In Washington, D.C., for example, lurid newspaper headlines following a rash of sexual assaults in July 1919 encouraged demonization of black men. "Negroes Attack Girl . . .White Men Vainly Pursue" blared the *Washington Post* after one episode. White servicemen stationed near the capital led in a frenzy of mob assaults on blacks, who were dragged off street cars, chased down alleys, and beaten brutally. With the Washington police doing little to protect the city's black citizens, African Americans began responding in kind, and for three days chaos ruled the city. Only the dispatch of 2,000 Regular Army troops restored order, after six people had been killed and more than one hundred injured. Other lethal episodes of white-instigated racial violence, often focusing on black incursions into previous all-white neighborhoods and on competition for jobs in a now-decelerating postwar economy, exploded in cities as diverse as Omaha, Indianapolis, Knoxville, and Longview, Texas.[27]

The most serious urban racial episode of 1919, however, erupted in Chicago, the Mecca of the Great War–era black northward migration. For months, blacks moving into white neighborhoods had been targets of bombings. Then on July 27, white youths killed a black youngster who had inadvertently strayed across an unofficial demarcation line separating the races at a Lake Michigan beach. For the next two weeks, gangs of young whites and young blacks surged through the streets of borderline neighborhoods in a festival of violence. The Chicago police did nothing to stop the mayhem and often collaborated with white mobs in attacks on blacks. By the time an uneasy order had been restored in August, at least thirty-eight people were dead, twenty-three of them African American, and arson and fire bombings left thousands homeless. These violent outbreaks were part of the country's long, sad history of racial violence, yet there was something new here as well. In the past, although blacks had often responded to attacks with armed defense, black leaders had always urged restraint and moderation. Now, however, voices of the "new" Negro, reflecting pride in blackness and refusal to be victimized, predominated. Poet Claude McKay caught the mood of defiance in his 1919 poem "If We Must Die": "If we must die, let it not be like hogs / Hunted and penned in an inglorious spot, / While round us bark the mad and hungry dogs."[28]

The Wilson administration had no response to this racial conflict. The only activity of federal personnel in the events of 1919 involved the cooperation of federal marshals and Bureau of Investigation agents with local white law enforcement authorities in the destruction of activist black organizations. In Arkansas, there were documented reports of federal troops that had been dispatched to restore order, machine gunning blacks. In Texas and Georgia, Bureau of Investigation agents identified outspoken blacks in behalf of local authorities, themselves working closely with private citizens and racially motivated gangs bent on violence. The Department of Justice and Military Intelligence planted informers in activist black organizations and circulated lurid stories of Bolshevik influence and preparations for armed uprisings among African Americans. According to MID sources, for example, the NAACP, in reality a white-financed, largely middle-class organization, was a "menace" because Bolsheviks "dominated" it. A Post Office report described widespread "Radicalism and Sedition among the Negroes" and falsely charged that prominent labor activist A. Philip Randolph "advocates Bolshevism among the negroes [sic] and the establishment in this country of Bolshevik rule."[29]

Neither the president nor his cabinet spoke out against assaults on fellow citizens of color. Wilson and Postmaster General Burleson regularly used demeaning language in references to African Americans and liked to tell offensive "darky" stories lampooning blacks. There was no discussion of the racial disturbances at cabinet meetings, and the president responded to expressions of concern from prominent citizens, black and white, with bland evasions. In his only public utterance in 1919 on the subject of racial violence, at a speech in September in Helena, Montana, largely devoted to foreign policy, Wilson expressed "shame as an American citizen at the race riots that have occurred," thus encouraging fellow citizens to regard blacks and whites as equally responsible. Wilson apparently never contemplated using the moral and political authority of the presidential office to condemn racial bigotry or direct public attention to the chronic perpetrators of racial violence.[30]

Neither the president nor his key advisers could be so indifferent toward another major postwar domestic problem, labor conflict. The years of the Great War occurred in the middle of a ten-year strike wave that made the 1910s one of the most consistently turbulent eras in U.S. history. From 1916 through 1920, the country experienced an annual average of more than 3,700 strikes. A rising proportion of these were "control" strikes, that is, strikes over union recognition, work rules, and disagreements over the nature, pace, and regulation of the work to be performed. Many factors combined to make labor conflicts of the Great War era particularly fierce. The huge influx of European immigrants and rural southerners into the industrial labor force created a volatile mix of workers. The rapid pace of technological development eroded traditional notions of workers' autonomy. New mass production industries such as electrical products, chemicals, and motor vehicles featured rigid workplace regimes and employers' determination to combat union efforts to limit their power at the point of production. The hectic demands of wartime heightened tensions, and in 1917 and 1918 strike indexes spiked upward.

Nor did the end of the fighting in Europe have a calming effect on labor relations. Quite the contrary, for 1919 proved by far the most strike-torn year ever. The number of workers involved was staggering. Almost four and a half million, a number equal to 22.5 percent of the labor force, hit the bricks, triple the average for the other years in the period 1916–22, a span notable for its high level of work stoppages. Moreover, many of these disputes were violent, bitter confrontations, involving fundamental issues of social justice, managerial control, and human rights. "'Worse than at any time in history'— that seems to be the only way to describe the present situation," wrote one careful observer. "The greatest of all wars between organized labor and capital seems to have begun," declared a journalist after the war.[31]

Several factors account for this postwar labor turbulence and for the savagery that often characterized it. The administration's refusal to plan for postwar readjustment, the abrupt cancellation of many contracts for military equipment and munitions, the continuing surge of inflation, and the war-aided growth of organized labor bolstered workers' resolve to improve conditions and establish permanent footholds of organization throughout the economy. Reinforcing these tangible reasons for expanded labor militancy, moreover, were powerful psychological and ideological currents. The Bolsheviks' seizure of power in Russia and their widely publicized call for uprisings in other countries lent even ordinary labor disputes an unusual portentousness. The relatively proworker wartime policies of the administration at once encouraged union ambitions and stiffened the resolve of employers to reassert control in their shops and factories.

Perhaps most contested of all was the very language of patriotism as it might be applied to industrial life. For thousands of new immigrants toiling in the packinghouses, steel mills, and factories of their adopted land, highly emotive wartime propaganda, often directed specifically at so-called hyphenated Americans such as themselves, urged them to support the war effort, buy Liberty bonds, and release their sons to the military. A powerful subtext of these official appeals offered inclusion in the American polity and in American culture even to people earlier despised or feared as alien by virtue of language, religion, or appearance. As workers, soldiers, and food-conserving housewives, officials told them, they were crucial to the project of "making the world safe for democracy." Liberty Loan posters featured dignified images of exotic immigrants dutifully saluting the flag and lining up to buy bonds. The CPI recruited respected figures in immigrant communities to carry the messages of loyalty and patriotism—and thereby to invite their listeners into the expanding definition of "American" that the war effort required.

Most new immigrants were working people. For them the workplace was the least democratic and most authoritarian aspect of their experience. Surely, if democratic and patriotic appeals meant anything, they meant eliminating the arbitrary authority of their bosses and employers. Thus the democratic message of inclusion and civic participation echoed powerfully in the nation's workplaces, and of course it reinforced the decades-old message of the trade union movement, whose spokesmen had always couched labor's message in the language of democracy. For countless immigrants, the most far-reaching effect of the Great War was that it forever eliminated the prospect, initially harbored by many, of returning to their native land after a money-earning stint in the United States. With no choice now but to regard America as their permanent home, immigrant workers translated the message of democracy, reinforced by the benign policies of the National War Labor Board, into union activism and industrial militancy. To be sure, employers also sought to appropriate the language of patriotism, using appeals to "Americanism" to foster acceptance of heightened work norms and managerial discipline. But workers, whether immigrant or native, often had their own definitions of "Americanism," which involved equity and self-respect rather than subservience and docility. For many, the union was not the initial object of their activism but merely the vehicle by which fair treatment, just compensation, and industrial democracy—surely "American" goals—might be achieved. One day in 1918, a government official asked an electrical worker why he was struggling so hard to build a union in his plant. "In a way," he replied, "I didn't have any [union sympathies], only—I might say I had an American feeling, that is all." "Millions of wage earners have been fighting for . . . democracy not only in government, but in industry," declared an Ohio steelworker.[32] For immigrant workers especially, the wartime appeals, combined with the growing understanding that their lives and those of their families were now permanently embedded in American conditions, fueled union sentiment and determination to achieve these "American" standards, both of material life and civic status.

In the past, organized labor, as particularly embodied in the American Federation of Labor (AFL), had not been responsive to immigrant workers or to mass-production workers generally. Decades of bitter struggle to achieve recognition and acceptance had encouraged the AFL's leaders to soft-peddle its putative claim to speak for all workers. Because immigrants increased the labor supply and threatened skilled workers' efforts to control job sites or entry into the various trades, AFL leaders and members alike had usually shown little sympathy for them and little inclination to organize newcomers. But the war opened up new possibilities to expand union membership, bring the labor movement as never before into such great mass-production industries as automotives, electrical goods, and meatpacking, and revitalize moribund unions in the steel industry. "Now is our time to build an industrial army," urged a veteran labor activist. "[We must] get behind this campaign for industrial democracy."[33] AFL President Samuel Gompers and other national officials saw in the social climate the war had generated the opportunity for organized labor to make a great breakthrough and to assert its determination, hitherto always latent, to move to the center of the American political economy.

Of the thousands of strikes that helped make 1919 so turbulent, it was the walkout in September of 250,000 steelworkers in cities across the country and the bitter and often violent course of their subsequent conflict with employers and government authorities that was the most significant and dramatic. Other struggles also captured headlines and fed public fears of a mass labor uprising. The Seattle General Strike in February raised the specter of revolutionary uprising, and a job action on the part of Boston's policemen in September seemed to call into question the very foundations of law and order. But it was the steel strike, which lasted through the fall of 1919 and into the early months of 1920, that most dramatically and significantly embodied the promises, aspirations, and eventually, the disappointments, of the Great War–era labor movement.

In the late nineteenth century, the iron and steel industries had been bastions of union strength. However, the consolidation of the steel industry, first under Scots-born entrepreneur Andrew Carnegie and then in 1901 with the creation of the nation's first billion-dollar corporation, United States Steel, was accompanied by relentless and successful attacks on the iron and steel-workers' union. By the time of the Great War, steelmakers had almost completely driven the AFL out of the industry and enforced an aggressively open shop (i.e., antiunion) policy. Steelmaking was the very epitome of advanced industrialism. Because steel employed as many as a half-million workers, a successful campaign to reestablish the AFL in the mills and blast furnaces would betoken a dramatic shift in the balance of power between labor and capital. For that very reason, of course, steelmakers, although forced to make grudging concessions to worker organization during the war itself, girded for no-holds-barred resistance to a massive postwar organizing campaign. "It has been my policy, and the policy of our corporation," Judge Elbert Gary, chief executive officer of U.S. Steel, told a U.S. Senate committee during the strike, "not to deal with union labor leaders . . . we do not believe in contracting with unions."[34]

The actual walkout began on September 22, 1919, when about half of the nation's steelworkers honored union picket lines in steel centers from Colorado to New York state. Unfriendly editorialists, conservative politicians, and steel company executives accused union leaders, notably AFL President Samuel Gompers, nominal steelworkers' organizing campaign chairman John Fitzpatrick, and day-to-day director of operations William Z. Foster, of dictatorial ambition in calling the walkout. In fact, however, union leaders had tried desperately to forestall a strike. Since the creation in August 1918 of a special AFL committee to conduct an organizing drive, union leaders had attempted to balance militancy and caution. Issuing fiery appeals to workers to join the union, they simultaneously made earnest approaches to President Wilson and other government officials to help them to convince steel company executives to negotiate. But this was a tough balancing act for the ill-financed and loosely coordinated National Committee for Organizing Iron and Steel Workers (NCOISW). Preoccupied with the war and then the peace conference, Wilson grew increasingly distant in his relationship with Gompers and other labor leaders. Meanwhile, steel manufacturers ignored appeals to meet with union representatives.

But NCOISW recruiting efforts were if anything too successful, with thousands of new members paying their $3 initiation fee and surging into local organizations. "You talk about spirit," an Indiana activist declared, "why, that is all these men out here are breathing. They have been hungering for the chance to get in." Huge crowds greeted organizing rallies, with immigrants leading the way. Through 1918 and into 1919, steelworkers defied their bosses and risked retaliation from foremen and managers to join the new organization. In the summer of 1919, NCOISW representatives reported that "the [local] organizations everywhere are experiencing an unprecedented growth . . . they are coming in by the hundreds daily."[35]

And that was the problem. Enthusiastic steelworkers, having taken the bold step of joining the union, now expected results and pressed national leaders to confront obdurate employers. In July 1919, the NCOISW issued a list of demands calling in effect for union recognition; elimination of arbitrary employment practices as related to discipline, layoffs, and promotions; a reduction in the steel industry's then-prevailing seventy-two-hour work week; and unspecified wage increases "sufficient to guarantee [an] American standard of living." The committee announced that it would poll the membership for strike authorization if the steelmakers failed to agree to bargain. The balloting, which took place through July and into August, itself spurred additional membership and militancy. Thus, when once again, the steel companies dismissed out of hand requests to enter into negotiations, rank-and-file pressure for strike action grew irresistible, even though national leaders, only too aware of the partialness of organization and the weakness of the union's finances, dreaded a direct confrontation with the powerful steel corporations. But with overwhelming support for a strike and with the employers' continued refusal even to receive union representatives, apprehensive NCOISW leaders gave the go ahead and the largest industrial strike in American history began on schedule.[36]

From the start, however, the strike was in trouble. The NCOISW had done a remarkable job in recruiting more than 100,000 members, and steelworkers had shown solidarity when at least an additional 100,000 who had not initially signed up joined the strike. Even so, probably more than half the country's steelworkers reported for work. In addition, ethnic and workplace rivalries compromised support for the walkout. African American workers, largely ignored during the organizing campaign and legitimately feeling themselves excluded by the same democratic language that united white workers, largely ignored the strike call. In some areas, skilled maintenance and repair workers, disdainful of the polyglot mass of nonskilled immigrant workers who made up the bulk of the NCOISW membership, haughtily crossed picket lines, although in other locales skilled workers provided valuable experience and leadership. At root of the National Committee's difficulties, however, was its own weakness. Forced to function with bare-bones financing, it received only sporadic support from fellow AFL unions and was plagued by awkward organizational and logistical arrangements.

Quite apart from these internal problems, however, was the uncompromising stand of the steel industry. Steelmakers resolved to crush the fledgling union. Appeals to workers of diverse ethnic backgrounds exploited the ever-present racism and xenophobia in the mill towns. Threats to oust workers from company-owned housing and to bar strikers from future employment had a telling effect. Nor did steelmakers neglect their own version of patriotic appeals, designed to cast the union as an evil foreign interloper. "America Is Calling You," read an advertisement in a Pittsburgh newspaper. The strike, it warned, was a "diabolical attempt of a small group of radicals. . . . Keep America busy, and prosperous, and American. Go back to work."[37] For thousands of steelworkers, the power of the company for which they worked was direct and tangible while the appeal of the union was remote and abstract.

Physical force played a key role in the course of the strike. These powerful corporations dominated the communities in which the strike was daily played out. Local police, state militias, and informal citizen "law-and-order" bodies assaulted strikers, broke up meetings, and smashed picket lines. The overwhelming support of the union on the part of immigrant workers made it suspect to many in authority, who readily merged their antiunion feelings with the prevailing antiradical hysteria. In Gary, Indiana, the commander of U.S. Army troops brought in to quell strike-related disorders there pledged to do "my part in the rounding of the Red element," which he equated with immigrant strike supporters. In Allegheny County, Pennsylvania, the sheriff deputized 5,000 citizens, whom the steel companies actually recruited, outfitted, and paid, ostensibly to preserve law and order. Along with well-trained state police, termed "Cossacks" by the strikers, these men launched a veritable reign of terror, turning western Pennsylvania into an armed camp.[38]

The campaign to organize steelworkers had originated in 1918, at a time when the NWLB and other government agencies were supporting workers' rights to representation. Labor leaders hoped for the continued goodwill and friendly offices of government officials in efforts to bring the steelmakers to the conference table and reach a settlement. But even before the strike, the indifference and impotence of the government, from the president on down, had become apparent. In the spring of 1919, for example, the Bethlehem Steel Company reneged on wage agreements made under the auspices of the NWLB during the war. With the disbanding of the Labor Board and the cancellation of military orders, the company now refused to honor agreements it claimed had been made under wartime duress.

In the run up to the strike as well, NCOISW leaders found the federal government of little help. They appealed to Wilson to persuade Judge Gary and his colleagues to meet with union representatives. Not only did Wilson decline to do this, he refused to publicize the steelmakers' stand (which in private he did criticize). Moreover, when at the last minute he did propose the holding of an industrial conference to discuss a broad range of labor and economic problems, he publicly called on unionists to order an abrupt halt to strike momentum and preparations. Wilson's tardy intervention seemed to throw the onus of the strike on the workers while leaving the steelmakers without public censure. Declared the NCOISW's head in a comment that perhaps misremembered the sequence of events but captured their essence, "We did not expect much consideration from any government agency for the reason that the steel trust has dominated the government."[39]

By December 1919, the strike was clearly being lost. In the key Pittsburgh area, by late November, strikebreakers and "loyal" workers had equaled pre-strike production norms. Although strikers and their families displayed continued commitment and tenacity, the combination of police harassment, reviving production, and employer solidarity proved too much. Groups of workers trickled back into the mills, hoping to avoid punishment and retribution. Employers circulated newspaper ads and posters printed in a dozen languages announcing the failure of the strike and calling on workers to abandon the union. Finally, on January 8, 1920, the NCOISW declared an end to the strike. The union had been defeated, its press release declared, by the "arbitrary and ruthless misuse of power" of the steel companies.[40]

By the time of the defeat of the steel strike, organized labor was in retreat everywhere. With returning soldiers claiming their previous jobs, abrupt cancellation of military orders throwing thousands out of work, and the inability of the AFL and other unions to translate their brief moment of war-generated power and influence into permanent strength and continued forward movement, union membership began to ebb. Hardest hit were the metalworking, automotive, and other mass-production sectors. Multiracial unions of packinghouse workers in Chicago fell apart in a bitter 1919 strike. Aggressive use of still-standing war emergency powers by federal agents, who resorted to wire tapping, espionage, and public denunciation, forced the briefly powerful United Mine Workers to abort a national soft coal strike in the fall of 1919. With Wilson ill, distracted, and increasingly apprehensive over the reported power of organized labor, the administration reversed its wartime prounion course and, with the exception of a few officials in the Department of Labor, joined in the postwar union smashing and Red baiting.

This turn from labor had consequences for Wilson's party and for his vision. Many progressives considered the labor question to be the key domestic issue and regarded a strong and vigorous labor movement as a central component of a just society. The administration's sudden rejection of workers' claims and its abandonment of a labor movement it had so recently cultivated deepened progressives' disillusionment with Wilsonianism. Doing the steelmakers' bidding in the great strike did the administration little political good even as it robbed the Democratic Party of working-class support that might have helped counterbalance the resurgence of corporate power in the postwar months. Labor's defeat in steel, meatpacking, and other mass-production industries, combined with the excesses of the Red Scare and the immigrant-bashing that characterized so much of domestic life in the postwar United States, aborted any possibility that the Wilsonian vision might have achieved ongoing institutional footing in a postwar America in which forces of xenophobia, intolerance, and authoritarianism seemed increasingly potent.

The Treaty Fight

On the eve of the steel strike, a Philadelphia newspaper criticized President Wilson for neglecting domestic concerns as he sought ratification of the Versailles Treaty. "While the Senate debates the league-of-nations covenant the people are talking about high prices, increased wages, shorter hours and the reorganization of industry," observed the *Public Ledger*. "This is the great divide between Washington and the nation."[41] But to the president, the struggle for the peace treaty and membership in the League was *the* crucial issue, far outweighing even the most turbulent strikes, the most savage racial assaults, and the most serious problems of economic readjustment. In calling so eloquently for a declaration of war in April 1917, he had not fully anticipated that thousands of Americans would fight in the trenches of France, nor had he foreseen that many thousands would be killed. A man who cared little for the display of weapons and the rhetoric of combat, Wilson felt a deep personal responsibility for leading his fellow Americans into the bloodshed. The men he had sent overseas had done their job; it now remained for him to do his job, to establish a new structure of peace that would justify their terrible sacrifice. On Memorial Day, 1919, Wilson dedicated the new American military cemetery at Suresnes, just west of Paris, even as the final version of the treaty and covenant were being hammered out. Looking out over the graves of men killed in the fierce fighting of a year before, he made a pledge: "Here I stand consecrated in spirit to the men who were once my comrades and who are now gone, and who have left me under eternal bonds of fidelity."[42] To this man, critics of the treaty and the covenant were not political rivals with whom bargains might be struck. Instead, they were deadly enemies who threatened to sever the bond that linked the president to his fallen comrades.

Indeed, obduracy and inability to compromise characterized Wilson's efforts to secure ratification of the treaty. Repeatedly, he rejected the counsel of even his closest advisers and other friends of the treaty that he bargain with senatorial critics of the treaty and covenant. In Paris, it is true, he had retreated from the Fourteen Points. The terms imposed on Germany were harsher than he would have preferred. Italy, Japan, Britain, and France gained concessions and advantages that he disliked. He staked much—in a sense, everything—however, on the League covenant and on its direct incorporation into the treaty, for in the councils of the League, wrongs perpetrated in 1919 could later be made right. Above all, the League provided a mechanism for the taming of the rivalries and hatreds of the nations and ridding the world of the scourge of war. Having compromised in Europe, he could not further concede in the United States. The treaty and the covenant that he carried in his breast pocket as he debarked from the *George Washington* on July 8, 1919, was, for him, a sacred document, not to be sullied by the sordid and provincial objections of his political enemies.

Wilson's fierce commitment to ratification of the treaty without significant modification derived from three strands of experience and character. First, his deep religious convictions reflected no mere bland, generic Christianity but rather rested on a stubborn Calvinist bedrock that sustained his resolve in matters that he deemed of fundamental moral or ethical significance. Second, his powerful sense that he had sent men to die and that their deaths, and the wounds that maimed so many thousands, had to be redeemed through his own personal efforts reinforced this deep religious impulse. And third, and perhaps most significantly, the Woodrow Wilson who battled for the treaty in the summer and fall of 1919 was gravely ill, afflicted with physical ailments that clouded his judgment, reinforced his natural stubbornness, and made the normal processes of political exchange and negotiation all but impossible for him.

The actual debate over the treaty was a protracted and complex exercise in public discourse and political maneuvering that lasted from the time of Wilson's brief return to the United States in February 1919 through the presidential election of 1920. From the beginning, two facts were clear to most close observers: A majority of the American people supported ratification of the treaty and participation in the League of Nations; significant partisan, ideological, and practical differences nonetheless sharply divided proponents as to the precise terms under which America should participate in the new world order. Apart from a handful of "irreconcilables," senators who flatly opposed the treaty, the members of the Senate publicly favored ratification. The problem was that many senators insisted on hedging U.S. participation with "reservations," statements of exception or interpretation that would trump the specific words of the covenant, imposing specific limitations on how America could act in League deliberations and in response to League policies.

Various senators offered various reservations. Indeed, at Paris after his mid-conference trip to the United States, Wilson had reluctantly agreed to several to be incorporated into the final draft of the League covenant. Thus, he acceded to provisions that allowed a country to withdraw from the League, that guaranteed that no domestic matters would be subject to League action, and that removed any implication that America's Monroe Doctrine would be affected by membership in the League. The need to appease domestic interests by including such special understandings in turn weakened Wilson's hand in resisting Japanese, British, and Italian claims for their own special concerns. Nonetheless, if incorporation of these provisions satisfied domestic critics and thus paved the way for ratification, the president was willing to bow to necessity. But further he would not go, particularly rejecting demands that the covenant be severed from the treaty so that debate on it could take place after the restoration of peace with Germany.

Through the summer and fall of 1919, Wilson grew ever more adamant in his insistence on ratification without further reservation. Because of the Republican victory in the 1918 congressional elections, the chairman of the Senate Committee on Foreign Relations, in whose councils debate over the treaty would focus, was now Henry Cabot Lodge of Massachusetts. A shrewd, partisan, veteran lawmaker, Lodge hated Wilson with the visceral hatred of many in the Republican Party. Wilson, in Lodge's view, was an arrogant, sanctimonious, reckless politician who masked his lust for power with empty, but impressive-sounding, rhetoric. A tool, Lodge believed, of the provincial southerners who dominated the Democratic Party, Wilson had gained the presidency only because of Republican division. In his moralistic appeals, as now embodied in the covenant, Wilson threatened to impose his imprint permanently on an ill-informed and distracted public and to bind the United States to his unrealistic and unworkable notions of world order. No isolationist, Lodge readily agreed that the United States must play an active role in the postwar world. He even supported in principle a treaty with Britain and France guaranteeing the latter from renewed German attack. He could even contemplate participation in a league of nations. But any such participation had to adhere rigidly to constitutional requirements regarding the separation of powers and the rights and prerogatives of Congress and had to square with the tangible realities of a world still dominated by autonomous nation states. And as chairman of the Committee on Foreign Relations, Lodge played a crucial role in determining the sequence of events and in shaping the debate.

Wilson reciprocated Lodge's hatred. Moreover, he had a low opinion of the wisdom and even the patriotism of most of the members of the Senate, regarding them as petty partisan politicians. In February 1919, shown for the first time his newborn grandson, the president remarked, "With his mouth open and his eyes shut, I predict that he will make a senator when he grows up." He treated senatorial allies, such as Minority Leader Gilbert Hitchcock of Nebraska, as veritable errand boys, ignoring their advice while expecting worshipful loyalty. As to the Constitution's requirement that the president secure the "advice and consent" of the Senate in treaty-making, Wilson had ignored the Senate in selecting the peace delegation and had not otherwise sought senatorial involvement in Paris. When advisers suggested that senatorial statements critical of the emerging treaty might jeopardize his grand project, Wilson responded that when he returned to the United States he would "lick those fellows in the Senate."[43]

Unfortunately for Wilson, he would have to face the battle to gain ratification of the treaty without the benefit of the solid liberal support he had enjoyed throughout his presidency. Previously pro-Wilson progressives remained critical of what they deemed the harsh treatment of Germany, the granting of territorial concessions to Japan in China, the imposition of reparations, and other features. Indeed, by mid-1919, progressives had become deeply disillusioned with Wilson and with the great crusade for a more fair and equitable society, both domestically and internationally, that had sustained their support for the war. Counterrevolutionary intervention in Russia; the brutal suppression of civil liberties in America; the abandonment of organized labor; and the rapid, almost frantic, dismantling of promising war-related social welfare and regulatory programs all combined with the disappointments of the peace treaty to turn the bellwether liberal magazine *The New Republic* against the president. The words of Randolph Bourne, an antiwar progressive who from the start had warned that the war would inevitably unleash forces of repression, militarism, and intolerance, now seemed ruefully prescient.

Some progressive senators, notably Robert M. La Follette of Wisconsin and George Norris of Nebraska, both with large German American constituencies, similarly linked opposition to the treaty itself with attacks on the domestic policies of the administration. Most of the debate in the Senate over the treaty, however, focused on the League covenant. Its provision for a new structure of world order and an unprecedented role for the United States in the affairs of nations, which Wilson and his supporters saw as harbingers of a new, progressive world order, raised profound and troubling questions. Many Americans adhered to more traditional notions of foreign policy and were anxious to preserve the nation's freedom of action in the wake of the Great War. And no one more articulately or tenaciously subjected the treaty and the covenant to scrutiny from this angle of vision than Senator Lodge.

Thus, the Massachusetts lawmaker resolved to subject the treaty to searching and protracted public debate. He worried that wartime habits of deference to presidential leadership would override detailed examination of the covenant. In addition, he feared that division within his own Republican Party would play into the wily Wilson's hands. On the one hand, Lodge had to accommodate internationalist-minded Republicans such as former President William Howard Taft who favored the treaty. On the other, however, there were the irreconcilables such as Senators Hiram Johnson of California and William E. Borah of Idaho, who saw the treaty and League as little more than a facade for preservation of the British Empire. Thus Lodge used his position as chairman of the Foreign Relations Committee to delay senatorial consideration and attenuate debate while building a GOP consensus. In July he consumed two full weeks of committee time by having the entire treaty read aloud and then scheduled no fewer than sixty witnesses to present testimony, most of it critical of Wilson's proposed league.

Even among those favorably inclined toward the treaty and participation in a league of nations, there were fears. The treaty, even some supporters worried, left America vulnerable to outside dictation of its foreign policies and perhaps even committed the country to the use of military force without the approval of Congress. Democratic senators, although generally loyal to the president, shared some of these concerns. Throughout the summer and early fall of 1919, pro-League members of both parties advanced various packages of reservations, designed to protect American prerogatives while committing the nation to partnership in the new world order.

Although senatorial and broader public debate addressed many of the specific features of the League covenant, it was Article 10 that dominated discussion and that most sharply divided Wilson from his critics. In the final draft of the covenant, it read this way:

> The Members of the League undertake to respect and preserve as against external aggression the territorial integrity and existing political independence of all Members of the League. In case of any such aggression or in case of any threat or danger of such aggression, the Council shall advise upon the means by which this obligation shall be fulfilled.

Here was a seemingly bold statement in behalf of "collective security," a new approach to the resolution of disputes among nations that sought to foster delay, debate, and accommodation while obviating the need for military alliances and secret understandings. If the death and the destruction of the Great War were to have any transcendent meaning, Wilson believed, it lay in the adoption of this new, hopeful method of conducting the affairs of nations.

But Article 10, for all the simplicity of its language, left the answers to key questions uncertain. Did these words mean that decisions of the League Council, consisting of the five major victorious powers as permanent members and four others chosen for specific terms, would commit the United States to go to war against another nation deemed an aggressor? If so, what of the U.S. Constitution's reserving of war-declaring powers to Congress? To be sure, the permanent members of the Council, which would include the United States, had the right of veto over any Council decision, but even so, in case of a divided government—such as the case prevailing in the wake of the 1918 elections—could a war-bent administration agree to military action even though a majority of Congress opposed it?

Critics also charged that Article 10 froze the international status quo, in effect outlawing challenges to colonial powers on the part of subordinated nationalist movements. Had Article 10 been in effect in 1776, critics claimed, King George could have called upon the League of Nations to impose economic sanctions and even wage war against George Washington and the patriot cause. The current effect of Article 10, claimed Senator Borah, was to align the United States with colonial powers such as Britain and France against the wishes of subject peoples. What, for example, of the revolt of the Irish Republicans against Great Britain, raging even as the Senate deliberated? Would Article 10 obligate the United States to join the British in suppressing this struggle for Irish independence? The fact that the British Empire had six votes in the League Assembly—one each for Canada, New Zealand, South Africa, India, Australia, and Great Britain itself—further fueled suspicion of the covenant as a tool of British imperial interests and provided grist for the mills of anti-Wilson and anti-League forces.

Many of these fears, doubts, and objections were exaggerated. Partisan determination to embarrass the president and his party, the pandering to large and influential electoral blocs of Irish American and German American constituencies, and dogged commitment to ill-understood national traditions of isolationism further clouded the issue. But Article 10 was genuinely problematic, as even Wilson implicitly acknowledged. Drafted with the intention of discouraging aggression and furthering the cause of collective security, Article 10 could be seen as meaning that the United States had a legal obligation to take action, including military force, at the behest of the League Council. To be sure, as Wilson never tired of pointing out, no one seriously believed that any American president would jeopardize the lives of American soldiers without first securing the support of Congress and the public. But in that case, was not Article 10 misleading and potentially embarrassing? Did not its language commit the United States to something its government would not, in fact, implement? Far better, Lodge and even those more sympathetic to the League concept argued, to declare forthrightly that Article 10 would not, in fact, bind the United States to any actions that its constituted governing bodies, notably Congress, did not independently endorse. Thus the words of a key reservation offered in November 1919 by Lodge:

> The United States assumes no obligation to preserve the territorial integrity or political independence of any other country . . . under the provision of Article 10, or to employ the military or naval forces of the United States . . . unless in any particular case the Congress . . . shall . . . so provide.

Such a reservation was, in fact, a realistic statement of what would inevitably be U.S. policy, whatever the text of Article 10 said. Wilson, however, believed that collective security was so important in the effort to scrap the old, war-generating world order—and that Article 10 was so critical to the furthering of collective security—that Lodge's "reservation" was in reality an attempt on the part of the Massachusetts senator to gut the covenant's central feature.

Wilson sought to answer the charge that Article 10 compromised American constitutional strictures by insisting that under its terms the country assumed not *legal* responsibilities to act in accordance with League policy but rather only *moral* obligations. Clearly, no power existed or could compel an American president to send troops to, say, Syria or New Guinea, or to compel Congress to give its approval or appropriate funds for such ventures. But the United States must willingly accept *in principle* the understanding that the success of collective security required the abridgment of national autonomy, even if in practical terms the normal constitutional forms would prevail. "Article X," Wilson declared in September, "is the heart of the enterprise. Article X is the test of the honor and courage and endurance of the world."[44] This being the case, even though he might acknowledge that *practically* congressional endorsement was necessary for the actual implementation of U.S. obligations under Article 10, "reservations" such as that offered by Lodge amounted to a substantive amendment to the covenant and thus could not be accepted.

Even critics friendly to the idea of a League found Wilson's logic elusive. Were not moral commitments, especially in the Wilsonian world view, more solemn than mere legal obligations? Would not the current acceptance of far-reaching moral obligations place future administrations in an impossible dilemma? They would have either to adhere to League dictates and thus violate the Constitution or, more likely, repudiate a solemn moral obligation. If, Senator Lodge insisted, "it goes without saying" that U.S. constitutional strictures in effect qualified our understanding of the meaning of Article 10, "there can be no harm in saying it."[45]

The objections of Lodge and his fellow "strong reservationists" raised legitimate questions about constitutional authority and national identity. This was no mere struggle between the "idealistic" Wilson and the "realistic" Lodge. The Massachusetts senator and his staunch, mostly Republican, allies did not lack a high-minded and "idealistic" vision of America and its role in the world. Valuing discipline, military valor, and national autonomy, Lodge and his more thoughtful adherents sought to make the covenant consonant with traditional, but by no means cynical or tawdry, conceptions of America's destiny. For his part, alongside his determination to create mechanisms for preventing war, Wilson believed that a prosperous, undamaged America was uniquely positioned to exert influence and to flourish commercially in a new world order that rejected traditional diplomatic maneuvering, military alliances, and secret arrangements. Both sides sought leadership roles for triumphant America and both projected high-minded, if nationally self-serving, conceptions of its future role. Thus declares historian John Milton Cooper, "Lodge sought to preserve power politics as the arena for exhibiting the finest traits of individual and national character" and Wilson "sought to weave together individual and national interest into a community of peace and happiness."[46]

Late in the summer of 1919, frustrated by the protracted hearings in the Committee on Foreign Relations and sensing that the initiative in the treaty fight was slipping from his grasp, Wilson resolved to appeal over the heads of the Senate directly to the American people. Convinced of the righteousness of his cause and of popular support for it, he mapped out a grueling speaking schedule in the belief that he could generate a groundswell of pro-League sentiment and break the logjam in the Senate. Thus, on September 4, 1919, he set out aboard a presidential train "to go out," as he told his first audience in Columbus, Ohio, "and report to my fellow countrymen concerning those affairs of the world which now need to be settled." The president's train described a wide arc, chugging from the Ohio capital to St. Louis and Kansas City by way of Indianapolis. He spoke in Des Moines, St. Paul, Minneapolis, Bismarck, Helena, and Coeur d'Alene before reaching Spokane and Seattle. Then down the coast to Portland, San Francisco, Los Angeles, and San Diego. To joint sessions of state legislatures, business luncheons, and huge public meetings held in auditoriums and fair grounds he drove home his message that the treaty, and especially the covenant, for all of their limitations, remained the best hope for securing a peaceful world. Repeatedly, he challenged the American people to honor the sacrifices of their fighting men by demanding that their senators ratify the treaty as presented, without significant reservation. America's soldiers and sailors had fought heroically, and now "There is only one honorable course when you have won a cause—to see that it stays won. . . . And that is the purpose of the much-discussed Article X," he insisted before a California audience.[47]

From the start of the tour, Wilson had shown signs of fatigue. Headaches, sometimes blinding ones, afflicted him. He had difficulty breathing and slept poorly. In San Francisco on September 17, his physician, Dr. Cary Grayson, feared a physical breakdown, but Wilson rallied to deliver a stirring speech. A week later in Utah, Grayson became more alarmed. "The President," he recorded, "was suffering very serious fatigue. . . . The trip was far too strenuous" and threatened "to exhaust every possible bit of vitality that the President had." At last, after speeches in Denver and Pueblo, Colorado, on September 25, Wilson's body gave out. That night, he could not sleep and Grayson found him "in a highly nervous condition." His facial muscles twitched and his breathing was labored. The next morning, Grayson and Wilson's personal secretary, Joseph Tumulty, persuaded the initially reluctant president to cancel the rest of his speeches. Eventually, even Wilson acknowledged the gravity of his illness, telling Tumulty "I seem to have gone to pieces. . . . I am not in a condition to go on." The presidential train then sped through the night, bound directly for Washington.[48]

A week after returning to the White House, the president suffered a massive stroke, paralyzing his right side and, for five weeks, keeping him in seclusion. Even after the crisis had passed, he lived as an invalid, able to work for only short stretches, in need of lengthy rest periods, and capable of seeing visitors only under the most tightly controlled conditions.

Meanwhile, the treaty debate was reaching a climax. On November 6, Lodge introduced fourteen reservations, the most significant of which concerned Article 10. Two weeks later, Wilson instructed Democratic senators to vote against the treaty with the Lodge reservations attached, which they did the next day, ensuring its defeat. Then the Senate turned down by a vote of 38 to 53 a Democratic motion to ratify the treaty as originally submitted. For the next four months, senatorial supporters of the treaty worked to arrange a compromise, proposing various packages of reservations and understandings. At last, on March 19, 1920, with the slightly recast Lodge reservations attached to it, the treaty once again came up for a Senate vote. Although British and French leaders made it known that they could accept the Lodge reservations and would welcome U.S. ratification on virtually any basis,

Wilson once again instructed Democratic senators to vote to reject. Twenty-one in fact defected, voting for the treaty despite the Lodge reservations, but enough remained loyal to Wilson to secure the treaty's defeat; this time it gained a majority of votes (49 to 35), but it fell victim to the Constitution's requirement of a two-thirds majority for treaty ratification. Undaunted and still believing that "the people" would punish his opponents for what he considered a betrayal of his fallen comrades, Wilson placed his hopes in the forthcoming presidential election, believing that his adversaries would be punished and the treaty vindicated by popular mandate.

It was in these final months that Wilson's illness was decisive. Until the time of his stroke, he might have been able to reach an agreement with a sufficient number of Republican supporters of the treaty to outmaneuver Lodge. In the past, Wilson had proved a skillful congressional operator, achieving passage of controversial legislation despite the slimness of his pre-1918 Democratic majorities. Perhaps his passionate, if sometimes confusing, appeals for a reservationless covenant might have rallied the public to his cause, as the enthusiastic audiences for his speeches throughout the West suggested. Perhaps, having demonstrated overwhelming public support for the League and having plausibly shown critics the danger they faced from an aroused electorate, Wilson might have been able, through Hitchcock and other proxies, to soften GOP support for Lodge and to steer a version of the original treaty—with, no doubt, some reservations—through to ratification. In his prime as a national leader, Wilson could be as calculating and as astute as any successful politician. Having played his trumps and having moved the opposition toward the center, a lucid and realistic leader might have emerged with the essence of the treaty and the covenant intact.

But Wilson's illness seemed to rob him of nuanced judgment. He grew increasingly bitter at Republican attacks and increasingly willful in imposing his views on the Democratic senators. It was almost as if ratification of the treaty and entry into the League of Nations had taken second place to his need for personal redemption. It would be better, he said on more than one occasion, to go down in defeat than to accept the quibbles and compromises that lesser men proposed. He even apparently entertained fantastic hopes of running for a third term, bringing the treaty and the covenant directly before the people in "a great and solemn referendum" in 1920. When in February he riposted, "Let Lodge extend the olive branch!" to aides who urged him to bargain, he appeared to have cut loose from his otherwise well-tuned politician's grasp of reality.[49] But an enfeebled, embittered, and perhaps martyrdom-seeking Wilson refused to realize that an exercise of judicious restraint and face-saving compromise might still win the day.

There was no "great and solemn referendum" on the treaty and covenant during the presidential election of 1920. Although Democratic candidates James M. Cox and Franklin D. Roosevelt dutifully charged their Republican opponents with sabotaging the peace treaty, there was no evidence that the treaty or the League played a major role in the outcome. Traditional sectional and party electoral alignments, temporarily shaken during the decade of the Great War, reasserted themselves. Republican candidate Warren G. Harding rolled to a landslide victory, carrying with him overwhelming Republican congressional majorities. In July 1921, Congress declared the war with Germany to be over and in October, the Senate ratified brief treaties with Germany, Austria, and Hungary.

Thus the American people's involvement with the Great War ended not with national commitment to a bold new adventure in international affairs but in perfunctory legal closure. Not long before his death in 1924, Wilson's daughter Margaret found the former president in a contemplative mood one day as they passed the afternoon hours together in the house in Washington, D.C., to which Wilson had retired. "I think," he confided, "it was best after all that the United States did not join the League of Nations" in 1919 or 1920. Surprised, she asked the reason. "Because," Wilson replied, "our entrance into the League at the time I returned from Europe might have been only a personal victory. Now," he continued, "when the American people [do] join the League it will be because they are convinced it is the only right time for them to do it." He concluded, "Perhaps God knew better than I did after all."[50] The United States never did join the League of Nations, of course, but at the end of another great war in 1945, it did help to launch the League's successor organization, the United Nations. Far less ambitious than the earlier League in its expectations and mechanisms for encouraging peaceful resolution of disputes, the United Nations nonetheless reflected important elements of the Wilsonian world view. It also, however, reflected the spirit of the Lodge reservations, carefully specifying the rights of independent nations and qualifying obligations to implement U.N. actions. In effect, the terms under which the United States embarked in 1945 on participation in the United Nations achieved the compromise between Wilsonian "idealism" and Lodge's "realism" that had proved so elusive in 1920.

EIGHT

Questions for Americans

For many years after the defeat of the Versailles Treaty by the U.S. Senate in 1919–20, the question of America's role in the Great War remained a vivid and lively matter of public debate and political controversy. In the 1920s and 1930s, questions as to whether Woodrow Wilson's decision for war had been right remained central in foreign policy discussions. The rejection of the Versailles Treaty likewise continued to be a source of bitter partisan and political debate. In entering the war when and how it did, was the United States following "the command of gold," as Senator George W. Norris had charged in 1917 and as revisionist historians and politicians argued in the 1930s? Had munitions makers and their financial backers maneuvered a naive president into launching his ill-advised crusade? Had wily British propaganda duped innocent Americans into demonizing Germany and sending American boys to fight in a war that brought in its wake only disillusionment and renewed international rivalry?

Countering these criticisms of Wilson and American involvement in the Great War were the arguments of those who believed that Wilson's great vision remained powerful and compelling. Historians such as Charles Seymour and critics of the isolationism of the 1930s contended that it was the narrow-minded and cynical opponents of the League of Nations who had betrayed the American people. Senator Henry Cabot Lodge and his Republican cohorts had fed the flames of the isolationism that prevented America from responding effectively to German, Italian, and Japanese aggression.

In the 1930s and 1940s, these debates over the meaning of U.S. participation and its failure to join the League of Nations continued to be acrimonious and intensely political. In 1934–35, widely publicized hearings conducted by North Dakota Republican Senator Gerald Nye were aimed at demonstrating the responsibility of profit-hungry munitions makers and conscienceless financiers for the decision to send troops to Europe. The committee's disclosures fueled an isolationist movement that was determined to avoid the errors of judgment and sentiment that had misled Wilson and the American people into a disastrous abandonment of their traditions of noninvolvement in European conflicts. At the end of World War II, from a diametrically opposite perspective, supporters of the new United Nations and advocates of an active foreign policy in response to the perceived threat of Soviet communism pointed to the rejection of the Versailles Treaty, failure to join the League of Nations, and retreat into sterile isolationism as critical factors in America's failure to respond until it was almost too late to the aggression that triggered another world war. For politicians such as Nye, Senators William E. Borah, Robert A. Taft, and Burton K. Wheeler; policymakers such as George Kennan and Dean Acheson; and Presidents Franklin Roosevelt and Harry S. Truman, controversy over the events of 1914–20 was no mere exercise in historiographical disputation but rather a vital component of contemporary public debate.

More recently, of course, the presumed lessons and warnings contained in the events of 1914–20 have receded from everyday political discourse. The isolationist–interventionist debates of the 1930s and 1940s have receded and with them public consciousness of the Great War era as an active factor in foreign policy determination. Issues such as military preparedness and intervention in the affairs of Europe, which were in the forefront of political conflict at the time of the Great War, have long since been resolved, continuing debate dealing only with the details.

Historians, however, have continued to address the events of the Great War era. Increasingly, they have been less concerned with direct judgments on the wisdom and legitimacy of U.S. policies both before and after the American declaration of war and more focused on the meaning and implications of these policies and actions. To be sure, Wilson still has his defenders and critics. Monographs, dissertations, and journal articles continue to add to the understanding of U.S.–British relations, the economic aspects of U.S. policy, relations between the president and his domestic constituencies during the treaty-making and treaty-debating process, and related issues.

Particularly since the 1960s, however, historians have tended to be less concerned with the details of Wilsonian diplomacy and more with its overall thrust and implications. Historians of foreign relations in the 1920s, for example, have persuasively challenged the view that isolationism reigned in the wake of the rejection of the treaty. They have pointed to the continuing importance of foreign trade and finance to the American economy, arguing that Wilson's postwar initiatives and the goals of his most bitter critics were alike in being predicated on growing American economic hegemony. Treaty or no Treaty, League or no League, argue such historians as Carl Parini and

William A. Williams, the United States emerged from the Great War with both a moral vision and economic ambitions that generated an active foreign policy. In this view, Wilsonian internationalism rested on and was implicated in America's extensive economic interests. It was merely one version of a generic American internationalism that, apart from a brief resurgence of classic isolationism in the mid-1930s, has continued to govern U.S. foreign relations from the era of the Great War until the present day. Scholar and activist Noam Chomsky has more recently promoted a particularly harsh version of this view of U.S. foreign policy, stressing the ruthlessness with which economic elites and policymakers have promoted U.S. interests behind a Wilsonian smokescreen.

To other historians, best represented by John Lewis Gaddis, however, the stress on economic developments and material interests, either during Wilson's era or more recently, reverses the central themes of American diplomacy. To be sure, Gaddis freely acknowledges, economic goals and related geostrategic interests played an important role in twentieth-century U.S. diplomacy, just as these factors always play important roles in any nation's foreign relations. But what was distinctive about America in the twentieth century was its consistent resistance to authoritarianism. In Gaddis's view, the Wilsonian vision has remained strong and has outpaced the Leninist vision that seemed such a compelling alternative in the wake of global conflict. True, there were gapping chasms between Wilson's (and America's) professions of freedom and equality, on the one hand, and the nation's often arrogant and high-handed treatment of smaller countries, on the other. But the United States was not unique in the gap between its proclaimed ideals and its failures. After all, what greater tragedy could there have been than the chasm between the communist dream of a new world and the unspeakable horrors of real existing communism? Thus, although the names of Woodrow Wilson and Henry Cabot Lodge are rarely heard these days on the political hustings, as they commonly were as late as the 1950s, broader historical perspectives on the meanings and implications of America's role in the Great War remain lively issues for those who think broadly about world order at the dawning of the twenty-first century.[1]

In comparison with political and historiographical debate over foreign policy, controversy over the domestic aspects of America's Great War has been more muted. It is not hard to trace the roots of what historian Ronald Schaffer aptly calls the "war welfare" state back to the policy innovations of the American war effort. Even though in the 1920s, government activism receded, in 1933 and 1934, when President Franklin Roosevelt's New Dealers sought precedents and examples of how government might respond to economic and social crisis, they instinctively turned to the experiments in social welfare, labor relations, and economic mobilization in which many of them had participated during World War I. To be sure, some historians continue to debate the precise relationship of wartime innovations to subsequent federal policies, and others focus attention on the wartime experiences of hitherto neglected groups, notably women and African Americans. Exploration of the meaning and implications of postwar domestic turbulence continues: Was the Red Scare a frightening aberration or were the instruments of government surveillance and repression, forged during the war, the signature features of the new and enduring National Security State?

These and other questions continue to make the era of the Great War of compelling interest to students of history. Although America's Great War exhibited less of the existential tragedy and the sense of futility and waste than did the experiences of the European powers, it was and has remained a crucial episode in the nation's modern history. The effort of historians to come to grips with that experience has rarely produced definitive answers. Indeed, final answers are probably not what should be expected of historians in any event. Perhaps what students can most fairly expect of the historians they read is, at minimum, identification and forthright discussion of the key questions and, occasionally, fresh ways of perceiving the people who lived and the events that occurred in the ever-shifting past that it is perilous to attempt to ignore or escape.

Some Central Questions

How representative and legitimate a spokesman for American values and interests was Woodrow Wilson during the era of the Great War?

Wilson's fervent and specific religious commitment separated him from his countrymen. Although his beliefs in American exceptionalism and in the beneficence of Providence with respect to America were commonplace, he brought to political life a degree of religious passion and a determination to apply his understanding of Christian beliefs that was rare among practicing politicians. Of all U.S. presidents, only Jimmy Carter has exhibited a similarly intense and specific notion of Christian identity as applied to public life. During the first part of his presidency, dealing as it largely did with domestic affairs, Wilson could square his sense of Christian mission with the give-and-take necessary for concrete legislative and political success. The war, however, raised the stakes, and his belief in America as the final epitome of Christian mission finally found an object worthy of this transcendent vision. His translation of broad religious beliefs into concrete policies and programs—notably with respect to the League of Nations covenant—cut him loose from the base of public support that was his so long as people could see his goals as generic rather than specific. His sense of sacred obligation, likely affected by his devastating illness, changed from a bracing determination to keep faith with the war dead to an intransigent adherence to a specific formula for U.S. involvement in the postwar world. This earnest personal application of his religious understanding to the complex problems of the postwar order made Wilson, in the end, unrepresentative and finally illegitimate as the would-be guide to America's postwar course.

Were U.S. policies from 1914 to 1917 unfairly weighted toward the Allies?

German statesmen should have considered the American factor before risking war with the Entente in 1914. Given the patterns of international trade and finance that then prevailed, the United States could not help but contribute to Britain's (and hence the Allies') war-making capacity. It was not Wilson's fault that the Germans opted to wage a two-front war; even if British statesmen are to be condemned for not earlier announcing their intent to enter the war, German leaders still merit criticism for unwillingness to contemplate a worst-case scenario. The contribution of American trade and finances to the Allied war effort was no more unneutral or unfair to Germany than a policy of denying trade to the Allies would have been to Germany's enemies. Although American trade with the Allies soon far surpassed prewar levels, although the trade in munitions was controversial, and although the scale of U.S. trade soon required immense financial lubrication, the fact of U.S. economic enmeshment with Great Britain was sufficiently well established before the war to have given prudent statesmen cause for caution and restraint.

Moreover, Wilson was right to distinguish between German U-boat warfare and British maritime restrictions. The latter, although extremely galling and obnoxious, did not take American lives. Torpedoes did. Since 1915, the world has become accustomed to all sorts of murderous attacks on civilians. Wilson's concerns over the rights of U.S. citizens to travel on neutral ships or passenger ships seem naive, even disingenuous. But Wilson quite legitimately saw himself as the one powerful voice in a world at war whose words and policies might moderate the savagery. And indeed for more than a year, it seemed that he had won the day and done something no other twentieth-century statesman has been able to do, namely place limits around the use of otherwise-effective weapons during wartime.

There is one aspect of the unfairness question, however, that remains troubling. The de facto British blockade of Germany likely took more civilian lives than did the entire U-boat campaign. Should not fairness have demanded that the United States be at least as energetic in seeking moderation of the blockade on humanitarian grounds as it was in condemning submarine attacks? Could not Wilson have used Allied dependence on American money and supplies to force moderation of the blockade, quite independently of his legitimate and, until 1917, successful effort to regulate submarine warfare? In implicitly regarding the blockade, with its widespread civilian suffering, as less heinous than instantly lethal submarine attacks, Wilson perhaps betrayed his reflexive (and hence "unfair") tilt toward Britain.

Was the United States justified in declaring war on Germany?

U.S. entry may have saved Europe from chaos and revolution, thus enabling Western civilization to draw back, at least temporarily, from the abyss. Whether Western civilization deserved to be saved is another question. Suffice it to say that if the positive features of life in the West—representative government, individual rights, the rule of law, freedom of conscience—were to be salvaged, it was up to America to do so, and this U.S. belligerency did. As the war brutally revealed, of course, the West was no paragon of wisdom or virtue. The history of the West's relations with the rest of the world before 1914 is marked by arrogance, racism, exploitation, and violence. Wilson showed little awareness of the crimes of Western imperialism, and in deciding to ask for a declaration of war, he pointed to the unwelcome rise of colored peoples, eager to benefit from Europe's agony, as a justification for U.S. belligerency. So was the West worth saving? Do Western achievements outweigh Western crimes? These are questions for individual rumination and are not subject to definitive answer. But if the responses are affirmative, the world owes a great debt to the doughboys.

Wilson's war message, high-minded and eloquent, actually is not very clear as the bases of U.S. belligerency. His formulation seems to have been along these lines: The renewed U-boat campaign revealed that an autocratic German government would stop at nothing to achieve its ends, namely military conquest and eventual political domination and economic exploitation of the rest of Europe. The United States must punish the German government for breaking its word and prevent it from realizing its broader aims. In the process of doing this, the United States must lead all the belligerents toward a safer, more democratic future through the creation of new instruments of international order. Only in achieving these ends could America be truly safe and secure in the modern world. This formulation was too concrete (punishment of Germany for maritime depredations), too partisan (because in truth, all the belligerents had ambitious territorial and economic aims), and too abstract (because success in the war could only be claimed when a new, American-led world order was in place). In this message and other statements, Wilson came close to defining the American mission in terms of rescuing Europe, but he never quite spelled out the mechanics and implications of this goal.

One other nagging question remains unsettled, namely the character of the German state, both during the Great War and in the "short" twentieth century more generally. Especially after the ascendancy of Erich Ludendorff as the de facto German military chief, Germany took on many of the attributes of a military dictatorship. Moreover, it is clear that as the war progressed, nationalist, military, and industrial forces in Germany advanced sweeping territorial claims, often couched in racist terms. Were these goals implicit in the character of Wilhelmine society? Was the Germany of 1914 the Germany of 1939 in embryo? Was the wartime German state in some essential way uniquely aggressive and aggrandizing? Was there a kernel of truth in Allied (and American) propaganda about the particular perniciousness of the German polity and German *Kultur*? The Treaty of Brest-Litovsk in March 1918 and the behavior of German military authorities in territories occupied by the army point in these directions. In his war message, Wilson made a careful distinction between the autocratic German government and the victimized German people, but by the end of the war he had come to impute an essential lust for power to the German people at large. Were the horrors and the excesses of the Third Reich implicit in the agenda and practices of the wartime Second Reich? If so, U.S. intervention came none too soon. If not, the case for intervention rests largely on more concrete questions of how best to bring the war to a conclusion and erect a new framework for international relations.

Was the settlement that Wilson brought home from France enlightened, or was it merely a victor's peace?

There are two parts to this question: what the Treaty of Versailles and League of Nations covenant specified and what they left out. With reference to the first part, what was specified, the answer to the question is positive. It is true that important features of the treaty were punitive and retrograde, notably the war guilt clause and certain territorial and political arrangements. On the whole, however, a peace settlement that established the beginnings of arms limitations and recognized, in however rudimentary and inconsistent a form, the claims of human rights was a positive step. The League, although smacking too much of a victors' club, provided a forum for the airing of grievances, including those distasteful to the great powers. Wilson was right to believe that League actions and deliberations could moderate some of the excesses and injustices of the treaty, although he was wrong to believe that those who drafted the covenant had created a transcendent new international order that no longer had room for traditional diplomatic and military concerns.

But the treaty and the League of Nations covenant were silent on key issues. Where the treaty and the covenant fell far short of enlightenment and assumed most blatantly the character of a victors' peace was in the area of colonialism. True, the mandate system, although far from a ringing affirmation of the rights of colonial peoples, did impose limits on military and economic exploitation of subject peoples and did substitute public international oversight for unchallengeable imperial prerogatives. But mandates, with all their limitations on protection of native peoples, applied only to former German colonies. The covenant said nothing about the subject peoples of the British, French, Italian, Japanese, and American empires, who were accorded no rights and no representation, either at Versailles or in the League of Nations. "The problem of the twentieth century," W. E. B. Du Bois wrote in 1906, "is the problem of the color line." Despite the sufferings and sacrifices of colored peoples in behalf of the Allied cause, despite the solemn invocation of democracy and national self-determination, neither the treaty nor the covenant offered anything to Indians, Senegalese, Filipinos, or Algerians. That the only influential voice asserting the claims of colonial peoples to come out of the Great War was that of the Bolsheviks is a telling indictment of the Wilsonian peacemakers.

Who was responsible for the failure of the U.S. Senate to ratify the Versailles Treaty and for the failure of the United States to join the League of Nations?

The blame for the defeat of the treaty and the League covenant rests squarely with Woodrow Wilson. As late as March 1920, a nod from him to his Democratic senatorial followers would have ensured ratification of the treaty and hence U.S. membership in the League. British and French acceptance even of the Lodge reservations removed the most compelling reason for Wilson's adamancy. Through the time of his speaking tour, a strong case existed for the course the president pursued. His intransigence at the outset of the ratification fight, along with his impressive ability to mobilize support for his views, had backed Lodge and his fellow Republicans into a corner. They would have found negotiations as to the precise wording and scope of reservations with a successful war president difficult. Wilson's impatient response to those who urged him in February 1920 to deal with Lodge—"Let Lodge extend the olive branch!"—is revealing. At this stage, Lodge could not have *avoided* compromising without facing the charge that his stand had been insincere from the outset. Wilson never played the cards dealt him by substantial Republican support for a version of the treaty, such as that voiced by former President William Howard Taft. In mounting his assault, Wilson believed that he was keeping faith with the soldiers he had sent to die in France. By going head-to-head with Lodge, however, an illness-weakened and judgment-impaired Wilson lost any chance of redeeming their sacrifice with American approval of the League covenant. As evidenced by his unrealistic dreams of running for a third term and his naive belief that an American presidential election campaign could be waged as a referendum on one issue, Wilson's political sense abandoned him when he most needed it.

Did the domestic wartime and postwar experience expose fatal flaws in the worldview of liberal progressives?

Writer and critic Randolph Bourne thought so. To this young New Jersey-born critic and writer, once a dedicated follower of Progressive icon John Dewey, the notion was absurd that war could bring social good in the form of regulation of business, public health programs, and amelioration of want and poverty. He ridiculed Dewey's bland confidence that wartime conditions would promote the progressive agenda by expanding "social control" (i.e., government regulation) over the country's chaotic economic system and reducing its festering poverty and injustice. War, Bourne countered, produced only intolerance, repression, and conformity. "War," he asserted in a posthumously published essay in 1918, "is the health of the state." Wartime government powers yoked citizens to the state's deadly apparatus; any steps toward social reform were temporary, inadvertent, and compromised. By the end of the war, even the editors of the *New Republic*, who had earlier disavowed their one-time colleague's antiwar stand, were acknowledging that the war-generated domestic repression and the disappointing character of the Versailles Treaty called into question their earlier optimism.

Indeed, evidences of the abuses of wartime agencies were plentiful. But Bourne shied away from important questions, ones that liberal progressives also relegated to the edge of their consciousness as they later sought to assimilate and learn from the Great War experience. Was it *ever* safe to rely on the powers of government to achieve social advance? Were the excesses of the Wilsonian wartime state aberrations traceable to the exigencies of war? Or were they endemic in *any* use of the state's ultimately terrifying power? Would the demands of the National Security State inevitably subsume those of the Welfare State even as they distorted and perhaps destroyed the liberties of the people? Was it possible to have a Welfare State without creating a Leviathan

State? Questions such as these, inchoately raised during America's Great War adventure, have remained central dilemmas for liberals throughout the twentieth century.

Where does the American people's experience during the Great War fit into the broader trajectory of the country's modern history?

With the onset of a new millennium, familiar and seemingly permanent chronological demarcations in American history seem to flatten out. Although, understandably, the events of 1914–20 seemed to those who experienced them as monumental in their intensity and importance, today they seem to merge into longer and more gradual trends. Where once, for example, the Russian Revolution of 1917 appeared destined to change forever the very bases of political, economic, and social life, today the wave of communism has receded, its monuments and mausoleums disdained and in ruins, even as the great cathedrals of the Middle Ages remain open and thriving.

In one important sense, the American Great War experience does seem to merge into the general twentieth-century experience of the people. Its most distinctive feature was perhaps its short duration, which lent to it a sense of impermanence and disjuncture. Whether the subject is military development, foreign policy, race relations, labor relations, women's status, or government functions, the Great War stimulated potentially powerful changes that were to end, abruptly, before they could take root. When, for example, did the vast U.S. military establishment, and the government and civilian agencies and institutions that undergird it, originate? In one sense, it originated during the Great War era, when Americans created an enormous army and first established the elaborate network of logistical, propaganda, research, and technical supports on which it depended. And yet, of course, over the next twenty years, that army atrophied, with only skeletal remnants of the imposing infrastructure associated with the American Expeditionary Force visible in the 1930s.

At very least, the American experience in the Great War raised for the first time in modern form profound and enduring questions about values, institutions, and ways of life that continue to reverberate into the twenty-first century. Is the price of domestic prosperity and security chronic military engagement abroad? Is it possible to create and sustain a government that provides social benefits without at the same time compromising the essential liberties of the people? Can a polyglot nation transcend its heritage of racism and exclusionism in the service of worthy national purposes? Can America, with its enormous wealth and power, truly foster a peaceful and prosperous world order without attempting to impose a Pax Americana? Can Americans cherish and develop what historian Richard Hofstadter once called "the native decencies" without succumbing to the fallacy of claiming special virtues and privileges? These are pressing questions today, just as they were to the generation of the Great War. The ways in which the men and women of 1914–20 confronted, evaded, and reflected on them remain part of America's common, contested legacy.

Notes

Chapter One

1. Newspaper quotes from David Kennedy, "The World Wars," *Encyclopedia of the United States in the Twentieth Century*, 4 vols., editor-in-chief Stanley I. Kutler (New York: Scribner's, 1996), vol. 2, 621–22; Department of State release quoted in Harry Scheiber, "World War I as Entrepreneurial Opportunity: Willard Straight and the American International Corporation," *Political Science Quarterly* 84: 3 (Sept. 1969): 493–94.

2. Paul A. C. Koistinen, *Mobilizing for Modern War: The Political Economy of American Warfare, 1865–1919* (Lawrence: University Press of Kansas, 1997), 127.

3. Straight quoted in Scheiber, "World War I as Entrepreneurial Opportunity," 496.

4. John Milton Cooper, *The Vanity of Power: American Isolationism and the First World War, 1914–1917* (Westport, Conn.: Greenwood, 1969), 27–29.

5. Manly quoted in Scheiber, "World War I as Entrepreneurial Opportunity," 501; Harding letter to Benjamin Strong, November 16, 1916, quoted in Koistinen, *Mobilizing for Modern War*, 133.

6. Wilson quoted in August Heckscher, *Woodrow Wilson* (New York: Macmillan/ Collier, 1991), 337, 340.

7. Edwyn A. Gray, *The U-Boat War, 1914–1918* (reprint; London: Leo Cooper, 1994), 18, 21, 22.

8. The *Lusitania* notes, including various drafts and related correspondence, are found in *The Papers of Woodrow Wilson*, 69 vols., ed. Arthur S. Link (Princeton: Princeton University Press, 1980), vol. 33, passim.

9. Wood quoted in Kennedy, "The World Wars," 623.

Chapter Two

1. Martin Gilbert, *The First World War: A Complete History* (New York: Holt, 1994), 257.

2. Paul A. C. Koistinen, *Mobilizing for Modern War: The Political Economy of American Warfare, 1865–1919* (Lawrence: University Press of Kansas, 1997), 133–34.

3. Quoted in Harry Scheiber, "World War I as Entrepreneurial Opportunity: Willard Straight and the American International Corporation," *Political Science Quarterly* 84: 3 (September 1969): 500.

4. Quoted in Koistinen, *Mobilizing for Modern War*, 129.

5. Villard quoted in John Patrick Finnegan, *Against the Specter of a Dragon: The Campaign for American Military Preparedness, 1914–1917* (Westport, Conn.: Greenwood, 1974), 122.

6. First two quotes from ibid., 110, 111, respectively; third from *Chicago Tribune*, June 3, 1916.

7. Baker quoted in John A. Thompson, *Reformers and War: American Progressive Publicists and the First World War* (Cambridge: Cambridge University Press, 1987), 174–75.

8. Quoted in Finnegan, *Against the Specter of a Dragon*, 107.

9. General Wood quoted in Edward M. Coffman, *The War to End All Wars: The American Military Experience in World War I* (Oxford: Oxford University Press, 1968; reprint, Madison: University of Wisconsin Press, 1986), 14; Grenville Clark quoted in Finnegan, *Against the Specter of a Dragon*, 67.

10. Amos Pinchot quoted in David M. Kennedy, *Over Here: The First World War and American Society* (New York: Oxford University Press, 1980), 146; Quin quoted in Finnegan, *Against the Specter of a Dragon*, 121.

11. Finnegan, *Against the Specter of a Dragon*, 133.

12. Wilson is quoted in ibid., 73, and Coffman, *The War to End All Wars*, 87.

13. Quoted in Finnegan, *Against the Specter of a Dragon*, 94.

14. Patrick Devlin, *Too Proud to Fight: Woodrow Wilson's Neutrality* (New York: Oxford University Press, 1975), 517.

15. Wilson quoted in ibid., 440–41.

16. Quoted in John Milton Cooper, "The Command of Gold Reversed: American Loans to Britain, 1915–1917," *Pacific Historical Review* 45 (May 1976): 225.

17. This account is based on August Heckscher, *Woodrow Wilson: A Biography* (New York: Macmillan/Collier, 1991), 399–400.

18. Quoted in ibid., 422.

19. Wilson address, January 22, 1917, *Papers of Woodrow Wilson*, vol. 40, 533–39.

20. Quoted in Cooper, "The Command of Gold Reversed," 220-21.

21. Lansing quoted in Arthur S. Link, *Wilson: Campaigns for Progressivism and Peace, 1916–1917* (Princeton: Princeton University Press, 1965), 291.

22. Wilson's State of the Union Address, December 7, 1915, as cited in Anthony Gaughan, "Woodrow Wilson and the Rise of Militant Interventionism in the South," *Journal of Southern History* 65: 4 (November 1999): 785.

23. Wilson's speech is quoted at length in Link, *Campaigns for Progressivism and Peace*, 424–26.

24. Lodge quoted in ibid., 426.

25. Du Bois is quoted in David Levering Lewis, *W. E. B. Du Bois: Biography of a Race, 1868–1919* (New York: Holt, 1993), 525.

26. Stone and Cobb are quoted in Link, *Campaigns for Progressivism and Peace*, 430 and 431, respectively. Wilson is quoted in Ray Stannard Baker, *Woodrow Wilson Life and Letters: Facing War, 1915–1917*, 8 vols. (Garden City, N.Y.: Doubleday Doran, 1937), vol. 6, 515.

Chapter Three

1. Quoted in George H. Nash, *The Life of Herbert Hoover*: Vol. 3: *Master of Emergencies, 1917–1918* (New York: Norton, 1996), 73.

2. Quotes, respectively, from David M. Kennedy, *Over Here: The First World War and American Society* (New York: Oxford University Press, 1980), 144, and Edward M. Coffman, *The War to End All Wars: The American Military Experience in World War I* (Oxford: Oxford University Press: 1968; reprint, Madison: University of Wisconsin Press, 1986), 8.

3. Clark quoted in John Whiteclay Chambers II, *To Raise an Army: The Draft Comes to Modern America* (New York: Free Press, 1987), 165.

4. Wilson quoted in Daniel R. Beaver, *Newton D. Baker and the American War Effort, 1917–1919* (Lincoln: University of Nebraska Press, 1966), 33–34.

5. *Ocala Banner*, June 6, 1917.

6. James R. Green, *Grass-Roots Socialism: Radical Movements in the Southwest, 1895–1943* (Baton Rouge: Louisiana State University Press, 1978), 359; *Chicago Tribune*, June 5, 1917; *New York Times*, July 22, 1917.

7. Foch quoted in Edward Robb Ellis, *Echoes of Distant Thunder: Life in the United States, 1914–1918* (New York: Coward, McCann, and Geoghegan, 1975), 352.

8. Quotes in this paragraph from Kennedy, *Over Here*, 157, 156, respectively.

9. Edison interview, *New York Times Magazine*, May 30, 1915, 7.

10. Quoted in Paul A. C. Koistinen, *Mobilizing for Modern War: The Political Economy of American Warfare, 1865–1919* (Lawrence: University Press of Kansas, 1997), 148.

11. Quoted in Robert H. Ferrell, *Woodrow Wilson and World War, 1917–1921* (New York: Harper and Row, 1985), 25.

12. Ibid., 25.

13. Robert D. Cuff, *The War Industries Board: Business-Government Relations during World War I* (Baltimore: Johns Hopkins University Press, 1973), 209.

14. Hoover is quoted in Elena Danielson, "United States Food Administration," in *The United States in the First World War: An Encyclopedia*, ed. Anne Cipriano Venzon (New York: Garland, 1995), 737; *New York Tribune* in James P. Johnson, *The Politics of Soft Coal: The Bituminous Industry from World War I through the New Deal* (Urbana: University of Illinois Press, 1979), 67.

15. Quoted in Ferrell, *Woodrow Wilson and World War*, 95.

16. Danielson, "United States Food Administration," 737; Ferrell, *Woodrow Wilson and World War*, 93.

17. Quoted in Kennedy, *Over Here*, 107, 108, respectively.

18. Ibid., 105–6.

19. Figures from Charles Gilbert, *American Financing of World War I* (Westport, Conn.: Greenwood, 1970), 220–37 and chapter 6, passim.

20. Root quoted in Wayne A. Wiegand, *"An Active Instrument for Propaganda": The American Public Library during World War I* (New York: Greenwood, 1989), 88.

21. Michael McCarthy, "Committee on Public Information," in *The United States in the First World War*, 162–64.

22. Quoted in Alfred E. Cornebise, *War As Advertised: The Four Minute Men and America's Crusade, 1917–1918* (Philadelphia: American Philosophical Society, 1984), ix, 33–34.

23. Barbara L. Tischler, "Four-Minute Men," in *The United States in the First World War*, 236.

24. Cornebise, *War As Advertised*, 20.

25. These paragraphs draw upon Carol S. Gruber, *Mars and Minerva: World War I and the Uses of the Higher Learning in America* (Baton Rouge: Louisiana State University Press, 1975) and George T. Blakey, *Historians on the Homefront: American Propagandists for the Great War* (Lexington: University Press of Kentucky, 1970).

Chapter Four

1. Edward M. Coffman, *The War to End All Wars: The American Military Experience in World War I* (Oxford: Oxford University Press, 1968; reprint, Madison: University of Wisconsin Press, 1986), 30–31, 67.

2. Ibid., 61; David M. Kennedy, *Over Here: The First World War and American Society* (New York: Oxford University Press, 1980), 157.

3. Coffman, *War to End All Wars*, 56–57.

4. Ibid., 68.

5. Baker quoted in Mark Meigs, *Optimism at Armageddon: Voices of American Participants in the First World War* (New York: New York University Press, 1997), 74.

6. Nancy K. Bristow, *Making Men Moral: Social Engineering during the Great War* (New York: New York University Press, 1996), 104–06.

7. Baker quoted in David F. Trask, *The AEF and Coalition Warmaking, 1917–1918* (Lawrence: University Press of Kansas, 1993), 12.

8. Quoted in Donald Smythe, *Pershing: General of the Armies* (Bloomington: Indiana University Press, 1986), 233.

9. Ibid., 134–35.

10. Ibid., 146.

11. The quotes of Pershing in this paragraph are found, respectively, in Russell Weigley, *History of the United States Army* (enlarged ed.; Bloomington: Indiana University Press, 1984), 389, and Smythe, *Pershing*, 187.

12. Bliss quoted in Daniel R. Beaver, *Newton D. Baker and the American War Effort, 1917–1919* (Lincoln: University of Nebraska Press, 1966), 44–45.

13. Quoted in Coffman, *War to End All Wars*, 222.

14. Teilhard de Chardin quoted in ibid., 246.

15. Ibid., 247; Martin Gilbert, *The First World War: A Complete History* (New York: Holt, 1994), 444.

16. Smythe, *Pershing*, 199–200.

17. Ibid., 207.

18. Ibid., 205.

19. Wood quoted in Kennedy, *Over Here*, 161.

20. Pershing quoted in Coffman, *War to End All Wars*, 319.

21. Arthur E. Barbeau and Florette Henri, *The Unknown Soldiers: Black American Troops in World World War I* (Philadelphia: Temple University Press, 1974), 121–36; q. 121.

22. "Rapist Division": Miles S. Richards, "Ballou, Charles Clarendon (1862–1928)," *The United States in the First World War: An Encyclopedia*, ed. Anne Cipriano Venzon (New York: Garland, 1995), 65; Bullard quoted in Barbeau and Henri, *Unknown Soldiers*, 138.

23. Barbeau and Henri, *Unknown Soldiers*, 153.

24. Quoted in Coffman, *War to End All Wars*, 320.

25. Ibid., 217; Michael J. Knapp, "'Lost' Battalion," *The United States in the First World War*, 353–54.

26. Quoted in Coffman, *War to End All Wars*, 324.

27. Father Francis P. Duffy, quoted in Gilbert, *The First World War*, 447.

28. Quoted in Ronald Schaffer, *America in the Great War: The Rise of the War Welfare State* (Oxford: Oxford University Press, 1991), 155.

29. Ibid., 155.

30. Ibid., 159.

31. Coffman, *War to End All Wars*, 363; David Kennedy, "The World Wars," *Encyclopedia of the United States in the Twentieth Century*, 4 vols., Stanley I. Kutler, editor-in-chief (New York: Scribner, 1996), vol. 2, 629–30.

32. Alfred W. Crosby, *America's Forgotten Pandemic: The Influenza of 1918* (Cambridge: Cambridge University Press, 1989; pub. as *Epidemic and Peace, 1918*, Westport, Conn.: Greenwood, 1976), 160–66.

33. Robert H. Ferrell, *Woodrow Wilson and World War, 1917–1921* (New York: Harper and Row, 1985), 61–62.

34. Schaffer, *America in the Great War*, 199–212; Meirion and Susie Harries, *The Last Days of Innocence: America at War, 1917–1918* (New York: Random House, 1997), 460.

35. Quote in Kennedy, *Over Here*, 368; G. Kurt Piehler, "The War Dead and the Gold Star: American Commemoration of the First World War," in *Commemorations: The Politics of National Identity*, ed. John R. Gillis (Princeton: Princeton University Press, 1994), 168–85.

36. Quoted in Frank E. Vandiver, *Black Jack: The Life and Times of John J. Pershing*, 2 vols. (College Station: Texas A&M University Press, 1977), 989.

37. Quoted in Coffman, *War to End All Wars*, 94–95.

38. Jellicoe quoted in ibid., 97; Ferrell, *Woodrow Wilson and World War*, 38–39.
39. Kennedy, *Over Here*, 205.

Chapter Five

1. Theodore Roosevelt to Carl Schurz, December 24, 1902, quoted in Robert H. Zieger, *Republicans and Labor, 1919–1929* (Lexington: University of Kentucky Press, 1969), 4.

2. David Montgomery, *Workers' Control in America: Essays in the History of Work, Technology, and Labor Struggles* (Cambridge: Cambridge University Press, 1979), 93, table, 94; Graham Adams Jr., *Age of Industrial Violence, 1910–1915: The Activities and Findings of the United States Commission on Industrial Relations* (New York: Columbia University Press, 1966).

3. Quoted in Joseph A. McCartin, *Labor's Great War: The Struggle for Industrial Democracy and the Origins of Modern American Labor Relations, 1912–1921* (Chapel Hill: University of North Carolina Press, 1997), 80.

4. Quoted in ibid., 78.

5. Ibid., 93.

6. Ibid., 93.

7. Ibid., 91.

8. Quoted in David M. Kennedy, *Over Here: The First World War and American Society* (Oxford: Oxford University Press, 1980), 29.

9. Quoted in Neil A. Wynn, *From Progressivism to Prosperity: World War I and American Society* (New York: Holmes & Meier, 1986), 114.

10. Wilson, quoted in Jane Lang Scheiber and Harry N. Scheiber, "The Wilson Administration and the Wartime Mobilization of Black Americans, 1917–18," *Labor History* 10: 3 (Summer 1969): 433.

11. Vincent Vinikis, "Specters in the Past: The Saint Charles, Arkansas, Lynching of 1904 and the Limits of Historical Inquiry," *Journal of Southern History* 65: 3 (August 1999): 541; Arthur E. Barbeau and Florette Henri, *The Unknown Soldiers: Black American Troops in World War I* (Philadelphia: Temple University Press, 1974), 21–23.

12. Quoted in Wynn, *From Progressivism to Prosperity*, 177.

13. Ibid., 180–81.

14. Quoted in ibid., 183, 114, respectively. See also Elliott M. Rudwick, *Race Riot at East St. Louis July 2, 1917* (Carbondale: Southern Illinois University Press, 1964).

15. Quoted in Wynn, 185.

16. Quoted in ibid., 175–76.

17. Theodore Kornweibel Jr., "Apathy and Dissent: Black America's Negative Responses to World War I," *South Atlantic Quarterly* 80: 3 (Summer 1981): 322–38.

18. Quoted in Scheiber and Scheiber, "The Wilson Administration and the Wartime Mobilization of Black Americans," 438.

19. Quoted in David Levering Lewis, *W. E. B. Du Bois: Biography of a Race, 1868–1919* (New York: Holt, 1993), 556.

20. Joel Spingarn, quoted in Wynn, *From Progressivism to Prosperity*, 176.

21. Scott, quoted in Nancy K. Bristow, *Making Men Moral: Social Engineering during the Great War* (New York: New York University Press, 1996), 143.

22. Quoted in Cindy Hahamovitch, *The Fruits of Their Labor: Atlantic Coast Farmworkers and the Making of Migrant Poverty, 1870–1945* (Chapel Hill: University of North Carolina Press, 1997), 110.

23. Quoted in Scheiber and Scheiber, "The Wilson Administration and the Wartime Mobilization of Black Americans," 449.

24. Quoted in Eric Arnesen, "Charting an Independent Course: African-American Railroad Workers in the World War I Era," in *Labor Histories: Class, Politics, and the Working-Class Experience*, ed. Eric Arnesen, Julie Green, and Bruce Laurie (Urbana: University of Illinois Press, 1998), 287.

25. Quotes are, respectively, in ibid., 289, and Eric Arnesen, "'Like Banquo's Ghost, It Will Not Down': The Race Question and the American Railroad Brotherhoods, 1880–1920," *American Historical Review* 99: 5 (Dec. 1994): 1631; McCartin, *Labor's Great War*, 116.

26. Quoted in McCartin, *Labor's Great War*, 115.

27. Quoted in Hahamovitch, *Fruits of Their Labor*, 112.

28. Quoted in McCartin, *Labor's Great War*, 116–17.

29. Susan Zeiger, "She Didn't Raise Her Boy to Be a Slacker: Motherhood, Conscription, and the Culture of the First World War," *Feminist Studies* 22: 1 (Spring 1996): 7–39; Kathleen Kennedy, *Disloyal Mothers and Scurrilous Citizens: Women and Subversion during World War I* (Bloomington: Indiana University Press, 1999), 18–23 (on O'Hare).

30. Barbara J. Steinson, *American Women's Activism in World War I* (New York: Garland, 1982), 400.

31. Quoted in Allen F. Davis, *American Heroine: The Life and Legend of Jane Addams* (New York: Oxford, 1973), 212.

32. Quoted in Harriet Hyman Alonso, *Peace as a Women's Issue: A History of the U.S. Movement for World Peace and Women's Rights* (Syracuse: Syracuse University Press, 1993), 68.

33. Quoted in Davis, *American Heroine*, 242.

34. Steinson, *American Women's Activism in World War I*, 397.

35. Annie Cothern Graves, quoted in ibid., 180–81.

36. D'Ann Campbell, "United States Army: Nurse Corps," in *The United States in the First World War: An Encyclopedia*, ed. Anne Cipriano Venzon (New York: Garland, 1995), 715–17.

37. Susan Zeiger, "Women in the American Expeditionary Force," ibid., 803–5.

38. Quoted in Maurine Weiner Greenwald, *Women, War, and Work: The Impact of World War I on Women Workers in the United States* (Ithaca: Cornell University Press, 1990; originally Westport, Conn.: Greenwood, 1980), 34, 20, respectively.

39. See the photographs in ibid., passim.

40. Quoted in ibid., 27.

41. Quotes in this paragraph, respectively, from Susan R. Grayzel, *Women's Identities at War: Gender, Motherhood, and Politics in Britain and France during the First World War* (Chapel Hill: University of North Carolina Press, 1999), 137, and William L. O'Neill, *Everyone Was Brave: A History of Feminism in America* (rev. ed.; Chicago: Quadrangle, 1971), 191.

42. Quoted in Valerie Jean Conner, *The National War Labor Board: Stability, Social Justice, and the Voluntary State in World War I* (Chapel Hill: University of North Carolina Press, 1983), 143.

43. Quoted in Greenwald, *Women, War, and Work*, 123, 127.

44. Ibid., 40; second quote from McCartin, *Labor's Great War*, 114.

45. Conner, *The National War Labor Board*, 156.

46. Anderson quoted in Greenwald, *Women, War, and Work*, 75.

47. Wilson quoted in Eleanor Flexner, *Century of Struggle: The Women's Rights Movement in the United States* (Cambridge: Belknap Press of Harvard University Press, 1959), 308–9.

Chapter Six

1. Gregory S. Butler, "Vision of a Nation Transformed: Modernity and Ideology in Wilson's Political Thought," *Journal of Church and State* 39: 1 (Winter 1997): 46.

2. Quoted in Lloyd Ambrosius, *Wilsonian Statecraft: Theory and Practice of Liberal Internationalism during World War I* (Wilmington, Del.: Scholarly Resources, 1991), 11.

3. The Wilson quotes are in ibid., 11, and Butler, "Vision of a Nation," 43, respectively.

4. The quotes are found in N. Gordon Levin, *Woodrow Wilson and World Politics: America's Response to War and Revolution* (London: Oxford University Press, 1968), 17, 18.

5. Ibid., 17.

6. Quoted from Thomas J. Knock, *To End All Wars: Woodrow Wilson and the Quest for a New World Order* (New York: Oxford University Press, 1992), 10–11.

7. Pershing is quoted in Byron Farwell, *Over There: The United States in the Great War, 1917–1918* (New York: Norton, 1999), 256; Roosevelt in Knock, *To End All Wars*, 176.

8. Philipp Scheidemann quoted in Klaus Schwabe, *Woodrow Wilson, Revolutionary Germany, and Peacemaking, 1918–1919: Missionary Diplomacy and the Realities of Power*, trans. Rita and Robert Kimber (Chapel Hill: University of North Carolina Press, 1985), 12.

9. Quoted in Levin, *Woodrow Wilson and World Politics*, 133–35.

10. The text of the Fourteen Points is most conveniently available in *Documents of American History*, ed. Henry Steele Commager. My references are to the 7th ed. (New York: Appleton-Century-Crofts, 1963), 137–43. The final quote is from Wilson's Third Liberty Loan address, April 6, 1918, cited in Manfred F. Boemeke, "Woodrow Wilson's Image of Germany, the War-Guilt Question, and the Treaty of Versailles," in *The Treaty of Versailles: A Reassessment after 75 Years*, ed. Manfred F. Boemeke, Gerald D. Feldman, and Elisabeth Glaser (Washington and Cambridge, U.K.: German Historical Institute and Cambridge University Press, 1998), 612.

11. Quoted in Knock, *To End All Wars*, 138.

12. Truman quoted in Farwell, *Over There*, 259; Martin Gilbert, *First World War: A Complete History* (New York: Holt, 1994), 501.

13. Paul Cambon quoted in Alan Sharp, *The Versailles Settlement: Peacemaking in Paris, 1919* (New York: St. Martin's, 1991), 19.

14. Quoted in ibid.

15. Quoted in Boemeke, "Woodrow Wilson's Image of Germany," 612.

16. Clemenceau quoted in August Heckscher, *Woodrow Wilson* (New York: Macmillan/Collier, 1991), 554.

17. The first quote in the paragraph is from Sharp, *The Versailles Settlement*, 29–30; others are from Knock, *To End All Wars*, 198–99.

18. Hankey quoted in Charles L. Mee Jr., *The End of Order: Versailles, 1919* (New York: Dutton, 1980), 190.

19. Wilson is quoted in Heckscher, *Woodrow Wilson*, 567; Mee cites the Italian reaction in *The End of Order*, 187.

20. Lloyd George in Sharp, *The Versailles Settlement*, 49; Clemenceau in Mee, *End of Order*, 62.

21. Quoted in Sharp, *The Versailles Settlement*, 62.

22. Quoted in Mee, *End of Order*, 142.

23. Quoted in ibid., 215.

24. Quoted in ibid., 216.

25. Quoted in ibid., 218, 222.

26. Quoted in ibid., 212, 225–26.

27. Quoted in Knock, *To End All Wars*, 250–51.

28. Quoted in ibid., 252.

Chapter Seven

1. Richard Polenberg, *Fighting Faiths: The Abrams Case, the Supreme Court, and Free Speech* (New York: Viking, 1987), 108.

2. Arno J. Mayer, *Wilson vs. Lenin: Political Origins of the New Diplomacy, 1917–1918* (Cleveland: Meridian Books, 1964; originally pub. 1959), 276.

3. Byron Farwell, *Over There: The United States in the Great War, 1917–1918* (New York: Norton, 1999), 273.

4. Ibid., 282, 283; Alfred W. Crosby, *America's Forgotten Pandemic: The Influenza of 1918* (Cambridge: Cambridge University Press, 1989; originally published as *Epidemic and Peace, 1918*, Westport, Conn.: Greenwood, 1976), 148.

5. Ibid., 276–77.

6. Ibid., 277; Polenberg, *Fighting Faiths*, 41.

7. Ilya Somin, *Stillborn Crusade: The Tragic Failure of Western Intervention in the Russian Civil War, 1918–1920* (New Brunswick, N.J.: Transaction Publishers, 1996), 123.

8. Quoted in ibid., 116.

9. Quoted in Theodore Draper, *The Roots of American Communism* (New York: Octagon Books ed., 1977; originally pub. 1957), 110.

10. Newspaper reproductions in ibid., following 212.

11. Quoted in Robert K. Murray, *Red Scare: A Study in National Hysteria, 1919–1920* (Minneapolis: University of Minnesota Press, 1955; McGraw-Hill ed., 1964), 63.

12. Quotations in ibid., 71, 79.

13. Ibid., 76.

14. Robert Goldstein, *Political Repression in Modern America: From 1870 to the Present* (Cambridge: Schenkman, 1978), 108.

15. Quoted in Melvyn Dubofsky, "Industrial Workers of the World," *The United States in the First World War: An Encyclopedia*, ed. Anne Cipriano Venzon (New York: Garland, 1995), 301.

16. Jorg Nagler, "Victims of the Home Front: Enemy Aliens in the United States during the First World War," in *Minorities in Wartime: National and Racial Groupings in Europe, North America and Australia during the Two World Wars*, ed. Panikos Panayi (Oxford/Providence, R.I.: Berg, 1993), 191–215.

17. Paul L. Murphy, *World War I and the Origin of Civil Liberties in the United States* (New York: Norton, 1979), 103.

18. Quoted in Stanley Coben, *A. Mitchell Palmer: Politician* (New York: Columbia University Press, 1963), 211.

19. Quoted in ibid., 230.

20. Ibid., 228, 229.

21. Dewey quoted in David M. Kennedy, *Over Here: The First World War and American Society* (New York: Oxford University Press, 1980), 50; clergyman in Burl Noggle, *Into the Twenties: The United States from Armistice to Normalcy* (Urbana: University of Illinois Press, 1974), 40.

22. Quoted in Noggle, *Into the Twenties*, 43.

23. Ibid., 50.

24. Du Bois quoted in ibid., 41–42.

25. Steven A. Reich, "Soldiers of Democracy: Black Texans and the Fight for Citizenship, 1917–1921," *Journal of American History* 82: 4 (March 1996): 1492 (quote); J. William Harris, "Etiquette, Lynching, and Racial Boundaries in Southern History: A Mississippi Example," *American Historical Review* 100: 2 (April 1995): 387–410; Stephen H. Norwood, "Bogalusa Burning: The War against Biracial Unionism in the Deep South, 1919," *Journal of Southern History* 63: 3 (August 1997): 591–628.

26. William M. Tuttle Jr., *Race Riot: Chicago in the Red Summer of 1919* (New York: Atheneum, 1970), 22–23; Dewey W. Grantham, *The South in Modern America: A Region at Odds* (New York: HarperCollins, 1994), 32.

27. Tuttle, *Race Riot*, 29–31.

28. Ibid.; McKay quoted in Noggle, *Into the Twenties*, 158.

29. Richard C. Cortner, *A Mob Intent on Death: The NAACP and the Arkansas Riot Cases* (Middletown, Conn.: Wesleyan Universiy Press, 1988), 30 and notes 24, 25; Theodore Kornweibel Jr., *"Seeing Red": Federal Campaigns against Black Militancy, 1919–1925* (Bloomington: Indiana University Press, 1998), 22, 23.

30. Wilson's address, September 11, 1919, *The Papers of Woodrow Wilson*, 69 vols., ed. Arthur S. Link (Princeton: Princeton University Press, 1980), vol. 63, 196.

31. Strike statistics in David Montgomery, *Workers' Control in America: Essays in the History of Work, Technology, and Labor Struggles* (Cambridge: Cambridge University

Press, 1979), 93, table, 94; quoted in Zieger, *Republicans and Labor, 1919–1929* (Lexington: University of Kentucky Press, 1969), 8.

32. The quotes are from Joseph A. McCartin, *Labor's Great War: The Struggle for Industrial Democracy and the Origins of Modern American Labor Relations, 1912–1921* (Chapel Hill: University of North Carolina Press, 1997), 67, and David Brody, *Steelworkers in America: The Nonunion Era* (Cambridge: Harvard University Press, 1960; Harper TorchBooks ed., 1969), 234.

33. Quoted in Brody, *Steelworkers in America*, 222.

34. Gary quoted in David Brody, *Labor in Crisis: The Steel Strike of 1919* (Philadelphia: Lippincott, 1965), 124.

35. Quoted in ibid., 69, 100.

36. Ibid., 96–105, quote 100–101.

37. Quoted in ibid., 158.

38. Ibid., 128–46, quote 135.

39. Quoted in Brody, *Steelworkers in America*, 249.

40. Quoted in ibid., 262.

41. Quoted in Gary Dean Best, *The Politics of American Individualism: Herbert Hoover in Transition, 1918–1921* (Westport, Conn.: Greenwood, 1975), 38.

42. Quoted in August Heckscher, *Woodrow Wilson* (New York: Macmillan/Collier, 1991), 574–75.

43. Quoted in Robert H. Ferrell, *Woodrow Wilson and World War, 1917–1921* (New York: Harper and Row, 1985), 175.

44. *Papers of Woodrow Wilson*, vol. 63, 432.

45. Quoted in Roland Stromberg, *Collective Security and American Foreign Policy: From the League of Nations to NATO* (New York: Praeger, 1963), 35 and attached note.

46. John Milton Cooper Jr., *Pivotal Decades: The United States, 1900–1920* (New York: Norton, 1990), 354.

47. Wilson's speeches appear in *Papers of Woodrow Wilson*, vol. 63. This quote appears on 403.

48. Grayson's notes are in ibid., 446, and passim; the quote from Wilson is in ibid., 519.

49. Ferrell recounts the episode in *Woodrow Wilson and World War*, 177.

50. Edith Gittings Reid, *Woodrow Wilson: The Caricature, the Myth and the Man* (London: Oxford University Press, 1934), 235–36.

Chapter Eight

1. The writers mentioned and the works alluded to in these two paragraphs are: Carl Parrini, *Heir to Empire: United States Economic Diplomacy, 1916–1923* (Pittsburgh: University of Pittsburgh Press, 1969); William Appleman Williams, *The Tragedy of American Diplomacy* (New York: Norton, 1988; originally pub. 1959); Noam Chomsky, *American Power and the New Mandarins* (New York: Pantheon Books, 1969); Noam Chomsky, *The New Military Humanism: Lessons from Kosovo* (London: Common Courage Press, 1999); and John Lewis Gaddis, "The Tragedy of Cold War History," *Diplomatic History* 17: 1 (Winter 1993): 1–16.

~

Bibliographical Note

The published literature on the Great War is truly staggering. No modest bibliographical listing that is possible here can begin to do justice to it. Nonetheless, the items indicated below provide introductions to most important subjects, especially as related to U.S. participation. Two excellent recent encyclopedias provide a wide range of up-to-date information: *The United States in the First World War: An Encyclopedia*, ed. Anne Cipriano Venzon (New York: Garland, 1995) and *The European Powers in the First World War: An Encyclopedia*, ed. Spencer C. Tucker (New York: Garland, 1996). For more detailed bibliographies, readers are referred to the "References" sections of these volumes and to the bibliographies and notes of the other items cited below. In addition, there are several splendid Web sites containing rich material on the Great War, including bibliographies, collections of documents, annotated lists of films and novels, maps, chronologies, photographs, and other invaluable items. I have found the following URLs of particular value: <http://www.mcs.net/~mikei/tgws/sr001.htm> (a good reading list covering all phases of the Great War); <http://www.lib.byu.edu/~rdh/wwi/> (an excellent archive of Great War documents); <http://raven.cc.ukans.edu/~kansite/ww_one/photos/greatwar.htm> (a splendid collection of photographs); and <http://raven.cc.ukans.edu/~kansite/ww_one/links.html> (links to many Great War sites).

Overviews and Interpretive Volumes

For a powerful and poignant overview of the Great War, with magnificent photos and much material drawn from diaries, letters, and personal accounts,

Jay Winter and Blaine Baggett, *1914–1918: The Great War and the Shaping of the 20th Century* (London: BBC Books, 1996), a companion volume to a splendid twelve-hour public television series by the same name, is matchless. Recent military histories of the war include Martin Gilbert, *The First World War: A Complete History* (New York: Holt, 1994), and John Keegan, *The First World War* (New York: Knopf, 1999). Another recent book, Niall Ferguson, *The Pity of War: Explaining World War I* (New York: Basic Books, 1999) provides a provocative, wide-ranging interpretation of diplomatic, economic, and military themes. Hew Strachan, ed., *World War I: A History* (Oxford: Oxford University Press, 1998) contains authoritative essays on key aspects of the Great War. Paul Fussell, *The Great War and the Modern Memory* (London: Oxford University Press, 1975) is an influential analysis of the imaginative literature of the war, and Modris Eksteins, *Rites of Spring: The Great War and the Birth of the Modern Age* (New York: Houghton Mifflin, 1989; Anchor Books ed.) offers provocative cultural perspectives.

The United States and the Great War: Surveys

By far the best single book on the American experience in the Great War is David M. Kennedy, *Over Here: The First World War and American Society* (New York: Oxford University Press, 1980). John Milton Cooper Jr., *Pivotal Decades: The United States, 1900–1920* (New York: Norton, 1990) is an excellent overview of the period. Other good, shorter surveys include Neil A. Wynn, *From Progressivism to Prosperity: World War I and American Society* (New York: Holmes & Meier, 1986), outstanding in its treatment of the home front; Ronald Schaffer, *America in the Great War: The Rise of the War Welfare State* (New York: Oxford University Press, 1991), containing excellent material on the combat experience and medical treatment of U.S. troops; Meirion and Susie Harries, *The Last Days of Innocence: America at War, 1917–1918* (New York: Random House, 1997), an engaging overview; Edward Robb Ellis, *Echoes of Distant Thunder: Life in the United States, 1914–1918* (New York: Coward, McCann, and Geoghegan, 1975), which places the war experience in a broad social and cultural context; and Robert H. Ferrell, *Woodrow Wilson and World War, 1917–1921* (New York: Harper and Row, 1985), a brisk and thoughtful analysis focusing on government, diplomatic, and military affairs. Frank Freidel, *Over There: The Story of America's First Great Overseas Crusade* (New York: McGraw Hill, 1990; rev. ed.) features a rich collection of photographs, and Byron Farwell, *Over There: The United States in the Great War, 1917–1918* (New York: Norton, 1999) is a lively account of military action. Frederic L. Paxson, *American Democracy and the World War* (3 vols.; Boston: Houghton Mifflin, 1936-48) contains much still-useful information.

Woodrow Wilson

There is a vast literature on the twenty-sixth president. Woodrow Wilson was a prolific correspondent who wrote many of his own speeches, statements, and working papers. *The Papers of Woodrow Wilson*, ed. Arthur S. Link (69 vols.; Princeton: Princeton University Press, 1965–94) is an essential source. Arthur Link's massive biography of Wilson [(especially vol. 3), *The Struggle for Neutrality, 1914–1915* (1960)], *Confusions and Crises, 1915–1916* (1964), and *Campaigns for Progressivism and Peace* (1965), all published by Princeton University Press, are standard. Several other volumes by Arthur S. Link, notably *The Higher Realism of Woodrow Wilson and Other Essays* (Nashville: Vanderbilt University Press, 1971); *Wilson the Diplomatist: A Look at His Major Foreign Policies* (Baltimore: Johns Hopkins University Press, 1957); and *Woodrow Wilson: Revolution, War, and Peace* (Arlington Heights, Ill.: Harlan Davidson, 1979), along with *Woodrow Wilson and a Revolutionary World, 1913–1921*, ed. Arthur S. Link (Chapel Hill: University of North Carolina Press, 1982) focus on foreign policy. Lloyd Ambrosius, *Wilsonian Statecraft: Theory and Practice of Liberal Internationalism during World War I* (Wilmington, Del.: Scholarly Resources, 1991) stresses the religious and historical dimensions of Wilson's political ideology. N. Gordon Levin, *Woodrow Wilson and World Politics: America's Response to War and Revolution* (London: Oxford University Press, 1968) is persuasive, and Frank Ninkovich, *The Wilsonian Century: U.S. Foreign Policy since 1900* (Chicago: University of Chicago Press, 1999) applies the Wilsonian worldview broadly. August Heckscher, *Woodrow Wilson* (New York: Macmillan/Collier Books, 1991) is a sympathetic recent biography. Kendrick A. Clements, *The Presidency of Woodrow Wilson* (Lawrence: University Press of Kansas, 1992) is an able overview of the period.

Specialized Studies

Below is a listing of the books that I found particularly helpful with reference to the significant topics addressed in *America's Great War*.

U.S. Policy, 1914–1917

Coogan, John W., *The End of Neutrality: The United States, Britain, and Maritime Rights, 1899–1915* (Ithaca: Cornell University Press, 1981).

Cooper, John Milton, *The Vanity of Power: American Isolationism and the First World War* (Westport, Conn.: Greenwood, 1969).

Devlin, Patrick, *Too Proud to Fight: Woodrow Wilson's Neutrality* (New York: Oxford University Press, 1975).

May, Ernest R., *The World War and American Isolation, 1914–1917* (Cambridge: Harvard University Press, 1959; Quadrangle, 1966).

The U.S. Military Effort

American Battle Monuments Commission, *American Armies and Battlefields in Europe: A History, Guide, and Reference Book* (Washington, D.C.: Government Printing Office, 1938).

Barbeau, Arthur E., and Florette Henri, *The Unknown Soldiers: Black American Troops in World War I* (Philadelphia: Temple University Press, 1974).

Braim, Paul F., *The Test of Battle: The American Expeditionary Forces in the Meuse-Argonne Campaign* (Newark: University of Delaware Press, 1987).

Bristow, Nancy K., *Making Men Moral: Social Engineering during the Great War* (New York: New York University Press, 1996).

Chambers, John Whiteclay II, *To Raise an Army: The Draft Comes to Modern America* (New York: Free Press, 1987).

Clifford, John Garry, *The Citizen Soldiers: The Plattsburg Training Camp Movement, 1913–1920* (Lexington: University Press of Kentucky, 1972).

Coffman, Edward M., *The War to End All Wars: The American Military Experience in World War I* (Oxford: Oxford University Press, 1968).

Finnegan, John Patrick, *Against the Specter of a Dragon: The Campaign for American Military Preparedness, 1914–1917* (Westport, Conn.: Greenwood, 1974).

Meigs, Mark, *Optimism at Armageddon: Voices of American Participants in the First World War* (New York: New York University Press, 1997).

Smythe, Donald, *Pershing: General of the Armies* (Bloomington: Indiana University Press, 1986).

Trask, David F., *The United States in the Supreme War Council: American War Aims and Inter-Allied Strategy, 1917–1918* (Middletown, Conn.: Wesleyan University Press, 1961).

Vandiver, Frank E., *Black Jack: The Life and Times of John J. Pershing* (2 vols.; College Station: Texas A&M University Press, 1977).

Political Economy, Labor

Breen, William J., *Labor Market Politics and the Great War: The Department of Labor, the States, and the First U.S. Employment Service, 1907–1933* (Kent, Ohio: Kent State University Press, 1997).

Conner, Valerie Jean, *The National War Labor Board: Stability, Social Justice, and the Voluntary State in World War I* (Chapel Hill: University of North Carolina Press, 1983).

Cuff, Robert D., *The War Industries Board: Business-Government Relations during World War II* (Baltimore: Johns Hopkins University Press, 1973).

Gilbert, Charles, *American Financing of World War I* (Westport, Conn.: Greenwood, 1970).

Hawley, Ellis W., *The Great War and the Search for a Modern Order: A History of the American People and Their Institutions, 1917–1933* (2d ed.; New York: St. Martin's, 1992).

Haydu, Jeffrey, *Making American Industry Safe for Democracy: Comparative Perspectives on the State and Employee Representation in the Era of World War I* (Urbana: University of Illinois Press, 1997).

Johnson, James P., *The Politics of Soft Coal: The Bituminous Industry from World War I through the New Deal* (Urbana: University of Illinois Press, 1979).

Kaufman, Burton, *Efficiency and Expansion: Foreign Trade Organization in the Wilson Administration, 1913–1921* (Westport, Conn.: Greenwood, 1974).

Kerr, K. Austin, *American Railroad Politics, 1914–1920: Rates, Wages, and Efficiency* (Pittsburgh: University of Pittsburgh Press, 1969).

Koistinen, Paul A. C., *Mobilizing for Modern War: The Political Economy of American Warfare, 1865–1919* (Lawrence: University Press of Kansas, 1997).

McCartin, Joseph A., *Labor's Great War: The Struggle for Industrial Democracy and the Origins of Modern American Labor Relations, 1912–1921* (Chapel Hill: University of North Carolina Press, 1997).

Nash, George H., *The Life of Herbert Hoover*: Vol. 3: *Master of Emergencies, 1917–1918* (New York: Norton, 1996).

Offer, Avner, *The First World War: An Agrarian Interpretation* (Oxford: Clarendon, 1989).

Propaganda

Blakey, George T., *Historians on the Homefront: American Propagandists for the Great War* (Lexington: University Press of Kentucky, 1970).

Cornebise, Alfred E., *War As Advertised: The Four Minute Men and America's Crusade, 1917–1918* (Philadelphia: American Philosophical Society, 1984).

DeBauche, Leslie Midkiff, *Reel Patriotism: The Movies and World War I* (Madison: University of Wisconsin Press, 1997).

Gruber, Carol S., *Mars and Minerva: World War I and the Uses of the Higher Learning in America* (Baton Rouge: Louisiana State University Press, 1975).

Mock, James R., and Cedric Larson, *Words That Won the War: The Story of the Committee on Public Information, 1917–1919* (Princeton: Princeton University Press, 1939).

Shover, Michele J., "Roles and Images of Women in World War I Propaganda," *Politics and Society* 4 (Winter 1975): 469–86.

Thompson, John A., *Reformers and War: American Progressive Publicists and the First World War* (Cambridge: Cambridge University Press, 1987).

Vaughn, Stephen, *Holding Fast the Inner Lines: Democracy, Nationalism, and the Committee on Public Information* (Chapel Hill: University of North Carolina Press, 1980).

Ward, Larry Wayne, *The Motion Picture Goes to War: The U.S. Government Film Effort during World War I* (Ann Arbor: University of Michigan Research Press, 1985).

Wiegand, Wayne A., *"An Active Instrument for Propaganda": The American Public Library during World War I* (New York: Greenwood, 1989).

Radicalism, Civil Liberties

Avrich, Paul, *Sacco and Vanzetti: The Anarchist Background* (Princeton: Princeton University Press, 1991).

Draper, Theodore, *The Roots of American Communism* (New York: Octagon, 1977; originally pub. 1957).

Dubofsky, Melvyn, *We Shall Be All: A History of the Industrial Workers of the World* (New York: Quadrangle, 1969).

Goldstein, Robert Justin, *Political Repression in Modern America: From 1870 to the Present* (Cambridge, Mass.: Schenkman, 1978).

Kornweibel, Theodor, Jr., *"Seeing Red": Federal Campaigns against Black Militancy, 1919–1925* (Bloomington: Indiana University Press, 1998).

Lasch, Christopher, *American Liberals and the Russian Revolution* (New York: Columbia University Press, 1962; McGraw-Hill paperback ed., 1972).

Murphy, Paul L., *World War I and the Origin of Civil Liberties in the United States* (New York: Norton, 1979).

Murray, Robert K., *Red Scare: A Study in National Hysteria, 1919–1920* (Minneapolis: University of Minnesota Press, 1955; McGraw-Hill ed., 1964).

Polenberg, Richard, *Fighting Faiths: The Abrams Case, the Supreme Court, and Free Speech* (New York: Viking, 1987).

Preston, William, Jr., *Aliens and Dissenters: Federal Suppression of Radicals, 1903–1933* (New York: Harper TorchBooks, 1966; originally pub. by Cambridge: Harvard University Press, 1963).

African Americans

Barbeau and Henri, *The Unknown Soldiers* (cited above).
Cortner, Richard C., *A Mob Intent on Death: The NAACP and the Arkansas Riot Cases* (Middletown, Conn.: Wesleyan University Press, 1988).
Kornweibel, Theodore, Jr., *"Seeing Red"* (cited above).
Lewis, David Levering, *W. E. B. Du Bois: Biography of a Race, 1868–1919* (New York: Holt, 1993).
Rudwick, Elliott M., *Race Riot at East St. Louis, July 2, 1917* (Carbondale: Southern Illinois University Press, 1964).
Tuttle, William M., Jr., *Race Riot: Chicago in the Red Summer of 1919* (New York: Atheneum, 1970).

Women

Alonso, Harriet Hyman, *Peace as a Women's Issue: A History of the U.S. Movement for World Peace and Women's Rights* (Syracuse: Syracuse University Press, 1993).
Davis, Allen F., *American Heroine: The Life and Legend of Jane Addams* (New York: Oxford University Press, 1973).
Flexner, Eleanor, *A Century of Struggle: The Women's Rights Movement in the United States* (Cambridge: Belknap Press, Harvard University Press, 1959).
Greenwald, Maurine Weiner, *Women, War, and Work: The Impact of World War I on Women Workers in the United States* (Ithaca: Cornell University Press, 1990; originally pub. by Westport, Conn.: Greenwood, 1980).
Kennedy, Kathleen, *Disloyal Mothers and Scurrilous Citizens: Women and Subversion during World War I* (Bloomington: Indiana University Press, 1999).
O'Neill, William L., *Everyone Was Brave: A History of Feminism in America* (rev. ed.; Chicago: Quadrangle, 1971).
Steinson, Barbara J., *American Women's Activism in World War I* (New York: Garland, 1982).

Postwar Diplomacy

Ambrosius, Lloyd E., *Woodrow Wilson and the American Diplomatic Tradition: The Treaty Fight in Perspective* (Cambridge: Cambridge University Press, 1987).

Bailey, Thomas A., *Woodrow Wilson and the Great Betrayal* (New York: Macmillan, 1945).

Boemeke, Manfred F., Gerald D. Feldman, and Elisabeth Glaser, eds., *The Treaty of Versailles: A Reassessment after 75 Years* (Washington and Cambridge, U.K.: German Historical Institute and Cambridge University Press, 1998).

Foglesong, David S., *America's Secret War against Bolshevism: U.S. Intervention in the Russian Civil War, 1917–1920* (Chapel Hill: University of North Carolina Press, 1995).

Gelfand, Lawrence E., *The Inquiry: American Preparations for Peace, 1917–1919* (New Haven: Yale University Press, 1963).

Knock, Thomas J., *To End All Wars: Woodrow Wilson and the Quest for a New World Order* (New York: Oxford University Press, 1992).

Levin, N. Gordon, *Woodrow Wilson and World Politics: America's Response to War and Revolution* (London: Oxford University Press, 1968).

Lowry, Bullitt, *Armistice 1918* (Kent, Ohio: Kent State University Press, 1996).

Mayer, Arno J., *Wilson vs. Lenin: Political Origins of the New Diplomacy, 1917–1918* (Cleveland: Meridian, 1964; originally pub. 1959).

Mee, Charles L., Jr., *The End of Order: Versailles, 1919* (New York: Dutton, 1980).

Schwabe, Klaus, *Woodrow Wilson, Revolutionary Germany, and Peacemaking, 1918–1919: Missionary Diplomacy and the Realities of Power* (Chapel Hill: University of North Carolina Press, 1985).

Sharp, Alan, *The Versailles Settlement: Peacemaking in Paris, 1919* (New York: St. Martin's, 1991).

Somin, Ilya, *Stillborn Crusade: The Tragic Failure of Western Intervention in the Russian Civil War, 1918–1920* (New Brunswick, N.J.: Transaction, 1996).

Stevenson, David, *The First World War and International Politics* (Oxford: Oxford University Press, 1988).

Other Topics

Best, Gary Dean, *The Politics of American Individualism: Herbert Hoover in Transition, 1918–1921* (Westport, Conn.: Greenwood, 1975).

Britten, Thomas A., *American Indians in World War I: At Home and at War* (Albuquerque: University of New Mexico Press, 1997).

Crosby, Alfred W., *America's Forgotten Pandemic: The Influenza of 1918* (Cambridge: Cambridge University Press, 1989; pub. as *Epidemic and Peace, 1918*, Westport, Conn.: Greenwood, 1976).

Noggle, Burl, *Into the Twenties: The United States from Armistice to Normalcy* (Urbana: University of Illinois Press, 1974).

~

Index

Acheson, Dean, 228
Addams, Jane, 138–40, 141
Africa, colonialism in, 54–55, 181, 188
African Americans: activism, 126, 129–31, 205–6; agriculture, 129, 132, 134–35; armed forces, 85, 102–6, 126, 141; conscription, 63; labor, 132–35, 205, 212, 214; migration, 126, 128–29, 144–45; postwar experience, 205–7; railroad industry, 132–33, 135; U.S. Army, 85, 102–6, 126; wartime experience, 3, 80, 115, 116, 126–35, 143, 205, 230; women, 142, 144–45. *See also* Du Bois, W. E. B.; lynching
African Blood Brotherhood, 129
Aisne-Marne offensive (July 1918), 97–98, 102, 107, 112. *See also* American Expeditionary Force; Foch, Ferdinand
Alaska, propaganda in, 80
Alexander II, 195
Algerians, colonial subjects, 234
Alien Enemies Act (1798), 198
Allegheny County, Pa., 213
Alsace-Lorraine, 8, 29, 45, 160, 162, 165, 174
American Alliance for Labor and Democracy, 124
American and Allied Ideals (CPI publication), 82
American Defense Society, 200

American Expeditionary Force (AEF), 85, 91, 93, 190, 236; African American troops, 102–6; casualties, 102–3, 105, 106, 107, 108–11; debate over role in war, 92–93, 94–97; logistics and supply, 100, 101, 107; military action involving, 97, 98–99, 99–102, 107, 112; military cemeteries, 112; morale and mentalité of troops, 85, 86–91, 95, 98, 99, 100, 102, 103, 105–6, 112–13, 145, 191; reliance on Allies for weapons, 93, 94, 96–97, 102; structure and command, 94, 96; role of women, 141, 142–43. *See also* Pershing, John J.; U.S. Army; U.S. Marine Corps
American Expeditionary Force, individual units: First Army, 96, 97, 100–102; Second Army, 96, 97; Third Army, 96, 98; 2nd Division, 112; 32nd Division, 107; 35th Division, 105; 42nd Division ("Rainbow Division"), 107; 77th Division, 106; 82nd Division, 106; 88th Division, 109; 92nd Division, 104–6; 93rd Division, 104–6; Marine Corps units, 102, 103, 107, 112, 142
American Expeditionary Force, North Russia (AEFNR), 191–92. *See also* Russia, Allied and U.S. intervention

259

~

About the Author

Robert H. Zieger is Distinguished Professor of History at the University of Florida. He previously taught at the University of Wisconsin–Stevens Point, Kansas State University, and Wayne State University. A native of New Jersey, he received his Ph.D. from the University of Maryland. His other books include *American Workers, American Unions*, a third edition of which is scheduled for publication in 2001, and *The CIO, 1935–1955*, which received the Philip A. Taft Prize for labor history in 1996. He and his wife, Gay, live in Gainesville.

~

Critical Issues in History
Series Editor: Donald T. Critchlow